Inside the FBI

Also by Andrew Tully

NOVELS:

The Brahmin Arrangement
The Time of the Hawk
Supreme Court
Capitol Hill
A Race of Rebels

NONFICTION:

The Secret War Against Dope
The Super Spies
White Tie and Dagger
The FBI's Most Famous Cases
Where Did Your Money Go? (with Milton Britten)
Berlin: Story of a Battle
CIA: The Inside Story
When They Burned the White House
Treasury Agent
Era of Elegance

Inside the
FBI

From the Files of the Federal Bureau of Investigation and Independent Sources

Andrew Tully

Author of *CIA—The Inside Story*
and *The FBI's Most Famous Cases*

McGraw-Hill Book Company

NEW YORK   ST. LOUIS   SAN FRANCISCO
DUSSELDORF   MEXICO   TORONTO

Certain passages in this book have been fictionalized to disguise investigative techniques and to protect informants still in place.

Andrew Tully

1 2 3 4 5 6 7 8 9 B P B P 8 7 6 5 4 3 2 1 0

LIBRARY OF CONGRESS CATALOGING IN PUBLICATION DATA

Tully, Andrew, 1914-
Inside the FBI.
1.   United States   Federal Bureau of Investiga-
tion.   I.   Title.
HV8141.T84   353.0074   80-14092
ISBN 0-07-065425-5

This book is for
my brother Stuart and my sisters Beatrice and Lucy

The author is indebted to FBI Director
William H. Webster for his sympathetic en-
couragement, and to Special Agent Robert
Blitzer for assistance given cheerfully and
with amazing patience.

CONTENTS

CONTENTS

THIS
IS
THE FBI

1

Ten Million Dollar Man

"I think your bank is missing about $10 million,"
Brown told Warner.
    It was Warner's turn to be flabbergasted. "What
do you mean?" he asked. "How do you know?"
    "I mean somebody stole $10 million from your
bank," Brown replied. "We know it because we're look-
ing for the man who stole it."

Everybody agreed that Stanley Mark Rifkin was a smart kid. He
breezed through California State University, Northridge, to pick
up a bachelor's degree in business administration, then took a
master's degree at the University of California, Los Angeles. He
had taught computer classes at Northridge, sold computer
software, and worked for an international energy conglomerate in
Geneva, Switzerland. He had married, and been divorced from,
his high school sweetheart and a German girl he met in Switzerland.
    Now, balding and growing pudgy at thirty-two, Rifkin was
doing pretty well in the fall of 1978. He owned his own computer
consulting company—Stan Rifkin, Inc.—and did business from a
three-bedroom apartment in Sepulveda, California, crammed with
computer equipment. Two years earlier he had been engaged by
Payment Systems, Inc., a subsidiary of American Express, to
assess the computer system at the Security Pacific Bank in Los
Angeles, with emphasis on the bank's security arrangements.
Earlier in 1978, on assignment from Incoterm Honeywell, Inc., he
had helped set up the bank's backup system for Fed Wire, a
bank-to-bank funds transfer system. Throughout the summer and
early fall, he made periodic visits to the wire transfer room to
check on its operations.

To those who knew him, Rifkin seemed on the way to becoming a *rich,* smart kid. So his attorney, Gary Goodgame, was not unduly surprised when Rifkin called on him early in October and asked the lawyer to put him in touch with a diamond broker who had European contacts. Goodgame arranged a meeting for Rifkin with Lon Stein, a reputable diamond salesman for Ambel Diamond Importers, Inc., of Los Angeles. Rifkin told Stein he represented a group of companies interested in buying "about ten million dollars' worth" of diamonds. It was a big order, but after all Rifkin had been recommended by Gary Goodgame, and Stein was accustomed to dealing in big money.

Stein also had done business with Russalmaz, a firm established by the Soviet Union in 1976 to sell its diamonds. He contacted Alexandre Malinin, director of Russalmaz operations in Geneva, by telex and told him of Rifkin's interest. Five days later, on October 14, Russalmaz received a second telex, this one signed by a Mr. "Nelson" of Security Pacific Bank. The message read: "Mr. Lon Stein is our representative and has access to U.S. dollars 10 million for small goods to three-carat-size commercial quality or better."

On October 16, Rifkin left his consulting business in charge of his secretary and several part-time workers from California State, Northridge, and took a job as manager of software (programming) systems development for National Semiconductor Large Computer Systems, Inc., in San Diego. He asked the apartment manager for permission to leave the equipment behind and to allow others to use it while he was gone.

Nine days later Rifkin took the afternoon off and drove to Los Angeles "to check the wire room" at Security Pacific. He entered an unmarked elevator in the 55-story building and descended to Operations Unit One on D level, where he exchanged pleasantries with a guard and was admitted to the wire room. His face and geniality were familiar; to the guard and employes in the wire room he was "the expert."

Rifkin did some apparently casual checking. On this day, however, he was memorizing the secret code numbers—changed daily as a security precaution—for transferring money between Security Pacific and other banks in the United States and abroad. Finished, he sauntered out, bestowing smiles here and there.

By this time it was almost 4:30 P.M., a time when wire room employes are relaxed. Once outside, Rifkin immediately telephoned the room and said he was "Michael Hansen," an executive with the bank's international division. He recited several security codes, then ordered that $10.2 million be transferred from an account to which he had given a fictitious number to a second falsely numbered account at the Irving Trust Company in New York City. The order went through without a hitch. Security Pacific handled about 1500 such transfers a day totaling up to $4 billion, so that $10.2 million was, relatively, peanuts. Besides, the caller had given the right codes. Next morning, before the transaction could be checked, Rifkin ordered the money transferred from Irving Trust to Wozchod Bank, a Swiss institution, with instructions to deposit it in the Russalmaz account.

Lon Stein, convinced of Rifkin's bona fides, arrived in Geneva and hurried to the Russalmaz office. When the Russians confirmed that the money was in their account, they sent the diamonds to Geneva where Stein examined the stones. Satisfied, Stein negotiated an $8,145,000 purchase with Russalmaz's Malinin for 6.04 pounds of diamonds.

Rifkin flew to Geneva to pick up the diamonds. Carrying the gems in his luggage, he flew back to the United States on October 29. That was a daring ploy, but Rifkin figured correctly that no U.S. Customs inspector would suspect such a display of effrontery. Rifkin simply said he had nothing to declare and was passed through the ever milling mob at New York City's Kennedy International Airport. Guile is all very well, but chutzpah is the gambler's game.

Back on the West Coast, Rifkin checked into L'Hermitage Hotel in Beverly Hills, a swank caravansary with sunken living rooms and wood-paneled fireplaces. Between entertaining friends and casual acquaintances in his suite, he found time to stuff a handful of diamonds into his pocket and take a cab to Le Vieux Paris jewelers, where he sold them for $6000. As required by law, Le Vieux filled out a police report on the purchase. Beverly Hills police, noting that the stones were loose—that is, not mounted in settings—began an investigation. Meanwhile, Rifkin paid his bill at L'Hermitage and checked out.

At about this time, an FBI agent undercover had a chat on a

Beverly Hills street corner with a small-time confidence man who had passed on occasional gossipy tips about life in the twilight world of the hustler. He claimed a pal employed by another jewelry firm had told him about a dude who was peddling loose diamonds.

"Peddling them where?" asked the agent.

"I dunno," said the con man. "The guy wouldn't tell me. All he said was he got it from a dame whose boyfriend pulls a heist, as you might say, now and then. Jokers like that get to know things."

The agent sighed. "See if you can find out more about it," he said. "Those diamonds are probably illegal."

"Yeah, must be," said the con man. "I'll try." He grinned. "Don't forget to bring money if I get anything."

The agent didn't grin back. "Just see what you can do, for now," he said. He strolled off, stopped in a doorway, and dutifully scribbled a few words on a piece of paper. Loose diamonds, he thought. Boy Scouts don't sell loose diamonds. It might fit in with something we've got.

But before the FBI or the Beverly Hills police took the first steps that could have identified Rifkin as the diamond salesman, Rifkin revealed both his braggadocio and his amateur standing in the big league of crime. On November 1, 1978, he visited attorney Goodgame and showed him a cache of $1 million worth of diamonds. That might not have been fatal, but Rifkin couldn't resist bragging that he had acquired a new identity and was headed for "places unknown." In case Goodgame's intelligence had fled him, Rifkin also told him, comfortably, that Security Pacific "could bear the loss of $10.2 million."

Goodgame was flabbergasted. But after Rifkin had departed, leaving three of the diamonds with Goodgame, the lawyer saw his duty as a citizen. He telephoned the FBI field office and told Special Agent Robin C. Brown about Rifkin's visit. That same day, an earlier Rifkin mistake surfaced. He had forgotten to tell his mother he was leaving town, and Mrs. Rifkin phoned the police and reported that her son was missing.

An FBI agent went to the mother's home and picked up a picture of the fugitive for national circulation. Then Robin Brown, by now the case agent in charge of the investigation, paid a call on Richard Warner, senior vice president of the Security Pacific National Bank.

"I think your bank is missing about $10 million," Brown told Warner.

It was Warner's turn to be flabbergasted. "What do you mean?" he asked. "How do you know?"

"I mean somebody stole $10 million from your bank," Brown replied. "We know it because we're looking for the man who stole it."

A quick check verified the theft, although Warner told reporters later the loss would have been discovered that same day without the FBI's help. He also told Brown that no one from the bank named Nelson had sent a message to Russalmaz, and that there was no one in the bank's employ named Michael Hansen, the name Rifkin had used to order the transfer of funds to his bank account in New York.

Unaware that Goodgame had alerted the FBI, Rifkin flew to Rochester, New York, to look up one Paul O'Brien, treasurer of the Rochester Telephone Corporation. Rifkin had met O'Brien two years before while working for Pay Systems, Inc., and he wanted to persuade O'Brien to open a diamond brokerage firm in New York City to sell several hundred thousands of dollars' worth of diamonds a year while Rifkin was living in Europe.

On the afternoon of November 1, O'Brien was deeply engrossed in public rate hearings for his company when Rifkin walked into the room and sat down in the back row of the spectators' seats. When the hearing was over, Rifkin walked up to O'Brien.

"Hello, I've come to offer you a job," Rifkin said.

"Well, hello," O'Brien replied. "But I already have a good job, a good career."

But Rifkin pressed him. He told O'Brien he had been in Europe and had gotten involved over there in land development. He said he was well paid and that his clients had plenty of financing. "They pay me part in cash and part in diamonds," Rifkin said. As a result, he said he had a cash-flow problem in turning diamonds into money. He wanted to set up a small firm in New York City to sell the diamonds. He needed someone over here he could trust to oversee the diamond business, since he would be in Europe for the foreseeable future.

The two men met for lunch the next day and discussed the matter further, but came to no agreement. At breakfast on the third day, O'Brien told Rifkin he might be able to take a month or so off from his current job to help set up the diamond brokerage firm. Finally, O'Brien got permission from his superior to take a month off, and Rifkin gave him $6000 in good-faith money to start setting up the business.

O'Brien was still mulling it over, however, as he sat watching the eleven o'clock news on television that night. Suddenly, there it was on the screen: Rifkin's picture and the voice of the commentator saying he was wanted for robbing a bank of $10.2 million.

"Oh, my God," O'Brien told his wife. "That's the guy I've been with for the last couple of days."

O'Brien called Security Pacific in Los Angeles and tried to get in touch with a bank official. He finally reached the head of the antifraud detail and gave him the whole story. O'Brien also said he'd contact the FBI. No, the official told him, he'd take care of that. But O'Brien called the Bureau's field office in Rochester, anyway, and spent the rest of the night answering agents' questions at his home. When daylight dawned, O'Brien and the agents drove out to the Rochester airport, hoping to confront Rifkin if he tried to take the early morning flight out, but Rifkin didn't show.

Back home, O'Brien's wife reported that Rifkin had telephoned and told her to tell her husband the deal was off and that he would call back that afternoon. With O'Brien's permission, FBI agents put a wiretap on his telephone. Rifkin did call that afternoon, but the conversation gave the FBI eavesdroppers no clue as to where he was. However, Rifkin did say he'd call again and tell O'Brien where to send the $6000 good-faith money back to him.

It was 4:30 P.M. on Sunday, November 5, when the O'Brien telephone rang. Rifkin was on the other end of the line.

"Stan, I've still got your money," O'Brien told him. "Where do I send it?"

Rifkin told him to mail the $6000 in cash to a post office box listed in the name of Dan Wolfson, a boyhood friend, who lived in Carlsbad, California. O'Brien argued against sending the money in cash, but Rifkin insisted and hung up. From the living room of the O'Brien home, an FBI agent phoned the Los Angeles field office and gave Agent Norman Wight Wolfson's name and the number of the post office box.

With that information in hand, the field office had no trouble tracing down Wolfson's address. Just after midnight on Monday, November 6—only 12 days after Rifkin's computer caper— Agents Wight, Brown, and Richard Dalton knocked on the door of the Wolfson apartment. At first Wolfson said Rifkin wasn't there, but Brown sensed that his "body language" contradicted his words. Moments later, Rifkin stepped out of a darkened bedroom. "Here I am," he said simply. So was a red bag containing the remaining diamonds, and $12,000 in cash. Wolfson, a photographer, took pictures of Rifkin, smiling broadly, with the three agents. He later sold one print to the Associated Press and another to a local newspaper serving the Carlsbad area.

II

Stanley Mark Rifkin's capture radically altered his reputation as a smart kid. In fact, he turned out to be a bungler who couldn't or wouldn't think things out. The Security Pacific theft was well planned, with the loot whisked out of the country and into a Swiss bank account in less than a day. Conversion of $8.1 million from the bank heist into a bag of diamonds went off without a hitch. But then the whole enterprise fell apart.

Lawmen like Robin Brown couldn't understand why Rifkin returned to the United States and then tarried in a Carlsbad condominium instead of trying to flee the country. In South America, there are countries in which a wealthy fugitive can— literally as well as figuratively—get away with murder. Rifkin's boasts to Goodgame and his sale of some of the diamonds to a Beverly Hills jewelry shop were bound to get him in trouble. And the climax came when he gave O'Brien the number of the post office box rented by the tenant of his hideaway.

"I don't know why he stayed here," Brown said. "Perhaps he was more comfortable in these surroundings. After all, he's pretty young. Perhaps he gave no thought to the kind of effort we could put into solving this case." Maybe Agent Dalton had the answer: "We're dealing with a computer specialist, not a professional criminal."

However, faculty members at California State, Northridge, were not surprised by what Rifkin had done. "Stan was always the kind of guy into a lot of things," recalled Jerry Boles, director of the Computer Center at Northridge. "My guess is that he got into this thing as a sort of intellectual exercise. But I would never have had any doubt he would get caught. Stan had a habit of jumping into a project, getting all wrapped up in it, and then moving on to something else without tying up all the loose ends." Dr. Gerald Smith, one of Rifkin's teachers, saw him as "a problem solver. He found a loophole and exploited it. He was arrested in Carlsbad, but he should have been in Rio."

Buying diamonds with the bank loot, of course, was an excellent tactic in Rifkin's strategy. That $10.2 million had to be laundered, that is, made usable. In an interview with the Los Angeles *Herald-Examiner,* Rifkin's investment in the gem market was explained by Donn Parker, author of *Crime by Computer*:

"When you've got $10 million in a bank, you don't just walk in and say, 'Give me $10 million in small bills.' What you have to do is transfer that money to other banks, keep it moving ahead of any suspicion. The idea, ultimately, would be to get it in a foreign bank, like a Swiss numbered account, where there would be no way to trace it. You want to leave a complicated trail that will give you time to spread it around and get it converted into cash. Then you have to get the money back into the financial system— as bonds, securities, diamonds or whatever—where you can use it as credit for purchases and so on."

But Rifkin ignored the commandment implicit in Parker's blueprint. He neglected to get lost. So on November 6, 1978, he was indicted by a Los Angeles grand jury on charges of fraud by wire, bank larceny, smuggling, and interstate transportation of stolen goods. A second count of fraud by wire later was included in a superseding indictment. Rifkin was held first on bond of $6 million, later reduced to $4 million. Then, on November 21, the bail was reduced to $200,000. Rifkin got up the money from family and friends and was released, under court orders to live with his parents and report daily to the Los Angeles Pretrial Services Agency.

No one, with the exception of Stanley Mark Rifkin, could have predicted what would happen next. What *did* happen next was that while awaiting trial he was arrested again by FBI agents on February 13, 1979, and charged with plotting to steal $50 million from the Union Bank in Los Angeles. Also arrested was

Mrs. Patricia Ferguson, president of Documentation Associates, a West Los Angeles information-peddling firm whose clients included several agencies of the federal government. Mrs. Ferguson, a pale, thirty-eight-year-old brunette, divorced mother of two children, had hired Rifkin as a consultant shortly before the Security Pacific robbery. She had put up $2000 and her house, valued at $97,500, as contributions toward Rifkin's $200,000 bail.

A sworn 11-page affidavit filed by FBI Special Agent Joseph T. Sheehan detailed the alleged conspiracy:

Working undercover, Sheehan posed as a business consultant who had been a loan officer at Union Bank. He was first approached by Mrs. Ferguson in a telephone call a week before. She told him she had been referred to him by someone who said he had "access to banks," and her proposal required the cooperation of a banker, someone who "must have larceny" in his heart. Rifkin, she said, wanted such a banker because he himself couldn't go near a bank but wanted to "do it again" and would "like to do it right." Mrs. Ferguson said that the wire transfer of the $50 million would be "a normal, everyday transaction, just like before," and that Rifkin would give the banker instructions on how to manipulate the transfer.

Arrangements were made for Sheehan, using an assumed name, to meet with Rifkin on Monday, February 12, at a Beverly Hills street intersection. It was at that meeting that Rifkin outlined his plans.

Rifkin told Sheehan he had two sources of bearer bonds, which are negotiable by anyone who holds them. One source involved a foreign holder of bearer bonds; another was what Rifkin said was "a large financial services firm." Rifkin favored use of the Union Bank because it was a big institution that "handles many wire transfers." He told Sheehan that once he bought the bearer bonds he would "go somewhere where no one would ever see me again" and that the banker Sheehan recruited would have to do likewise.

Still according to the affidavit:

Rifkin said the authorities would know almost immediately that he had fled jurisdiction, and that he would like to accomplish transfer of the money before his trial started. But he said the caper could be postponed because even if he were convicted, he expected to remain free on bail for about six more weeks pending sentencing. In any case, Rifkin said, he had every reason to avoid getting caught because he couldn't play "the good little boy in trouble game" again. He described Mrs. Ferguson as "up to her eyeballs in this thing, and also on the other thing."

Trial in the Security Pacific Bank case had been scheduled to start two days after the arrests of Rifkin and Mrs. Ferguson, but the government agreed to a continuance granted by United States District Court Judge Matt Byrne. Meanwhile, Rifkin and Mrs. Ferguson were held in $1 million bond each on the new charges.

There was, however, more to come. On March 21, 1979, the New York *Times* published a page one story quoting sources inside and outside the government as reporting that the alleged Rifkin plot to steal another $50 million had been orchestrated by a prisoner at the Metropolitan Correctional Center in San Diego, under the direction of the Federal Drug Enforcement Administration. The object, said the *Times,* was to obtain the release of the prisoner so he could work as an informant for the agency after infiltrating organized crime.

Rifkin had been confined to the prison while trying to raise bail, and he and the prisoner became confidants, the *Times* said. According to the newspaper, the DEA plan was for the prisoner to encourage Rifkin to commit a second, larger bank theft, and for the prisoner to keep the authorities posted. That way, said the *Times* story, federal agents could cite his cooperation to a judge and to local authorities and thereby establish his credibility as a cooperative undercover agent worthy of freedom.

The DEA forthwith issued a statement saying that "as an organization" it did not originate plans for the aborted $50 million heist. An Agency spokesman admitted the prisoner had discussed the robbery with Rifkin and had kept the DEA informed, but said the Agency had acted only as a conduit of information about planning the robbery between the prisoner and the FBI. That Bureau hastened to deny any role in a possible entrapment. A spokesman said that by the time the FBI had been brought into the case by the DEA, the plan for the Union Bank theft was well along and that Rifkin was a willing participant and conspirator.

That seemed to be that, although some DEA sources suggested that California agents had in fact encouraged the prisoner to help Rifkin plot the crime, probably without the knowledge of their superiors in Washington. In any case, Rifkin pleaded guilty to two counts of wire fraud, and prosecutors agreed to drop the charges stemming from the second bank theft conspiracy. That, said Rifkin's defense lawyers, made moot the question of whether their client had been illegally entrapped to commit a second crime.

Finally, on March 25, 1979, Stanley Mark Rifkin stood before Judge Byrne for sentencing. He asked the judge to place him on probation so he could teach bank officials how to prevent computer fraud, but Judge Byrne turned him down. Remarking that a prison term would be a "far more effective deterrent than all the lectures you could give," he sentenced Rifkin to eight years' imprisonment on the two charges.

Earlier, Judge Byrne had listened to a 40-minute pleading by Rifkin's lawyer, Robert Talcott. Talcott urged the judge to show mercy, asserting that his client was a brilliant, if troubled, man who had "an unconscious, merciless desire to destroy himself." But at the sentencing, Judge Byrne mentioned several times that he had considered the second arrest in his sentencing decision. That arrest, he said, had changed his mind about accepting Talcott's sympathetic characterization of the defendant.

After being freed on bail, Judge Byrne said, Rifkin "chose again to involve himself in the same kind" of crime, "in total disregard for the law; there was no showing at all of any remorse." The judge also dismissed Rifkin's contention in a letter to him that he had had no intention of actually going through with the second theft, that he was merely gathering information to write a book about bank fraud.

It was not until the following June that Mrs. Ferguson appeared in Los Angeles federal court. With tears in her eyes, she pleaded guilty to charges of conspiracy to commit wire fraud, to engage in the interstate transportation of stolen property, and to her part in Rifkin's plan to default on his bond.

Although Mrs. Ferguson had been indicted on charges of attempting to steal between $1 million and $50 million from the Union Bank, she told Judge Robert Firth that no set amount had ever been decided on by her and Rifkin. She said FBI Agent Sheehan had insisted she specify an amount, so she made up the $50 million figure.

Mrs. Ferguson could have drawn up to five years in prison

and a $10,000 fine. But on July 2, 1979, she was sentenced to two years in prison, with 18 months of the term suspended. She was also placed on five years' probation and ordered to put in 2000 hours of charity work after her release from custody.

Meanwhile, Dan Wolfson, in whose apartment Rifkin was apprehended, had been arrested on charges of aiding and abetting and harboring a fugitive. Prosecution was deferred, and Wolfson in effect was placed on probation. Finally, on January 7, 1980, the charges against him were dismissed on recommendation of the United States Attorney's office in San Diego.

Still behind bars, of course, was the young man who as a senior at Francis Polytechnic High School in Sun Valley, California, had been voted "most likely to succeed." For the FBI, the Rifkin case had produced new and sensational headlines for Director William H. Webster's crusade against the phenomenon called computer crime, which was costing the American people more than $500 million a year. Webster's only regret was that up to a point Rifkin had made the swindle look too easy.

III

More than a year before the Rifkin caper, in June 1977, Democratic Senator Abe Ribicoff of Connecticut introduced Senate bill 1766, "to make a Federal crime the use, for fraudulent or other illegal purposes, of any computer owned or operated by the United States, certain financial institutions, and entities affecting interstate commerce." It was six days lacking of a year later, on June 21, 1978, before Ribicoff got a chance to testify for his bill before the Criminal Laws and Procedures Subcommittee of the Senate Judiciary Committee. If the bill were enacted into law, he said, it would serve as an incentive to encourage corporate victims of computer crime to report their losses to the authorities.

"A gunman walks into a bank and pulls off a $10,000 robbery and the bank officials have no hesitation about calling in the police," Ribicoff told his peers. "Nobody blames the bank for the robbery. But a slick white-collar criminal manipulates that same bank's computers and steals $500,000—and all too often the bank officials have nothing to say. They would rather absorb the loss than call in the police. They are fearful of the bad publicity.

Consequently, computer crimes, which are very difficult to detect to begin with, often go unreported. Justice Department officials inform me that there are hundreds of big computer crimes that are not reported—and the fear of bad publicity is the reason."

Ribicoff put his finger on the problem. Because there was no specific computer crime statute in the United States Code, it was not always immediately apparent that a crime had been committed. As a result, banks and other businesses—and United States government agencies—could rationalize their unwillingness to report the crime by referring to it as an administrative error, or a bookkeeping mistake. With the passage of the Ribicoff bill, there would be little doubt that the law had been broken, and thus the victims would be obliged to report a fraud when the law described it as a crime in unmistakably clear language.

Ribicoff's bill didn't get off the ground, although it was cosponsored by several other senators, including Massachusetts Senator Edward Kennedy, Democrat, and Illinois Senator Charles Percy, Republican. It died when the 95th Congress adjourned without taking any action. So Ribicoff and his colleagues tried again in January 1979, reintroducing the bill, with minor changes, as S. 240. Entitled the Federal Computer Systems Protection Act, the bill was endorsed by the Justice Department, the FBI, and that congressional watchdog, the General Accounting Office.

Ribicoff described the bill as one which would give federal prosecutors "a weapon against the four main categories of computer crime: 1. The introduction of fraudulent records or data into a computer system; 2. The unauthorized use of computer-related facilities; 3. The alteration or destruction of information or files; 4. The stealing, whether by electronic means or otherwise, of money, financial instruments, property, services, or valuable data."

Under the Ribicoff bill, long prison terms and stiff fines would be imposed on electronic burglars; the penalty could be 15 years in prison, a $50,000 fine, or both. Moreover, the bill would be the first law enacted by Congress aimed directly at controlling crime by computer or computer-related crime. Under Title 18 of the United States Code, there are 40 statutes the government can use to combat computer-related crime. But all 40 statutes were written to prosecute abuses other than computer crimes, and thus federal prosecutors had been handicapped because they had to construct their cases on laws that did not envision the technical aspects of computer crime. The Ribicoff bill would make virtually all unauthorized use of federal computers and computers used in interstate commerce a federal offense. There would be no requirement that telephones or other forms of illicit computer penetration across state lines be used in order to qualify as a crime.

Ribicoff did not produce the bill from the top of his head. It was the fruit of a 300-page study by the Senate Government Operations Committee staff, which concluded that computer security in federal programs was frighteningly inadequate, that felons incarcerated in a federal prison were writing computer programs involving the disbursement of millions of dollars in public funds, and that Internal Revenue Service computers were vulnerable to tax fraud schemes that resulted in refund checks being issued to individuals filing fictitious returns.

As an extreme example, the staff study reported a curious situation at Leavenworth Penitentiary in which prisoners—some with white-collar crime backgrounds, some with relatively high rates of recidivism, and some with convictions for murder and kidnapping—were writing computer programs for the Agriculture Department's Commodity Credit Corporation and the Agricultural Stabilization and Conservations Service. Those programs disbursed hundreds of millions of dollars in public funds through loans and farm emergency assistance.

A senior Internal Revenue investigator found evidence that convicts at Leavenworth involved in the computer rehabilitation program had figured out IRS computer tolerance levels, or "discriminate function" tables. This would enable the prisoners to learn when the IRS computer would flag a tax return that ordinarily would not be reviewed by human beings. Thus, filing bogus tax returns to get tax refunds was made as easy as crossing the street. The IRS investigation revealed that tax frauds emanating from Leavenworth probably had risen from an average refund of $600 to an average refund of $10,000. And inmates could take their knowledge into the outside world when they were paroled or otherwise released.

The Department of Health, Education, and Welfare, with computers transacting a minimum of $84 billion in public fund payments, was one of the worst offenders. At the time of the staff's inquiry, HEW didn't have a single criminal investigator knowledgeable in computer-related crime. Prodded by the Senate committee, HEW finally began to train its own criminal investigators to uncover computer-related crimes.

Indeed, only the CIA and the Department of Defense and their "helper" organizations involved in national security were working to secure their computer systems against compromise. All continuously monitored their own computer security procedures, and frequently initiated exercises to deliberately penetrate their systems. The natural assumption was that foreign intelligence agents were constantly involved in trying to crack the systems.

The U.S. Civil Service Commission urged that computer programmers in federal programs involving privacy data, the disbursement of public funds, and economically valuable information be subjected to full field background investigations as a condition of employment. Only at the Department of Defense, the CIA, and its associated agencies were such programmers required to have security clearance.

Liberal critics complained of the Ribicoff bill's failure to distinguish between major and minor computer abuses. They argued that one effect of passage of the bill would be to make serious felony crimes of many pervasive practices among computer personnel. For example, it was common practice for programmers, computer operators, and other computer users to make unauthorized use of computers for such activities as "game-playing," printing "Snoopy" calendars, calculating bowling scores, and maintaining church mailing lists. Under the Ribicoff bill, said the critics, such practices no longer would be ethical issues, winked at or ignored by management, but federal crimes.

Nonsense, replied Phil Manuel, an investigator with the Senate Permanent Subcommittee on Investigations. He said the critics' arguments had very little merit, "when one considers that: (1) the same type of browsing and manipulation which creates a 'Snoopy' calendar could facilitate a major fraud; and (2) the Wire Fraud Statute, after which this bill is patterned and which has been consistently upheld by the courts since 1934, is broader than S. 240 and allows for as much prosecutorial discretion in its application." And at the Justice Department and FBI, officials scoffed at the idea that the majesty of the United States government would waste time and money prosecuting anybody for playing tictactoe on a computer. Joseph Henehan, chief of the FBI's White-Collar Crimes Section, said the law's approach would have to be selective. "It would be impossible for the FBI to enter the field of computer fraud in wholesale fashion," Henehan said. "Instead, it was likely the FBI would seek prosecutive criteria from local United States Attorneys limiting the matters to be investigated."

Meanwhile, the FBI had launched a recruiting drive to enlist more accountants into its special agent corps, while training present agents to investigate computer and other white-collar crimes. The Bureau was getting top people from the accounting profession's so-called Big Eight firms, and FBI Director William H. Webster ranked accountants third in the Bureau's hiring priorities—after minorities and women. Like all other FBI recruits, accountants got their orientation at the FBI Academy in Quantico, Virginia, where they were assigned to the "Financial Crimes Training Unit."

"In my view, an accountant is of more value to the FBI than any lawyer they ever had," said Nicholas Wultich, a former FBI agent with the House Small Business Committee. "Never in 28 years with the FBI did I ever have a case taken away from me—an accountant—because it was too complex. There is much more being stolen at the point of a pen than at the point of a gun." He noted that FBI statistics for 1978 showed that losses through bank fraud and embezzlement totaled $85 million, compared with losses of only $29.5 million in bank robberies.

In any case, by mid-1979, 1528 FBI agents were assigned to white-collar crime, an increase of 402 since Webster took over as the Bureau's director in February 1978. And during a 19-month investigation of Bert Lance, former head of the Office of Management and Budget, the FBI created the largest computer program ever used in any federal investigation, dispatching to the Justice Department for review the lending records of 40 banks. Similar computer detection was put to work reviewing the finances of President Carter's family peanut warehouse. In short, Webster had moved the FBI into the late twentieth century's techniques for catching unarmed crooks in business suits.

2

Healing a Legend

In the year after Webster arrived at the mausoleum-like J. Edgar Hoover Building on Pennsylvania Avenue, the number of FBI women special agents increased almost 50 percent–from 91 to 143. The number of black special agents rose from 143 to 172. At the same time, the special agents unit counted 170 Hispanics, 17 American Indians, and 38 "Asians." In August 1978, 39 budding agents entered the new training class at the FBI Academy in Quantico, Virginia. Of those 39, 17 were from minorities and nine were women.

The similarity is striking.

When twenty-nine-year-old J. Edgar Hoover, a Department of Justice lawyer, was appointed director of the Bureau of Investigation (later renamed the Federal Bureau of Investigation) in 1924, the Bureau was a shambles. It was a catch-all for political hacks and incompetents. Many agents took an active part in the election campaigns of sitting members of Congress, for pay. Promotions were dictated by White House hangers-on, senators, congressmen, and fat-cat campaign contributors. The public held the Bureau in contempt. Newspaper editorials demanded that the Bureau be abolished and its work distributed throughout other branches of the federal government. Hoover threw out the incompetents and the political pets, established a policy of promotion based on merit, recruited smart lawyers and accountants to fill the ranks of his special agents, and made of the FBI what most authorities called the most efficient government investigative agency in the world.

In February 1978, when William H. Webster, a Republican, became the sixth director of the FBI, he found the Bureau still shaken from the effects of Hoover's misuse of its functions as a siege complex seized him during the last two decades of his life. Before Hoover died at age seventy-seven on May 2, 1972, he had waged a bizarre vendetta against the Reverend Martin Luther King, Jr., used his office as a means of gathering information about the personal lives of members of Congress and other government officeholders to protect himself against public criticism, and ordered or sanctioned illegal or questionable tactics against political dissidents.

But perhaps the most tragic victim of Hoover's abuse of his enormous power was a tiny actress from Marshalltown, Iowa, named Jean Seberg. At seventeen, Miss Seberg was chosen from among 18,000 young women to play the role of Saint Joan in a motion picture produced by Otto Preminger in 1957. Fame followed and, eventually, tragedy. Jean Seberg took an interest in the American civil rights movement and became a regular contributor to the Black Panther party. The FBI had already begun its "intelligence" campaign against people who J. Edgar Hoover—and Richard M. Nixon—believed were on the "wrong" side. In 1970 the Bureau leaked false information that Miss Seberg was pregnant by a Black Panther leader. When she saw the report in print, Miss Seberg went into premature labor and delivered a baby girl who died shortly after birth. She took the body home to Iowa in a glass coffin, so all could see that the dead infant was white. On each anniversary of the baby's death, Miss Seberg attempted suicide. In September 1979 she finally succeeded; she was found dead in her car of an overdose of barbiturates. The new FBI could not bring her back to life, but Webster promptly confirmed the story of her destruction by the Hoover regime as revealed by FBI documents turned over to her former husband, French author Romain Gary, two years earlier. The Bureau, Webster said, was "out of that business."

In April 1978 indictments were issued against L. Patrick Gray, former acting director of the FBI, and two former high-level Bureau aides—W. Mark Felt and Edward S. Miller—on charges that they authorized illegal break-ins at the homes of relatives and acquaintances of radical Weather Underground fugitives in the early 1970s. Meanwhile, 61 other Bureau employes were under investigation for alleged involvement in the break-ins and illegal wiretaps and mail openings during the same period.

History, as is its wont, had repeated itself.

The fate of Gray, Felt, and Miller was in the hands of the courts, of course. But the cases of the 61 other FBI people, all special agents, were dumped in Webster's lap for adjudication. It seemed fitting as well as systemic. Webster, who turned fifty-four six days after he moved into the director's office, had had a distinguished legal and judicial career. He had been an attorney with a St. Louis law firm and a United States Attorney. He had been a judge of the United States District Court for the Eastern District of Missouri, and had come to the FBI from his seat on the United States Court of Appeals for the Eighth Circuit. He was low-key, soft-spoken, but firm, businesslike, and impatient with self-serving rhetoric at staff meetings.

Webster studied the cases of the special agents for several months. Then, on December 5, 1978, he announced that two FBI supervisors would be dismissed, another demoted, and one suspended because of their roles in illegal surveillance of the Weather Underground. He said that no administrative action would be taken against 58 street agents involved in the cases because they had acted on orders from higher authorities. But he did censure two street agents who, he said, had entered persons' homes without such approval from superiors.

Citing the "climate of the times" and great pressure from the Nixon White House to apprehend the Weather fugitives, Webster declared in his report to Attorney General Griffin Bell: "It seems clear to me that to discipline the street agents at this late date for acts performed under supervision and without needed legal guidance from FBI headquarters and the Department of Justice would wholly lack any therapeutic value either as a personal deterrent or as an example to others. It would be counterproductive and unfair."

Three weeks later Webster announced a reversal of his decision to fire an agent who had approved illegal investigatory actions while leading a New York squad. He said that because the agent had cooperated with internal investigations of FBI improprieties and had "conducted himself throughout the administrative inquiry with unusual candor," he would demote the agent to a nonsupervisory rank instead of dismissing him. Recognizing such candor and cooperation, Webster said, "serves as an incentive to others to cooperate with legitimate administrative inquiry."

In that case, as in the others, the operative word in Webster's decisions was *fairness*. It was a quality the general public might well have applied to the entire FBI structure during the furor over the scandals. When Webster took office the FBI admittedly had major problems. But what Hoover and others had done to the Bureau produced a feeling among many citizens in the mid-1970s that the FBI was populated largely by closet criminals, political hustlers, and witch hunters. In fact, the Bureau's improprieties allegedly had been committed by a small minority of its top people and a smaller minority of its total personnel.

As of January 31, 1979, the total number of FBI employes, including special agents and so-called support personnel, was 11,110—about the same as at the time of the illegal incidents. Of that approximate number, only 64 were charged with involvement in the misdeeds the courts and Webster were called upon to adjudicate.

That, of course, might be called too many. It could be rationally argued that *one* would be too many in an organization as sensitive as the FBI. But Webster, no softheaded patsy, was correct in citing the "climate of the times" as an extenuating circumstance. The Weather Underground claimed "credit" for a series of bombings, including those at the Capitol and the Pentagon. Several of its leaders became fugitives in 1969, and lawmen across the country mounted an intensive campaign to apprehend members of the only organization in the country that threatened international terrorism. As a result, many law enforcement people felt they were justified in occasionally violating civil liberties in this pursuit. True, there were rotten apples in the FBI barrel. But history has demonstrated that even men who are basically good can be adversely affected by the social and political atmosphere in which they find themselves living and working. And Richard Nixon was telling the forces of law and order to bring in the Weather people by any means necessary.

President Gerald Ford provided the medicine to heal this sickness. Under his direction, Attorney General Edward H. Levi in 1976 established guidelines for the FBI's counterintelligence corps. In part, the guidelines are classified, but in dealing with the terrorist threat the Bureau has to have information that an organization or its members are engaging in—or are planning to engage in—acts of force or violence directed against the United States. If there is no such information, there is no investigation.

As a result, hundreds of investigations begun in the past have been closed. In December 1979, the FBI was investigating only 13 domestic organizations, and from 40 to 60 individuals associated with those organizations. (The number changes almost weekly.) There is a certain risk that unless a closer watch is made, a terrorist group will organize with impunity. But, as Webster put it, that risk is consistent with the American tradition. Domestic organizations have the right to form and people have a right to express their views without fearing that the FBI will put informants in place to find out what's going on. Webster (he prefers to be addressed as "Judge") liked the guidelines. He found that the Bureau was better off with them because agents in the field now knew what they could legitimately do, and that they could act aggressively, without risk of criminal or civil sanctions.

In the spring of 1979, terrorist bombings around the country had been averaging about 100 a year. But for Webster there was a slender silver lining. It was that subversive or rebellious groups in America did not believe that causing injury to people was "the way to achieve support for political causes." So most violent protest had been directed against property, such as banks and public utilities. What the judge called that "tradition" had kept American homegrown organizations from engaging in mindless assaults on human beings. Indeed, the FBI tended to believe that the only organization in the United States that could be considered internationally terrorist was the Weather Underground, which as 1979 passed into springtime had about 60 members.

Under Webster, the Bureau reordered its priorities to put more effort and manpower into the investigation of white-collar crime, organized crime, and foreign counterintelligence. Its prime targets in the field of white-collar crime are government frauds, public corruption, and major bank embezzlement cases. Within a few months after a payoff and kickback scandal rocked the government's "storekeeper," the General Services Administration, the FBI had produced 41 indictments. In February 1978, the

Bureau was investigating 574 cases of corruption at all levels of local, state, and federal government. A year later, that number was close to 900. The FBI has identified 27 "families" engaged in organized crime. But it doesn't confine itself to those traditional operations; it looks at all ongoing criminal enterprises which have continuity as their essential ingredient and involve large numbers of people as organized crime. So the Bureau is training its young agents to enable them to deal with computer frauds and other techniques unknown 20 years ago. Meanwhile, a statute known as RICO—the Racketeer Influenced and Corrupt Organization Law—is being used more and more. The statute covers any criminal enterprise; it is possible for a city council to be a criminal enterprise if it's operating as such. And the law not only carries a maximum sentence of 20 years in prison but also provides for seizing the assets of the convicted "business."

Computer crimes, such as the Stanley Mark Rifkin caper, have been increasing apace. There is great potential for abuse in the fact that by January 1979 more than 90,000 general-purpose computers were in use by American businesses, plus another some 12,000 in the federal government. More than 2.5 million persons work with the new technology, and not all of them are immune to temptation. Moreover, a Federal Bar Association study committee estimated the chance of an electronic criminal going to jail if convicted to be only one in 1000, because of the vague or otherwise inadequate laws applying to the problem.

One problem facing both big and small companies is controlling access to the data in a computer system that uses "distributed data processing"—a network of computers and terminals in different locations linked by telephone lines. While the number Rifkin used to tell the system which account was being tapped for $10.2 million was false, the Security Pacific Bank didn't discover this until tipped off by the FBI that the money was missing. At Security Pacific, as at many other big banks, fund transfers were not immediately matched against other bank records. And, of course, Rifkin had the money transferred to the Russian account in Switzerland as soon as Security Pacific opened its doors the next morning.

Dishonest employes can use the system to order delivery to a confederate of merchandise that the computer will say was paid for, or they can use it to issue checks to pay nonexistent bills. Employes can "snoop" on the data to change their own records on payroll information and thus give themselves a raise. A disgruntled worker can wipe out information in a computer and never be caught.

Foreign espionage becomes a bigger problem every year. In late 1979, there were 1900 Soviet-bloc officials and their families in the United States. In 1978, there were 65,000 visits by foreign nationals from "hostile" states. Merchant seamen from such countries regularly stop over here, and there are visiting trade association groups and exchange students. The establishment of diplomatic relations with the People's (Communist) Republic of China meant the arrival of some 1200 additional Chinese officials and their families, and hundreds of students and trade groups. Then there are the thousands of foreign diplomats and their aides stationed at United Nations headquarters in New York City. One FBI estimate is that it takes at least nine agents to shadow a diplomatic suspect, often with a backup crew of as many as a score of technical experts. In some cases, as many as 40 FBI people have been involved in surveillance alone. Visits by trade groups and students are all very well, but the FBI cannot overlook the possibility that they may be thieves bent on stealing technological secrets.

J. Edgar Hoover was accused of squandering the Bureau's resources on the sort of activities that built imposing statistics—minor bank robberies and stolen cars, for example. Webster moved to reduce the number of relatively petty crimes that occupied so many agents. He asked Congress to transfer to other law and order agencies responsibility for enforcing laws against such "crimes" as the illegal wearing of a Civil Defense insignia and the interstate transportation of unsafe refrigerators.

At the same time, Webster pushed new technological approaches to criminal investigations. Among them was something called psycholinguistics, used with considerable success in tracking down suspects, especially in hostage situations. An expert in the science, a kind of psychiatric medicine, can arrive at a "profile" of the offender by appraising words used in ransom notes, and pronunciation of words in cases where the offender has made verbal contact with authorities. Given such raw material, the expert practitioner can establish the age, sex, race, ethnic background, and education of the suspect—even his propensities.

There was, for example, the case of a man who stole two barrels of low-grade enriched uranium from a General Electric plant in Wilmington, North Carolina. Such uranium is lethal if inhaled, and the man threatened to send samples of it to members of Congress unless he got $100,000 in ransom. Psycholinguistic examination of the handwriting on the ransom notes enabled the FBI to solve the case in 72 hours when it led agents to the employment files at the GE plant and then to a disgruntled employe.

FBI computers gobble up the thousands of words in agents' notes and hundreds of documents, take note of patterns and similarities identified by electronic means, and come up with evidence of suspects' movements and their links with other organized crime figures. Hostage negotiators, trained in how to talk terrorists into surrendering, are assigned to all field offices, on call from their routine assignments in the event of a skyjacking or other terrorist crisis within the wide slice of geography for which the office is responsible.

Meanwhile, the FBI had sent many more of its agents—all volunteers—underground. Its budget for fiscal year 1978 included an undercover item of $3 million, triple the amount appropriated in fiscal 1977. Most of these members of the "Unkempt Club" are directed against organized and white-collar crime, public corruption, suspected terrorist groups, and those employed in foreign counterintelligence activities.

It was quite a change. In Hoover's day, as Jeremiah O'Leary of the Washington *Star* remarked, "Going undercover was loosening your tie." But the relatively few "spies" reluctantly activated by Hoover had convinced him just before his death that the strategy worked. It has worked for Judge Webster, too; in 1977 such operations recovered more than $100 million worth of property. In recent years, the "Unkempt Club" has done some notable work:

FBI agents undercover exposed a manufacturers' ring that was selling pirated cassettes and soundtrack tapes of such movies as *Star Wars* by setting up a distributorship and identifying the pirates. There were six convictions.

Agents in New York City set up a small garbage collection company and learned that organized crime dominated the trash-hauling industry. As a result, two organized crime figures were convicted.

In Baltimore, undercover agents posed as contractors and formed a corporation. They infiltrated the inner circle of city officials and exposed a public works official who was extorting kickbacks from contractors who maintained municipal buildings. He was convicted, along with several other city officials and a number of contractors.

But as might be expected, the informant system does beckon to abuse and corruption. In late 1978, a New York agent named Joseph Stabile pleaded guilty to lying about taking a $10,000 bribe and drew a prison term. Then, in October 1979, two agents were removed from their posts when they were charged in an FBI affidavit with stealing funds budgeted for informants and then orchestrating a cover-up of the thefts. The affidavit said that Agents Alan H. Rotton, supervisor at Washington headquarters, and Stephen S. Travis of the Kansas City field office made payments of thousands of dollars in cash to informants who denied ever getting paid as well as to nonexistent tipsters. Tragedy intervened in this case: Rotton shot himself to death in the garage of his suburban Virginia home three days after the charges were published. Travis pleaded guilty and was sentenced to four years in prison.

Then on February 3, 1980, news leaks to reporters nationwide revealed to the American public the most sensational undercover operation in the FBI's colorful history. Code-named Abscam for Arab Scam, the investigation covered twenty-three months, involved about 100 agents, and cost more than $800,000. When the story of Abscam seeped out, 31 federal, state, and local officials were identified as subjects of the gigantic ''sting'' caper aimed at collecting evidence of large-scale bribery payments by FBI agents dressed as phony Arab sheiks seeking to buy political influence to protect their ''investments'' in New Jersey gambling casinos, an American titanium mine, and East Coast port facilities.

Headquarters for Abscam was an elegant town house in Washington, where the agents took television pictures, complete with sound tracks, of the accused officials accepting or discussing the acceptance of bribes for lending their political clout to the "Arabs' " various financial dealings. According to the news leaks, Justice Department sources maintained that their hidden-camera tapes would provide powerful proof of bribery. Among those named in the investigation were Senator Harrison H. Williams, Jr., Democrat, of New Jersey, who allegedly accepted stock in a titanium mine; Democratic Congressmen John M. Murphy of New York, Frank Thompson, Jr., of New Jersey, Raymond F. Lederer and Michael O. Myers of Pennsylvania, and John W. Jenrette, Jr., of South Carolina, each of whom allegedly took $50,000 in cash; and Republican Representative Richard Kelly of Florida and Democratic Representative John P. Murtha of Pennsylvania. Murtha was described as willing to accept $50,000, although he didn't take the money, and authorities said Kelly took $25,000.

There was consternation, and anger, on Capitol Hill. "It was a setup, a goddam setup," roared House Speaker Thomas P. (Tip) O'Neill. Other members of Congress complained that the story had been aired by the media before a single piece of evidence was presented to a grand jury. Civil libertarians thundered their indignation at the investigators for leaking their findings to the media, irreparably damaging the reputations of public officials before anyone had been formally accused of a crime.

Both the FBI's Webster and Attorney General Benjamin Civiletti—relatively new on the job as Justice Department chief after succeeding Georgian Griffin Bell several months earlier—were outraged by the news leaks and vowed to find and expose the offending tattletaling officials. But Webster rejected the accusation that his Bureau had targeted individual public officials "just to see what they were up to." Abscam, Webster said, grew instead out of leads produced by an undercover operation designed to recover stolen art and securities in New York's Long Island suburbs. Webster said he was confident that Congress and the FBI had compatible interests. Members of that body, he said, "want to get the rotten apples out. They're proud of what they are doing and are angered by anybody that is bringing discredit upon them by association."

Meanwhile, on May 23, 1980, a federal grand jury in Philadelphia indicted three members of the City Council and an alleged middleman in the Abscam operation. Grand juries in Washington and New York heard evidence against others involved. And the debate continued over whether Abscam was the product of FBI "rogue elephants" running wild to polish the Bureau's image.

However, from all the evidence, undercover FBI agents have been a big asset. Webster has called them "a remarkably elite cadre of volunteers. . . . These are people who have a certain talent and the psychological capacity to deal effectively with role playing and still accept the tough discipline of the FBI." But given the Bureau's visible workload, it could never spare enough of its agents for this type of work. It still must depend mostly on the services of outside espionage operatives—"informants" in official nomenclature, "informers" to critics of the system. They are referred to elsewhere in this work as informants, for the same reason it would be a gratuitous dismissal of official usage to describe a White House secretary who can type as a stenographer.

In May 1980 Webster disclosed that the FBI had 2891 private informants—1789 gathering general criminal information, 1060 assigned to organized crime, and 42 in the field of domestic intelligence and terrorism. It was the first time the Bureau had revealed the number of its active informants, but Webster's position was that the public should know the scope of the FBI's operations. He had not been amused by gossip that the Bureau was employing as many as 50,000 "snitches."

These informants move easily in the underworld of crime, many of them paid employes of the various rackets. They are not the kind of people encountered in drawing rooms or at community chest meetings. None of them will ever make archbishop or Eagle Scout. But the type is vital to the operation of any investigative agency. An informant is not casually hired nor instantly trusted. Certain tests are applied before hiring, and after the informant is in place, tests are conducted to check his credibility. Overall, the record of informants is as good as can be expected of people working with mutilation and sudden death looking over their shoulders.

But the system has been threatened by a statute with the high purpose of making certain that federal agencies are truthful with the American people. It is called the Freedom of Information Act.

Consider the situation: The FBI must have reliable sources of information. But most such sources insist upon confidentiality, and properly so. They don't want to be turned out into the cold and be on the wrong end of a submachine gun or sawed-off shotgun. In the past, law enforcement was always able to safeguard informants' identities. The Freedom of Information Act and court orders open the way for disclosure of those identities.

As a result, some informants are unwilling to supply information; they're not convinced the Bureau will be able to keep it confidential. Agents developing informants have trouble doing so in good conscience because they are doubtful about their ability to guarantee confidentiality. So the number of informants has been shrinking. They know that a prisoner can request and receive information about his prosecution that may tell him who was responsible for sending him to prison.

Shortly after he took office, Webster called the Freedom of Information Act "the greatest threat to effective law enforcement today." He pointed out that 12 percent of the information requests under the law were coming from prisons. Organized crime figures regularly demand information on their cases, and so have some foreign intelligence agents. It is all very well to operate an open government, but where lives and personal safety are involved, that value should be balanced against a law enforcement agency's obligation to keep accurate records and at the same time safeguard the confidentiality of its sources.

Indeed, the flood of information requests all but submerged the FBI. In February 1979, Webster reported there were 4600 Freedom of Information requests pending, and a backlog of four to six months. He said the Bureau could not, in the foreseeable future, comply with the law's time limit requiring a response to requests within 10 working days, plus a 10-day extension in "unusual circumstances." Because of budget constraints, however, Webster said he couldn't seek any additional funds or personnel to handle the flood.

(Have a parenthetical lunacy: There is also something called the Privacy Act of 1974. Fred Graham, law correspondent for CBS News, ran into this well-meaning statute. He discovered that the Justice Department would not tell him whether John Ehrlichman, the Nixon White House aide involved in the Watergate scandal, had ever been convicted of a crime. Ehrlichman, of course, was found guilty of various Watergate crimes on New Year's Day, 1975, but the Justice Department would not release such information because to do so would "constitute an unwarranted invasion" of Ehrlichman's privacy.)

If the Freedom of Information Act (and, to a lesser extent, the Privacy Act) confronted the FBI with a vexing problem, the Bureau finally emerged (blinking?) into the light of the Republic's Egalitarian Age. That is to say, it has gotten around to recognizing that its operations would not be damaged by the infusion of women and blacks into its prestigious corps of special agents. Hoover was not so much antiblack and antifemale as he was convinced that to recruit them into the corps would be meddling with perfection. Besides, he honestly believed women and blacks were happier in lower-level jobs.

First, a definition: A special agent is a sworn federal law enforcement officer. As such, he is charged with the duty of investigating violations of laws of the United States, collecting evidence in cases in which the United States is—or may be—a party in interest, "and performing other duties imposed upon him by law." As of January 31, 1980, the FBI had 7918 special agents, most of them outside Washington in 59 field offices, each headed by a special agent in charge. The so-called SAC is responsible for operations in his entire region, aided and abetted by a special deputy, his "number two man." Below these two officers are supervisory agents, each with his own squad of street agents.

In the year after Webster arrived at the intimidating J. Edgar Hoover Building on Pennsylvania Avenue, the number of FBI women special agents increased almost 50 percent—from 91 to 143. The number of black special agents rose from 143 to 172. At the same time, the special agents unit counted 170 Hispanics, 17 American Indians, and 38 "Asians." In August 1978, 39 budding agents entered the new training class at the FBI Academy in Quantico, Virginia. Of those 39, 17 were from minorities and nine were women. (In the fall of 1979, one of the firearms instructors at the Bureau's firing range in Quantico, Virginia, was a woman, Christine Kaporch. Webster called her "the best shot in the FBI.") Meanwhile, in February 1979 Webster had appointed the first black to head an FBI field office. The appointee was John D. Glover, a 12-year veteran of the Bureau, and as special agent in charge of the Milwaukee office, he had responsibility for operations throughout the state of Wisconsin.

It was not a record calculated to cause dancing in the streets by women and minorities, but it was a start. The FBI had punched a hole in what some younger agents called "Hoover's Maginot Line." And the future of equal rights in the Bureau was brightened by Judge Webster's pronouncement that "Hiring minorities and women is more than simple justice; it is important to our operation." King Hoover was dead. The latest of his successors was pledged to face up to a uniquely American fact of life.

Meanwhile, Webster struck a blow for what an aide described as "a form of thinking-man's independence" among his corps of agents outside Washington. He appointed Neil J. Welch, the special agent in charge in Philadelphia, to take over as SAC of the New York office, the Bureau's largest. Welch was widely respected by agents everywhere, but he had openly feuded with headquarters in the past over Hoover's emphasis on solving bank robberies and other relatively "cheap" cases, while giving much less attention to white-collar crime, political corruption, and organized criminal syndicates.

Now the man who once snapped that the FBI would be better off if someone put sandbags around the J. Edgar Hoover Building and disconnected its telephones became a member of the lofty executive council. Webster was only incidentally widening the distance between him and the old Hoover era crowd, a necessary tactic in the long-range strategy of cleaning up the FBI's image. He was rewarding Welch for 27 years of distinguished, often brilliant service to the Bureau in such "provinces" as Buffalo and Detroit. He saw New York as a training ground for his agents and wanted an SAC there who, as he said, "could re-program an office, get into quality work, and inspire his men to want to be in that work."

Although some of the Hoover holdovers at headquarters were shocked by this promotion of a man they felt had strayed off the reservation too much and thus couldn't be "trusted," they might have foreseen it. Webster was looking for more competence in the Bureau, special agents who had shown over a period of time that they were capable of making solid contributions to Bureau strategy. Moreover, Welch was the only FBI man on the list of five candidates for FBI director when President Carter's task force completed its job of screening prospects. The task force studied the records of 235 nominees and interviewed 48 of them. Welch was rated "top quality" by every member of the panel. Webster simply looked at the record and liked what he saw. At the same time, he was telling his agents that henceforth they would be rated solely on performance even if they occasionally differed with the Washington hierarchy.

But Webster's housecleaning was not an indiscriminate thing. He came under heavy criticism in certain liberal quarters early in his tenure when he promoted James G. Adams from his post as assistant director to associate director—the number two man in the Bureau. Adams had risen to power under Hoover and had been charged with giving false information to Congress about the infamous break-ins. Adams said he hadn't known the information was misleading, and Webster believed him.

Then, when Adams retired in April 1979 to become head of criminal justice planning on the staff of Texas Governor William Clements, Webster issued a strong statement praising him and clearing him of any involvement in the alleged cover-up. The investigation, Webster said, "has produced no evidence that [Adams] participated in, condoned or had knowledge of any such activities. Jim Adams has had a long and honorable career and I shall miss his wise and candid counsel."

One of Adams's more recent accomplishments was his direction of the successful FBI effort to trace the source of a 1977 leak of information from confidential Bureau files to James T. Licavoli, which described him as the head of the Mafia in Cleveland. The job took some doing, but in February 1978, Adams's men arrested Geraldine Rabinowitz, a longtime FBI file clerk, and her husband, Jeffrey, for passing the hot documents to the Cleveland mob for $15,900. Both pleaded guilty, and three months later each was sentenced to five years in prison for accepting bribes.

The leak was only the second in the FBI's history. The first—in 1974—involved a nineteen-year-old Bureau clerk named Irene Margaret Kuczynski of Newark, New Jersey, who sold some material from FBI files to another organized crime syndicate. Miss Kuczynski was sentenced as a young adult offender to five years' unsupervised probation on a charge of conspiring in the theft of government property.

In Webster's place, J. Edgar Hoover would never have promoted Neil Welch to head the prestigious New York office. As Webster's successor, Hoover would have purged all such close-to-the-throne barons as Jim Adams. Hoover was regal, not to say dictatorial. He seldom sought opinions from his palace guard; he stated his own position as a sort of divine right law. Courtiers avoided bringing him bad news as they would the pox. Doing so, they might save their heads, but their bodies would wind up in Montana. One did not disagree with the king—or be caught nursing an independent thought.

Webster the man and the FBI Director is understated. Perhaps because he was educated at Amherst College, that citadel of the determinedly casual, he encourages quiet discussions. He seems to have no side. One would never take him for the near-millionaire he is. His conversation is quiet and frugal, and he is capable of the common touch. In an interview while this work was in gestation, he called lugubrious attention to the fact he was wearing one black and one blue sock. "I do it all the time," he said. "I'd better switch exclusively to one color or the other." It was not in J. Edgar Hoover to descend to such self-deprecating humility; besides, by royal right, his socks always matched. When some old-timers at the Bureau objected to opening the FBI building's courtyard to open-air concerts, Webster told them calmly: "It's the public's property. Let some of the public use it."

As might be expected, Webster's dress is also understated, Amherstlike. He wears calm striped or white shirts with button-down collars, rep ties, and dark conservative suits or occasionally country tweeds. He plays early morning tennis at least three times a week. He told a reporter for the Washington *Post* that he had mowed his own lawn for twenty-five years and saw no reason to stop now that he lived in Washington. If that sounded just a bit much, it did fit the man's personality, his wonted unpretentiousness. No such claim could have been entered by J. Edgar Hoover. His passion for neatness dictated that his lawn be replaced by Astro Turf.

Indisputably, Judge Webster's personality, reflecting a quiet strength of purpose, has wrought changes in the FBI. While making the prestigious investigative Bureau a better place to work, he has also emphasized the personal accountability of its agents. As one veteran agent put it: "We now know exactly what we *can't* do. That's a comfortable feeling." But in its day-to-day operations, the FBI is unchanged. As the cases that follow make clear, the Bureau's function remains what it always was, namely, the investigation of crimes against the laws of the United States. Whether such an investigation took place in 1968 or 1979, the Bureau's responsibility has remained the same. John Edgar Hoover described it in street-corner language many years ago. "Our job," he said, "is to find out who did it."

THE
ESPIONAGE
TRADE

3

Have Cloak, Will

Kampiles was given an elaborate script to follow before he left the United States. First, he was ordered to send a coded message—disguised as a "Happy Birthday" greeting—to the Russian contact at an "accommodation address" in Athens that Michael had sent him. If Kampiles had written "Happy Birthday, I'm well," that would have meant he was coming. "I'm not well" would have meant he couldn't make it.

One way or another, the Central Intelligence Agency had been collecting information about missile emplacements in the Soviet Union since the years of the cold war. As technology improved, much of this information was gathered by spy satellites in space. Then in 1975, a new instrument was put into use to observe the emplacements. Called the KH-11, the satellite's cameras were so sensitive they could distinguish between civilians and uniformed military personnel from several hundred miles above the earth. But in the spring of 1978 certain CIA experts noticed that the Russians were trying to evade the agency's monitoring, and the FBI was asked to investigate the possibility that there had been a leak of intelligence within the United States.

At about the same time, there was a scheduling specialist for the International Communications Agency (formerly the U.S. Information Agency) named Anastasia Thanakos. This was the story she told under oath eight months later:

A young friend and protégé who had worked briefly as a clerk at the CIA called her in Washington from Chicago shortly after returning from a trip to Greece. His name was William Kampiles,

-three. She was amused by what she believed was a fantasy
piles unfolded to her.

He told her of meeting a "foreigner" on his February flight to
Athens. His account was rather garbled, but it appeared that
Kampiles had told the foreigner he was hoping to get a job in
Greece; the foreigner told him to go straight to the Soviet Embassy there. Kampiles did so, and gave the Russians "information
you could pick up anywhere—such as in *Newsweek* magazine."
She knew that Bill Kampiles was always making up stories, and
she questioned him about this one. He insisted he had wound up
with $3000 for the information he had delivered. In any case, at
Kampiles' request, Ms. Thanakos conveyed his story to another
mutual friend, a CIA officer named George Joannides. It seemed
that Kampiles wanted to return to the CIA as an undercover
agent.

This was Joannides' story, also told under oath:

He and Kampiles sat on a bench outside CIA headquarters in
Langley, Virginia, on April 29, 1978, and Kampiles told him about
his trip and his dickering with the Russians in Athens. Kampiles
said he had crashed a garden party at the Soviet Embassy one
night in February and struck up an acquaintance with a Russian
named "Michael." He said he convinced "Michael" that he was
still with the CIA by showing him some sort of "identity documents" he had used as a watch officer.

A reference was made to Kampiles returning to Greece in late
summer, 1978. Kampiles said "Michael" had given him an address in Athens where he could be contacted. He said he was
"playing the Soviets along" and that he had received $3000 from
them. Joannides, who worked in the CIA office of legal counsel,
told Kampiles he ought to be talking to someone from the Soviet
Section of the Agency. Kampiles agreed to wait on the bench,
near a statue of Nathan Hale, America's martyred spy of the
Revolutionary War, while Joannides went back inside to try to
find the right audience for Kampiles' story.

Joannides talked to a Soviet-bloc expert named "Ron," who
not only declined to talk to Kampiles but refused to send a
colleague. "Ron" gave as his reason Presidential orders governing the CIA's operations. He said it might be improper for the
Agency to contact "a U.S. person." (This was curious. An
executive order issued by President Carter in 1977 contained

some restrictions on domestic surveillance of "U.S. persons," but no prohibitions against voluntary interviews.)

Joannides argued briefly with the expert. He emphasized that Kampiles had been in touch with the Soviets in Athens and that he might be a "U.S. person" but he also was a former Agency employe who had come forward and who might be able to identify "Michael" from CIA photographs. Unable to make any headway with the expert, Joannides finally suggested that Kampiles write a letter to the Agency, and "Ron" agreed. He went back to the bench and told Kampiles that it was late Friday afternoon and he couldn't get anyone to "come down and see you." Kampiles agreed to write the letter.

Kampiles wrote and mailed the letter late in May to Joannides' home. Joannides had been recovering from a heart attack, and he stuck the letter in a zippered briefcase that he took to the office along with doctor bills and insurance forms. Because there had been changes in his assignments and status at the CIA, Joannides didn't "address" himself to the briefcase until late July. Only then did he open the envelope with Kampiles' return address on it.

In the letter, Kampiles wrote that in meetings with "Michael" they discussed "the use of a camera and my role in delivering the information." He enclosed a 50-drachma ticket, apparently to a Greek sporting event. On the ticket, ostensibly in the handwriting of the Soviet agent who was trying to enlist him, was the address of a proposed summertime rendezvous in Athens. Kampiles wrote: "If you think there might be Agency interest, I would be willing to discuss this experience in full detail."

Joannides turned the letter over to the CIA's Soviet Section, and at the request of an official there, one Vivian Sacos, he called Kampiles to ask him to come to Washington to discuss the matter. Kampiles agreed but said he was due to go to Athens on August 18. He said he would try to make arrangements to come to Washington before then. When he did so, and phoned Joannides, it was once again Friday afternoon (apparently a rest period for CIA hands) and Joannides' secretary "erroneously refused to put it through, saying I was in conference." Joannides called Kampiles back and arranged for a subsequent visit to Washington for interviews with CIA and FBI officials.

William Kampiles was arrested in Hammond, Indiana, on August 17, the day before he was due to leave for Athens. The charge was espionage. Kampiles was alleged to have removed a top-secret document entitled *KH-11, System Technical Manual* from CIA headquarters while employed there, and eventually to have delivered it to the Russian "Michael" on or about March 2, 1978, in Athens, for a payment of $3000.

Indeed, as it later turned out, the FBI was confident it had all the evidence it needed. That evidence, the Bureau announced, was a "full confession" by Kampiles, obtained on August 19 after three days of interrogation by an FBI team.

Meanwhile, on the day Kampiles was arrested, CIA officials searched the headquarters area where Kampiles had worked and couldn't find copy no. 155 of the KH-11 manual which had been kept there. Obviously, no one had missed it during the nine months since Kampiles quit the CIA. Obviously, too, no one at the CIA had thought of checking to see if *any* secret document was missing after Joannides' first encounter with Kampiles way back on April 29.

Predictably, Capitol Hill made known its ever brooding preoccupation with national security matters. Senate Intelligence Committee members sharply questioned a passel of CIA officials, seeking to find out how Kampiles, a low-level watch officer, could have walked off with a top-secret document without it being noticed for nearly a year. Republican Senator Malcolm Wallop of Wyoming said about the CIA: "They're forever telling us how weak the Congress is in protecting secrets. To my knowledge, nothing close to this has come out of either house of Congress."

While the CIA started an internal review of its security procedures, others in the intelligence community expressed surprise that a watch officer had access to a document describing what they called the most secret intelligence satellite built by the United States. Normally, such documents "are kept in a safe and are never kept anywhere near a watch office," said an official at the Pentagon. "The whole thing sounds a little like sloppy secrecy."

Actually, the watch office—or Operations Center— traditionally had been used as a training ground for inexperienced junior officers. In his capacity as watch officer, Kampiles received and relayed top-secret messages, most of them in code. He also read reams of newspaper and magazine articles, both domestic and foreign. None of these chores was what he had in mind when he was recruited by the CIA off the campus of the University of Indiana in 1976 and finally put on the payroll a little less than a year later. Most of all, he wanted to use the fluent Greek he had learned from his Greek immigrant parents to work for the CIA overseas.

Washington officialdom unanimously agreed that the loss of the KH-11 manual was a serious matter. Around the Justice Department, high-level experts said that the country had been done irreparable harm and called the loss "a real disaster" that could enable the Russians to hide their missile sites from detection. "It's significant, it's not trivial," FBI Director William H. Webster said. "But I'm not wringing my hands about it." Anyway, he said his agents had compiled "a very convincing case against Kampiles."

In fact, it was difficult to measure how much the Russians profited, assuming they got the manual from Kampiles—or from someone else. The Russians couldn't build such a satellite of their own from the manual, but they probably could identify weaknesses in the 12-ton satellite and protect their secret installations accordingly. But the Russians knew the satellite had been in orbit taking pictures of their country for some time. Getting their hands on the manual didn't give them the ability to stop the KH-11 from taking pictures.

However, the loss of the manual had indisputably compromised one of the most amazing devices ever built by man. More than a dozen of the KH-11 satellites had been put into orbit, and they were still sending back photographs whose detail boggled the imagination. One picture, for example, revealed the make—and even the license plates—of automobiles in a Soviet parking lot. Another, taken during a coup in Afghanistan, showed soldiers in tanks so clearly, it was possible to detect whether they had shaved.

There also was speculation after a closed hearing of the Senate Intelligence Committee that the manual's disappearance had imperiled prospects for ratification of a new strategic arms limitation treaty (SALT). Speaking off the record, officials involved feared that America's "collection capability" had been damaged. That is to say, the KH-11 provided a big fraction of the information the United States gathered—things that could be judged by seeing. Thus, the loss affected a key program that could verify Soviet compliance with SALT limitations. The fear was that the Soviet Union had been "instructed" in how to cheat by improving their camouflage techniques.

At that point, a familiar expert was heard from—Richard M. Helms, former director of the CIA. Helms wrote in *New York* magazine that the Kampiles case "raises the question of whether or not there has been infiltration of the United States intelligence community or government at a significant level." Helms was referring to what spy shops call a "mole," a master spy who joins a foreign intelligence agency in order to work from within, a worry that is always with the counterintelligence people at the FBI. Was Kampiles merely a fall guy for a mole, used to lead investigators down a false trail?

The FBI's Webster and CIA Director Stansfield Turner responded in the only way possible. Webster said he had no information that the mole talk was well founded, "or even likely to be so." Turner told CBS's "Face the Nation" that "I have no knowledge or indications that there is a mole, or secret agent, inside the Central Intelligence Agency. But for me to sit here and tell you that I was utterly confident that there was none would be foolish." If either man suspected the existence of a mole, of course, it would have been half-witted to admit it and thus tip off his prey.

By the summer of 1979, CIA officials were still being questioned by members of relevant congressional committees on the state of the Agency's internal security. Every time the question was raised, those witnesses assured their interrogators that measures had been taken to tighten security and that those measures were working. For one thing, steps had been taken to make certain that no low-level employes had access to any secret documents. Meanwhile, both Webster and Turner denied there was or had been any feud between the CIA and the FBI. But some officials within the FBI were still concerned that the CIA was not as airtight as they could wish.

II

Because the alleged crime took place on foreign soil, William Peter Kampiles went on trial on November 6, 1978, in Hammond, Indiana, where he was arrested.

As he walked calmly into the courtroom to face the jury of eight women and four men who would hear his case, he might have been anyone's son, two years out of college and taking the first steps in a career. His youth showed in his almost chubby face, in his thick dark hair, not overly long, and in the tailored lines of his sports jacket. William Peter Kampiles had come a long way, in a frighteningly short time, from his roots.

He had grown up in the home of his Greek parents in a predominantly Polish, Slovak, and Greek neighborhood called Hegewisch in Chicago's southeastern corner—a neighborhood George Lardner, Jr., of the Washington *Post* called "an improbable breeding ground for spies." As Lardner wrote, it was a neighborhood that remembered how many boys it had sent off to fight during World War II.

"My brother identifies himself as an American," Lardner was told by Michael Kampiles. "He loves his country, he's conservative personally—yes, my-country-right-or-wrong. I believe him to be innocent."

William Kampiles was only nine years old when his father died of cancer in 1964. His mother, Nicoleta, supported the family by working in the cafeteria at the Ford Motor Company's assembly plant in their neighborhood, and at the time of the trial she was still earning her wages there at sixty-three years of age. As a child, William was an altar boy at the neighborhood Catholic church, had a paper route, and worked at other odd jobs. And as a youth, he put himself through college by delivering groceries, driving a cab, and working at a steel mill. He joined the CIA in March 1977, at just under $15,000 a year, but he grew tired of the paperwork and frustrated by his superior's repeated pronouncements that he was too inexperienced for promotion to the position of case officer, so he left the CIA eight months later. People liked him, but he wanted to be an instant Nathan Hale.

In the courtroom, Kampiles' lawyer, Michael D. Monico of Chicago, was a kind of symbol of the government's preoccupation with the security of national defense secrets. The Justice Department was doing everything possible to protect details of the KH-11 manual. So Monico was under court order to keep his notes in a 600-pound General Services Administration "Approved Security Container" installed in his office several days before the trial's opening.

Ironically, United States Attorney David T. Ready gave the defense ammunition for suggesting that secrecy was not all that sacred. In his opening statement, Ready acknowledged that at least 13 other copies of the KH-11 handbook were missing. In pretrial documents filed the day before, the Justice Department admitted it had not made an inventory of the outstanding copies until after Kampiles' arrest in August.

Monico pounced. In his opening statement he noted that: "Last week there were 17 of those manuals missing. Now there are 13. Maybe they'll find No. 155 and we can all go home." In effect, he was asking the jury how its members could convict Kampiles of stealing the document when so many other copies had disappeared. Did somebody else steal copy no. 155?

Ready had said in pretrial pleadings that the government had no information "regarding the possibility that the Soviet Union gained its knowledge of the KH-11 satellite from a source other than the defendant." He admitted the FBI's investigation had developed other suspects but said a check of those suspects proved fruitless. As for Kampiles, said Ready, the government's case was based heavily on his own admissions to FBI agents. As Ready told the story, Kampiles took the manual home with him to Chicago, where he cut off the "Top Secret" markings. Then he sold the manual in Athens to a Soviet military attaché named Michael Zavali. Ready said Kampiles had told the FBI agents he "needed money badly" and finally settled on a price of $3000. Those 13 copies that were still missing, Ready said, "will not hamper the government's case."

Monico was more dramatic. A former assistant United States Attorney in Chicago, Monico's demeanor and language suggested that he was acquainted with prosecutors' tactics as he painted a picture of a young man obsessed with the romantic dream of spying for his country.

Monico brought the jury back to Kampiles' stay in Athens in February, when he was seized with an opportunity "to beat the Soviets at their own game." So, said Monico, the defendant marched into the party at the Soviet Embassy.

"He had a crazy notion, a wild and unbelievable notion," Monico told the jurors. "He wanted to test himself, to test his fantasies and dreams, so he walked in. It was the worst decision he had ever made in his life up to that point." He pictured

Kampiles strolling up to the Embassy's bar and trying to convince everybody that he still worked for the CIA and possessed some interesting secrets.

"His brain was pounding," Monico said. "Here was Bill Kampiles in the Russian Embassy doing exactly what he'd always wanted to do. . . . He thought he could return to the United States, be accepted by the CIA, and return to Greece as an undercover man." In any case, said the lawyer, after several meetings with the Russians, Kampiles got $3000 for nothing but promises.

Monico also had an explanation for his client's "confession." He said that one of the agents, James Murphy, "had learned Bill's vulnerability—the fact that Kampiles had put the $3000 in a joint account with his mother. He [Murphy] told Bill if he didn't change his story, his mother would be implicated, his relatives in Greece would be implicated. . . . Bill Kampiles is a young, patriotic boy that got involved in a bizarre notion . . . they turned him into a criminal."

The government had its own color man, with a story that might have been plucked from a spy novel. He was Cornelius G. Sullivan, an FBI counterintelligence expert, who told the jury about the intricate arrangements made for Kampiles' return trip to Greece and a rendezvous with the Russian, Michael Zavali. In undisputed testimony, Sullivan went into fascinating detail:

Kampiles was given an elaborate script to follow before he left the United States. First, he was ordered to send a coded message—disguised as a "Happy Birthday" greeting—to the Russian contact at an "accommodation address" in Athens that Michael had sent him. If Kampiles had written "Happy Birthday, I'm well," that would have meant he was coming. "I'm not well" would have meant he couldn't make it.

Once back in Athens, Kampiles was to have gone to the Athens Stadium, walked up a cobblestone path to a certain telephone pole, and stuck a red thumbtack in it. The tack would have been the clandestine signal to Michael to meet Kampiles the following Saturday night at a nearby pizzeria. This showed that Kampiles was a fully "recruited agent," because in the game of espionage spy shops do not make "probationers" privy to any part of their *modus operandi*.

Sullivan scoffed at the defense's argument that Kampiles had conned the Russians out of their money by promising them important secrets without actually giving them any. He said experience had taught him that the Russians in particular never paid out any money without getting solid information in return. Their policy was COD, he told the jury. "The Soviets are a very pragmatic, cynical people," Sullivan said. "They will not buy a pig in a poke."

As for the importance of the KH-11 manual, another government expert explained its value to the Soviet Union. Leslie C. Dirks, CIA Deputy Director for Science and Technology, testified that one page of the document described the limitations in the satellite's geographic coverage, and another page bore an example of the quality of its photographs.

Knowledge of the geographic limitations, said Dirks, could put the Russians "in a position to avoid the satellite's surveillance altogether," and knowledge of the quality of its photographs could enable the Soviets to devise "effective camouflage."

Such information in the manual was acknowledged by United States District Court Judge Phil M. McNagny, who admitted an unexpurgated copy of the handbook into evidence. Reporters at the trial had petitioned the judge to permit all documents admitted into evidence and shown to the jury, particularly the KH-11 manual, to be made public in light of the constitutional guarantee of a public trial. Judge McNagny denied the petition. He said an expurgated copy of the manual, with some "extraordinarily sensitive" numerical tables and geographical references, would be shown the jury, but "under no circumstances" would he let the press see even the censored version. The judge said he saw no reason why the government couldn't prosecute someone for espionage without revealing classified secrets.

Then the government presented its star witness—FBI Special Agent James Murphy. An operative who usually investigated bank robberies and kidnappings, Murphy had been called in to "reinterview" Kampiles when the defendant, after two days of interrogation, stuck to the story that he was conning the Russians. According to Murphy:

It was late in the afternoon of August 19, 1978, in an FBI interview room in Washington. Murphy had just told Kampiles he didn't believe his story. "I told him that if I didn't believe it, nobody in the whole world would believe it." Kampiles slumped down in his chair and buried his head in his hands. After several seconds, Kampiles looked up at Murphy.

"You're right," he said. "I haven't told you the truth. I actually stole a document and sold it to the Russians."

Kampiles told Murphy he had taken the KH-11 handbook from the CIA Operations Center and stuffed it into the left-hand pocket of the sports jacket he was wearing. "He stated that particular document interested him and he had some vague idea of selling it to the Soviets. He stated he was aware it was a violation of the espionage laws."

Kampiles finally broke down after being confronted with a number of inconsistencies in his account, involving an identification card Kampiles said he showed the Soviet agent, a receipt he said he signed when given the $3000, and a package of clippings from technical magazines Kampiles said he was going to prepare to fool the Russians. About the ID card, Kampiles had said he didn't want the Russians to know his real identity because "it was just a lark and he wanted to be able to cut it off when the time came and he didn't want to be blackmailed in the future." But in almost the next instant, Kampiles said he gave the Russian an ID card bearing his photograph and true name. Kampiles first said he had signed the receipt for the money, using the name "Robert Jackson," which was not the name on the card. Russian agent Michael Zavali suggested Kampiles smuggle information into Greece on film and recommended a specific Japanese camera. Yet Kampiles told Murphy he had planned to prepare a package of clippings that he would have turned over to the Russians in exchange for $10,000, plus expenses.

After purloining the manual, Kampiles took it to his apartment in Vienna, Virginia, and put it in a dresser drawer. When he quit the CIA, he carried the manual back with him to his mother's home in Chicago and again put it in a dresser drawer. Several weeks later, he cut off the "Top Secret" designation in case his mother came across the manual and also because it would be easier to get it past Greek Customs.

Murphy's testimony was supported by Donald E. Stukey, who directed the Kampiles investigation as chief of the Washington-based FBI counterintelligence squad. Stukey testified that he was called into the interview room by Murphy after Kampiles' alleged confession.

"I think Bill has something he wants to tell you," Murphy said to Stukey.

Kampiles, Stukey said, looked at him for a moment and then blurted out: "You're right. I didn't get the $3000 for nothing. I sold them a document."

Stukey said he showed Kampiles a hardcover copy of the KH-11 manual that was not exactly like the one Kampiles had mentioned to Murphy.

"Mr. Kampiles looked at me and said, 'That's it,' " Stukey told the jury. "I handed him the document. He leafed through it and said, 'That's it. That's the one I gave Michael.' "

But Kampiles took the stand in his own defense to flatly and uncompromisingly deny his guilt. His voice was a hoarse monotone as he swore that the only document he ever gave the Russians was a fake CIA identification card.

Asked by Monico if he had ever taken a document out of CIA headquarters, Kampiles replied: "Yes, sir, I did. It was a blank ID card."

"Anything else?" Monico asked.

"No, sir, I did not," Kampiles said.

"Did you ever give any Soviet, any person, a CIA document?"

"I did not."

Monico went to the evidence table, retrieved hardbound and soft-cover copies of the *KH-11, System Technical Manual,* and held them aloft. Had Kampiles ever given any Soviet or any person a copy of the manual?

Kampiles turned his dark, limpid eyes upon the jury. "No, sir," he said. "I swear it."

What about the blank ID card he'd taken from CIA headquarters?

"It was just a souvenir, something to remember the CIA by," he said. "I think I may have shown it to some friends."

Kampiles said, however, he doctored the card with a photograph, his signature, an expiration date in 1980, and the fake countersignature of a CIA security officer, then gave it to Michael as proof he was still with the CIA. Michael, he said, was so impressed that he recommended him to Soviet superiors who agreed to give Kampiles $3000 and pay him $10,000 per trip for future deliveries of secret documents.

Kampiles was not asked why he would have let the Soviets keep his CIA identification card or why they would want to keep it when they expected him to return to CIA headquarters and start spying for them. He also never got a chance to support the defense's claim that his "confession" was the result of threats and coercion. Monico was just beginning to question Kampiles about this claim when Judge McNagny halted the proceedings. The next morning, the judge issued a sealed ruling that inhibited Kampiles' counsel from asking the youthful defendant about whether he had been intimidated.

There were reports then that the judge held that this line of questioning would open the door to an even more damaging counterattack by the government. It was common gossip that Kampiles had taken two lie detector tests when he tried to retract the confession in August and had failed them.

So when Kampiles was cross-examined by James Richmond, the co-prosecutor, he had to admit time after time that he indeed had told FBI agents that he had stolen the manual and sold it to the Russians for $3000. "That's what I said, yes," Kampiles kept saying in response to Richmond's questions.

In an emotional final argument, Monico tried to repair the damage. He urged the jury to disregard the confession as "untrue, unreliable, and incredible." He declared that the government was in "such a rush to prosecute this case" that no effort was made to find out whether anyone at the CIA Operations Center had seen the manual after Kampiles quit the Agency in November 1977.

"Just because you get a kid to admitting to something he didn't do, that doesn't make a case," Monico protested in a near-shout. "He wants to scream out his innocence. Don't convict him on statements that came out of his own mouth that day [August 19]. He told them it wasn't true on the 17th. They paid no attention. Please! Pay attention! End the nightmare!"

United States Attorney Ready reminded the courtroom, however, that Kampiles actually told "three stories about what went on in Greece last winter—one to Anastasia Thanakos, his patroness, one to George Joannides, the CIA lawyer, and one to the FBI."

The jury deliberated more than 10 hours before returning to

the courtroom. Then, as some of its members blinked back tears, it returned a verdict of guilty on all six counts lodged against the young man who had dreamed of working secretly in the world of the cloak and dagger. Kampiles' mother burst into the well of the courtroom to hug her son to her breast and cry, "My darling, my darling!" And then, "Nobody had mercy on him, nobody had mercy on him." She followed her son as he was led into a nearby office, where the youth began sobbing. His mother cried out: "I want to kill myself! I want to kill myself! I've worked 16 years for what? How could America do this to my son?" ·

Not until then was there an explanation of the judge's ruling that the defense could not explore Kampiles' claim that he had been intimidated by the FBI. With the guilty verdict in, Ready confirmed that Kampiles had failed two polygraph tests.

If Monico had pursued that defense, Ready said, the government would have been permitted to present testimony regarding the tests, though not the results. "Monico discovered this judge is a very fair man, to both sides," Ready went on. "The judge wasn't going to allow Monico to raise that defense and not allow the government to at least put in that Kampiles had taken the polygraph tests." Kampiles, he said, didn't like the questions put to him in the first test, and the FBI permitted him to approve the questions in the second test. "When he failed the second test, he confessed," Ready said.

William Peter Kampiles stood before Judge McNagny for sentencing on December 22, 1978. He told the court: "First of all, Your Honor, I'm sorry for everything that has happened. Not at any time did I want to injure my country in any way. I only wanted to serve my country."

Then, after Ready asked the judge to impose "a substantial sentence" on a youth who "chose to callously disregard the safety and well-being of 200 million Americans," Judge McNagny sentenced Kampiles to 40 years in prison. "This case is a complete tragedy for a young man who has never been in trouble before," the judge said. On the other hand, he said, "The United States has suffered a severe setback because of the sale to the Russians."

McNagny recommended that Kampiles serve his term in a minimum security prison and said he would point out to federal parole officials Kampiles' clean record before his espionage conviction. "The court does not believe he will ever commit any similar offense again, nor any offense, for that matter," McNagny said. He also ordered federal prison officials to keep Kampiles in Chicago through the Christmas holidays so his family could visit him.

It had been, in lawman parlance, "a nice clean case" from beginning to end. William Kampiles was not a career criminal. He had not been a neighborhood bully, nor a petty crook. He was simply a young man who yielded to the temptation to speed up the fulfillment of a boyhood dream and, having done so, found himself in terrible trouble. Thus, it seemed understandable that Michael Monico should be moved to put a friendly arm on his client's shoulder when he announced that he would appeal the conviction to the United States Court of Appeals for the Seventh Circuit. The appeals court upheld Kampiles' conviction on October 15, 1979.

4

Operation Magic Dragon

"I'm a proud, loyal American besides what has happened here. I disgraced myself and my family by some bad judgment. With God as my witness, I am not a spy. I have never done anything to intentionally hurt my country and I never will."

After Griffin Bell took over as Attorney General of the United States in 1977, it didn't take him long to subscribe to the Somerset Maugham theory: When someone leaves a telephone message urging you to call back as soon as possible, the matter is often more important to the caller than to the person called. Still, there had been two callers on that afternoon in late May 1977, and both were very important people—FBI Director Clarence Kelley, and Deputy Secretary of State Warren Christopher—and they had stressed that the matter they wanted to discuss with the Attorney General was urgent. Everything is urgent in this town, Georgian Bell told himself. However, he had his secretary put through a return conference call to Kelley and Christopher. The matter just might be urgent to his domain, too.

It was. A meeting of the three was arranged for the next day, and Bell was told then that an FBI counterintelligence operation, code-named "Magic Dragon," had uncovered "one of the worst leaks in the history of the State Department."

Christopher and Kelley asked Bell for his assistance in their attempt to find out who in the government had taken secret documents and passed them on to a spy for the Communist Vietnamese regime. They informed him that the FBI investigation was concentrated on the activities of a Vietnamese antiwar crusader named David Truong, thirty-two, whose father ran against President Nguyen Van Thieu as a peace candidate in 1967 and wound up in jail. To Bell, the name David Truong rang a bell; he had been a source of information to antiwar members of Congress on the inside story of the war from the viewpoint of the Vietnamese people.

"This is a serious case, not only for us, but diplomatically," Christopher told Bell. "Those documents could endanger the lives of foreign embassy people in Hanoi who have supplied the United States with information in the past."

It was not known at the time how many of the documents were genuinely secret—because whoever had taken them had removed such information from them. But Bell found the situation serious. As he said later, "I thought in my own limited way that something had been done wrong to our country." Later, at a court hearing, he would say: "When I became Attorney General, I didn't know the Attorney General engaged in counterintelligence activities."

The government had three choices. It could put a suspect in a position where access to classified information was limited. It could persuade the suspect to work for United States counterintelligence. Neither of these steps would produce any flak from civil rights groups. Christopher and Kelley wanted to prosecute, once they had a case.

To aid the investigation, therefore, Bell was asked to authorize a warrantless wiretap on Truong's telephone. The Attorney General realized the very real conflict between his duty to protect the nation from espionage and his duty to protect the people's Fourth Amendment guarantee of privacy. The President, through the Attorney General, could proclaim his "inherent power" to authorize searches and wiretaps without a court order, but the misuse of this power during the Watergate scandal was still a national issue. Indeed, the Carter administration was putting the finishing touches to legislation that would require secret warrants. And an FBI agent in New York was indicted for illegal wiretaps and burglaries conducted in 1972. The investigation of that case eventually led to the indictment of the former acting FBI director, L. Patrick Gray III.

Bell pondered the program. Meanwhile, he spent a weekend

in Louisville for the Kentucky Derby. The day he returned to Washington he used the President's "inherent power," authorizing a tap on Truong's phone.

He also called on President Carter to acquaint him with the case, including the involvement of a Vietnamese woman code-named "Keyseat" by her bosses at the FBI and the Central Intelligence Agency. Posing as a spy for the Vietnamese, she had received batches of documents from a man she identified as Truong. She had then flown with them to Paris, where she turned over the documents to representatives of the Hanoi government.

This was heavy stuff. The United States was holding talks with American diplomats in Paris about United States-Vietnamese relations. The mood was one of conciliation. The Vietnamese were identifying the remains of Americans missing in action. A trial involving acts of espionage by the Hanoi regime could mess things up.

But time was of the essence, Bell told the President. "Keyseat" was due back shortly with a letter to Truong from a Vietnamese official in Paris. Bell persuaded the President to authorize the FBI to open and read the letter.

In the FBI translation, the letter said: "I applaud your business plans." Then it went on to note that "very often there are efforts to swindle and deceive one another."

Hanoi's man in Paris had a right to be suspicious. The wiretap on Truong's telephone began its listening job on May 11, and eventually it recorded 551 conversations. As it turned out, however, the FBI got what it wanted two days after the operation was launched. At 6:33 P.M. on May 13, Truong was overheard asking someone named Ron to stop by his apartment on Washington's F Street, Northwest.

A balding man arrived at the apartment a little after ten o'clock, and two FBI men watched. When the man emerged from the apartment building an hour later, an FBI agent followed him through the streets near George Washington University. The man walked past the World Bank, went into the building housing the U.S. Information Agency (later renamed the International Communications Agency), and stepped into an elevator. The agent watched as the elevator's indicator showed that it stopped on the seventh floor. On the sign-in register in the lobby, the agent found the man had signed the name "R. Humphrey."

"R. Humphrey" was found to be Ronald Louis Humphrey, age forty-two, a USIA watch officer with top-secret clearance. Now the FBI wanted—and received—more help. After carefully going over the methods that would be used, Attorney General Bell authorized the FBI to plant a microphone in Truong's apartment—without a court warrant. From May 27 on, every sound made in the apartment was overheard by listening agents.

Moreover, President Carter authorized television surveillance of the USIA office in which Humphrey worked. Two TV lenses were installed in the office's ceiling so that cameras could observe every move made in the room.

As 1977 passed from spring to summer, documents were still being leaked to Truong, and then given to "Keyseat," as the FBI pursued its electronic surveillance, seeking to wrap up a solid case. On the afternoon of June 22, "Keyseat" arranged to meet Truong at the Landmark Shopping Center in Alexandria. She didn't want to go too far from her home in nearby Springfield, and she was afraid to drive around Washington at night.

Truong arrived at the rendezvous in a borrowed car. While three FBI agents recorded the scene on three cameras, Truong gave "Keyseat" a grocery bag full of papers. Inside the bag were 33 State Department documents, 28 of them clearly labeled "Confidential," and one Defense Intelligence Agency paper marked "Secret."

But there was considerable official opposition from within both the State Department and the supersecret National Security Agency to proceeding with the prosecution. The State Department balked at having to tell nearly 20 foreign nations that the documents compromising foreign embassy personnel in Hanoi might have to be made public during a trial. The CIA wanted dearly to hang on to a valuable agent, whose cover would be blown at a trial.

Meanwhile, Vietnamese-American relations were souring. During negotiating sessions in May and June, the United States agreed to back Vietnam's admission as a full member of the United Nations, and it appeared the way might be cleared for the exchange of diplomatic missions by the two countries. But Hanoi insisted that President Nixon had promised Vietnam a few billion dollars to "heal the wounds of war." The American team said it was no sale, and the sessions became increasingly acrimonious.

Finally, during the December talks in Paris, the State Department gave the "necessary approval" for prosecution of Truong and Humphrey. Then Bell & Co. persuaded a reluctant "Keyseat" to testify at the trial in exchange for a payment of $11,800 for her "relocation" outside Washington. The government now had corralled its most important witness.

Truong and Humphrey were arrested on January 31, 1978, and charged with "crimes of espionage." They faced three lifetimes in prison. The indictment also named Vietnamese Embassy officials in Paris and Dinh Ba Thi, Vietnamese Ambassador to the United Nations, as unindicted conspirators. A few days later, a furious Thi was ordered out of the United States—the first UN ambassador ever to be deported.

At the time, the Supreme Court had never ruled on the use of warrantless electronic surveillance in a foreign intelligence investigation. The District of Columbia's United States Circuit Court of Appeals had questioned the procedure's legality, but federal courts in Virginia generally had been more tolerant. Predictably, then, the Justice Department arranged to try the case in Alexandria, across the Potomac from Washington.

In the interim, Humphrey's lawyers scoffed at the indictment as a fantasy. They claimed that at the time Humphrey was charged with conspiring to damage the national security he was preoccupied with efforts to get his Vietnamese woman friend and her five children out of Vietnam, where they had been trapped since the fall of Saigon. His efforts finally succeeded when the woman and four of the children were released in July 1977, a month after the FBI informed Attorney General Bell that Humphrey was the man who could be stealing confidential documents from the USIA. The fifth child was believed to be still in Vietnam.

It all seemed what the British are fond of calling inapropos. Central Casting would have fastened Humphrey into the role of an honest insurance salesman, working just a little harder to put his children through a good private school. He was, a neighbor remarked, "the kind of man you expect to see presiding over a grill smoking with hamburgers" at a backyard cookout. Humphrey was suburbia with a house that could stand a coat of paint, and *au pair* girls; a family man with an eye on the next-highest bureaucratic grade with its extra income and fatter pension.

Thus, when the trial opened on May 1, 1978, spectators were treated to an unusual sight. Humphrey's woman friend and her three little girls and little boy were on hand, and so were Humphrey's parents. So, too, was Humphrey's licensed wife, Marylou. From his seat in the well of the courtroom, Humphrey frequently looked over at his families and smiled wistfully.

In his opening statement, Truong's attorney, Michael E. Tigar, characterized the "secret" documents involved as "diplomatic chit chat," and announced that Truong "is nobody's agent and nobody's spy." The government's job, he said, was to "go out and ensnare, entrap others in compromising situations" in an effort to destroy the normalization of relations between the United States and Vietnam. He demanded to know how the government could send the material on to the Vietnamese in Paris if the information was so critical.

Humphrey's lawyer, Warren L. Miller, acknowledged to the jury that for months Humphrey had supplied Truong with wire service copy, cables, and other documents classified at the lowest level, confidential. Humphrey loved his Vietnamese mistress so much, Miller said, that he delivered what he thought were innocuous diplomatic cables to Truong, thinking it might improve relations between the United States and Vietnam and thus help secure her release from a Vietnamese prison camp.

"My client's case is that of a man who loved too much and trusted too much," Miller said. "He knew his conduct was wrong, but passing of these items was not a crime."

Miller also seemed to be putting some distance between Humphrey and Truong. He said the defense would prove that there never was "a meeting of minds" between Humphrey and Truong, and that his client thus had no criminal intent in supplying Truong with government documents. Humphrey did not know Truong was a spy—"if indeed he was," Miller announced.

Truong sat listening intently, in a trim dark suit, his cheeks just missing chubbiness, his intelligent eyes peering through oversize horn-rimmed glasses, his body so still it might have been riveted in place. Humphrey, his baldness seeming more pronounced, occasionally made a nervous movement, his obvious weariness draped about him like an old cloak.

"Keyseat" was the first witness for the government when the

trial got under way before a jury of six men and six women. She identified herself as Dung Krall, born in Vietnam, the daughter of a Communist official who became ambassador to the Soviet Union, and married to a commander in U.S. Naval Intelligence. She had been, and still was, employed by the CIA as a double agent, she said, and in that role she had cultivated an acquaintance with David Truong.

Eventually, she went on, she delivered packages given her by Truong to Communist Vietnamese officials who called Truong "one of our people in Washington." But first she had various rendezvous with an FBI agent. For example:

"After I left him [Truong] on June 19 or 20, 1977, at the Landmark Shopping Center, I went to a parking lot of a Holiday Inn at Springfield and met FBI Agent [William] Fleshman and gave him the package Truong had given me. When I came back from vacation on July 8, I met the FBI agent at a Ramada Inn and he gave me the package back. . . . Mr. Fleshman usually photographed the material."

Then, she said, she flew to London with her family and there wrote to Phan Phanh Nam, a Vietnamese intelligence attaché in Paris, to tell him that she had Truong's package. In Paris she found that Nam was concerned because her husband had come with her. Later there was a discussion in which Nam asked if there was anything her husband could get for him from the Navy. Finally, Nam gave her a letter to take back to Truong in Washington, but he ordered her to use the Paris Métro and take a roundabout route to get back to her hotel.

"On September 10, I returned to Washington and gave the letter to Mr. Fleshman," Mrs. Krall testified. "Then I called Mr. Truong and told him I had a letter for him from Nam." Her presumption was that the FBI examined the correspondence going both ways.

Mrs. Krall also linked to what the government called an international espionage ring the then Vietnamese Ambassador to the United Nations, Dinh Ba Thi. She said she went to New York City in February 1977 to deliver one of Truong's packages to Thi, and on that occasion she asked the Ambassador if there was anything she could do to help his government. She went on:

Thi's reply was that "what my father did was enough because

my father was a Communist and Vietcong ambassador to the Soviet Union.'' She told Thi she wanted a visa to visit her family in Vietnam, and she asked him if her husband would have to steal secrets for Vietnam. The reply was that "Mr. Truong would do that. . . . He volunteered to do that." She then asked Thi if he had any message for Truong, and he replied: "Tell him to send the same things he's been sending.''

She described a conversation she had with Truong in a Dupont Circle cafeteria in Washington on April 19, 1977. She said Truong told her he had a friend "who stole a pass to the State Department. He can walk up . . . and get anything he wants.'' She said, "That must be very helpful to the Vietnam government, and Mr. Truong was smiling.''

There followed a parade of witnesses from government officialdom to talk about the contents of the papers the prosecution charged Humphrey with passing to Truong and that Truong allegedly transmitted to the Vietnamese regime. The government's case rested heavily on its claim that giving the documents to a foreign power—especially to one not particularly friendly toward the United States—did damage to America's national security. The defense sought to convince the jury that the papers' contents were so trivial in nature they could not have caused such harm.

Thus, counsel for both Humphrey and Truong repeatedly challenged testimony by Kenneth M. Quinn, a middle-level State Department official, that about 100 United States diplomatic cables allegedly stolen by an espionage ring seriously breached the national security, compromised secret sources, and tipped off the Vietnamese to American diplomatic strategy. But Quinn stood firm throughout four hours on the witness stand. He declared that disclosure of any classified material—even material that is publicly known—is dangerous because it violates agreements made with sources who provided the information, because it reveals information given in confidence about other countries, and because it gives enemies of the United States insight into the government's bargaining strategy.

For example, he cited cables that merely stated a widely reported assertion that Soviet relations with Vietnam were deteriorating. The cables, he said, identified the source of the information as "a Third World source living in Hanoi," but bits of information in the cable narrowed the possibilities of who the source could be to "probably an [East] Indian." Quinn noted that there were few Indians in Hanoi; thus, the source might be identified by a careful, expert process of elimination. The chronic release of classified information, he said, would cause sources around the world to dry up.

Quinn also gave substance to the government's claim that Truong and Humphrey tried to affect, in Hanoi's favor, the 1977 American negotiations with Vietnam on normalizing relations. He said nine cables relating to the negotiations were passed on to Hanoi. Four revealed confidential information from governments in Singapore, Thailand, Japan, and Malaysia, he testified. He also reported that one of the documents was a secret assessment by the United States consul general in Hong Kong on the relationship between progress on American negotiations with Vietnam and Vietnam's closeness to Red China—information, he said, that was "valuable to the Vietnamese in bargaining."

"What about diplomatic gossip?" asked one of Humphrey's defense attorneys, Mark L. Foster. "Like the cable which remarks about how the Finnish Ambassador to Hanoi is probably henpecked by his wife."

Quinn didn't smile. "That type of information," he said, "is used by us in biographical data—if they're strong people, weak people, the effects their wives have on them. Then the Finnish Ambassador sees it and says 'If that's what the Americans think of us, then I won't talk to them anymore.'"

Foster prodded Quinn with another example, a cable that quoted a Vietnamese official complaining of an increased number of prostitutes in Saigon. Quinn said such a statement, of itself, would never be classified. But he said the revelation of the statement's source probably would discourage that source from giving information to the United States again.

Truong's counsel tried to make the point that government documents may be overclassified. Quinn wouldn't buy it. "It's my assumption that [classified documents] are always properly classified," he said sharply.

Quinn did admit that when he assessed the documents in the summer of 1977 he had given them only a "cursory" review and that he had not been given all the documents under discussion at the trial. He said he had judged the documents he did see as causing only "minor" damage, but said the word "minor" was used "in comparison to the problems that would have resulted if more sensitive documents had been leaked."

Donald W. Marsland, chief of a counterintelligence unit in the FBI Washington field office, told of his annoyance at another "light" assessment of 63 cables allegedly given to "Keyseat" by Truong. Marsland said he protested to the State Department that the evaluation "was not consistent with the pressure we were receiving" from the Department to stress the importance of the documents. "The thing I recall," he said, "is that it was not consistent with what I'm being told Mr. [Warren M.] Christopher [Deputy Secretary of State] said of the penetration [extent of espionage]."

Finally, the prosecution called on a military man to buttress its claim that Humphrey and Truong had dealt in real national secrets. Air Force Gen. Billy B. Forsman, Deputy Director of Current Intelligence for the Defense Intelligence Agency, testified that although the information in some of the documents seemed innocuous to laymen, the documents' contents were useful to the United States in predicting possible threats and protecting the national security. And he repeated other witnesses' statements that release of the cables could "identify Defense Intelligence sources abroad."

Humphrey testified for more than six hours in the course of admitting that he gave confidential State Department documents to Truong because of his desperate love for his Vietnamese mistress and her five children, who were trapped by the Communists in Vietnam. He said his love for the woman, whom he called Kim, caused him to lose his judgment. "I had one preoccupation and that was to get them out of Vietnam," he said. "I knew I owed my life to Kim. . . . I felt that whatever I was doing in life wouldn't be fulfilled unless I got that family."

But Humphrey told the court the material he took from the USIA was not intended as a bribe to get Hanoi officials to release "my family." He said he thought the documents might help Truong and members of Congress to normalize relations between the United States and Vietnam, and that if this occurred he would have a better chance of getting the family released.

Humphrey opened his testimony by recounting how he met twenty-four-year-old Nguyen Thi Chieu, or Kim, in 1969, when he was sent to Vietnam as a Foreign Service officer. Kim had been widowed and left with three children at the age of nineteen, he said. Shortly thereafter, she met an American, "fell in love," and had two children by the man, but he deserted her. Humphrey and Kim lived next door and at first they were just friends, but soon "I began to fall in love with them"—Kim and her children.

In 1970, he said, he was about to leave on a mission when Kim tipped him off to an impending attack by the Vietcong. "Don't worry about me, worry about the Vietcong," Kim told him. "They know you're coming and they're waiting by the bridge." Two South Vietnamese soldiers went on the mission anyway, Humphrey said, and were blown up by a land mine. "I'm alive today because of her," he told the jury.

Humphrey testified that he met Truong while trying to rescue Kim and her family from Vietnam. He said he was under the impression that Truong had influential friends on Capitol Hill who might be able to help him free "my family." They became friends and met often to discuss Humphrey's family and Truong's ambition to start an export-import business between the United States and Vietnam, Humphrey said.

Humphrey admitted he cut off the "Confidential" labels on the documents he gave to Truong. "It wasn't the right thing to do," he said. "But I didn't want him to stroll up to Capitol Hill and drop the classified documents on some senator's desk." He insisted he didn't consider what he was doing a crime, but a security violation. "I thought it was merely leaking. He would give it to his friends on Capitol Hill." He said he continued to give Truong documents after Kim's release, but only unclassified cables he figured Truong still needed to use in setting up his export-import business.

In cross-examination, the assistant government prosecutor, Frank W. Dunham, stressed part of the government's case: Although the information in the stolen cables may not in itself have seemed sensitive, the documents named sources that had to be protected to maintain national security operations abroad. Humphrey claimed he gave Truong only papers that did not name sources.

He denied giving Truong four cables the government had introduced against him that were classified as secret. He claimed he wasn't even at work when the cables were sent to the USIA, and he offered his work schedule to support his claim. He said it was "highly improbable" that he gave Truong 27 cables which the government had accused him of passing on to his codefendant, but said he "probably" did give Truong 67 others. He said he was sure he gave Truong four of the cables.

To Humphrey, the information he gave Truong was a "rehash" of publicly known information. He testified that "to the best of my knowledge, just about everything I gave him had been sourced to [revealed in] some publication—newspapers, magazines, wire services."

Most of the day, Humphrey testified in a flat monotone, relieved by the small smiles he directed at his parents and Vietnamese family seated in the front row. But he spoke up loudly and clearly when asked if he was a Communist.

"No!" he declared. "I'm a proud, loyal American besides what has happened here. I disgraced myself and my family by some bad judgment. With God as my witness, I am not a spy. I have never done anything to intentionally hurt my country and I never will."

Later, when Prosecutor Dunham asked him why he didn't divorce his current wife and marry Kim to get her out of Vietnam, Humphrey responded wearily: "Procrastination, procrastination."

On the witness stand in his own behalf, David Truong represented himself as a patriotic Vietnamese, grateful to an America that had given him refuge, whose twin goals in life had been to end the war in Vietnam and then to bring Americans and Vietnamese together.

During the 1960s, he testified, he collected information, advised government officials on Vietnam affairs, and lectured extensively as an anti–Vietnam war activist. He said he increased his activities after his father, an unsuccessful peace candidate for the presidency of Vietnam in 1967, was imprisoned by the regime of President Nguyen Van Thieu, who had the support of the United States. But he insisted he didn't hate the United States because of what had happened to his father.

Truong said he passed on the information he collected to United States senators, foreign policy experts, and university professors in the United States, as well as to his family in Vietnam and to Vietnamese friends in Paris. But he denied that he ever directed that such information be given to the Vietnamese Embassy in Paris; he said he was never paid by anyone in Vietnam for passing information, that he had no friends in Hanoi, and that he never asked Humphrey to give him classified information.

"I strongly feel in my position I should help to rebuild Vietnam," he said. "Americans and Vietnamese should get together. After 30 years of war and a lot of things that happened to divide families . . . and all of the suffering each of us has gone through, it's time to turn a new page and do something more meaningful than fighting."

Truong acknowledged that he knew that at least seven State Department cables he was accused of funneling to Communist diplomats in Paris were marked classified, but he maintained that all of the cables contained information that was well known, and none could be considered confidential.

"Did any of these cables give you any news?" asked his lawyer, Michael Tigar.

"This?" Truong asked, holding up a document. "No, sir."

Although government testimony showed that the FBI found five classified documents in his apartment, Truong said he believed the cables had been declassified. Anyway, he said, he had learned from other sources the information in the cables.

In cross-examination, Assistant United States Attorney Justin W. Williams asked Truong why he kept five classified documents in his apartment. "No particular reason," Truong replied.

Williams entered the claim that some of the cables involved in the case had nothing to do with Truong's avowed aim of helping the United States and Vietnam develop normal relationships. One such cable discussed Russian military advisers in Vientiane, the capital of Laos.

"What does that have to do with normalizing relations with Vietnam?" asked the prosecutor.

"Nothing, sir," Truong replied.

Williams asked if another cable, entitled "The Ethiopian

Request for Arms," had anything to do with United States-Vietnamese relations.

"No, sir," Truong replied.

"Well, did you ever ask for [Socialist Republic of Vietnam] material to give to the U.S.?" Williams asked.

"No, sir," said Truong.

Truong's testimony also came under a surprise attack from Humphrey's lawyer, Warren L. Miller, who earlier had suggested that if Truong indeed was a spy he had deceived Humphrey.

Miller elicited the information that Truong had once kept extensive notes on how to recruit spies. Under withering questioning, Truong claimed that the notes were part of his Asian studies related to the Central Intelligence Agency. Miller held up note cards on which Truong had written that an agent should use rank, influence, deception, friendliness, and other means "to penetrate the opposition's secrecy apparatus." Another excerpt from the notes read: "The most desirable situation is where the source does not know he is in fact providing information to a foreign intelligence network."

Miller wanted to know what the note meant. Truong replied that it would be of "very little use." But Miller remarked that such advice might be aimed at influencing another to be an "unwitting agent." Clearly, as Miller put it in a final question, the lawyer was trying to prove that Humphrey was "an unwitting dupe, unwitting agent" in the alleged spy network.

But Truong replied calmly that "when I wrote this down I was really interested in learning how the CIA operated in post–World War II. I was trying to find out how the CIA operates between here and Vietnam." He said he copied the material from a book on World War II.

This little *contretemps* done with, lawyers for both defendants insisted that the only question for the jury to decide was one of intent. Humphrey, the jury was told, acted out of love for a Vietnamese woman and never thought of himself as a spy. Truong was pictured as a patriot who sought to lend a hand to his native Vietnam by passing on what he believed was innocuous information.

"Absurd!" retorted United States Attorney William B. Cummings. His final statement concentrated on trying to link documents and people. "As the documents went in," he said, "[Humphrey's] girl friend would come out."

The jurors accepted the Cummings thesis that Humphrey and Truong had done damage to the national security. After almost 14 hours of deliberation, they found both defendants guilty of espionage, theft of government documents, and "conspiracy to injure the national defense of the United States." As the jury's verdict was read, relatives and friends of the two men wept silently, and as the jurors filed out of the courtroom, Humphrey's father leaped from his seat and addressed Judge Albert V. Bryan, Jr., in a shout.

"Your Honor," Louis Humphrey pleaded. "May I please take my son's place in jail tonight? He will need love and understanding tonight. May I please take his place, Your Honor?"

"No, you may not," replied Bryan.

Later, the jury foreman expressed sympathy for the defendants. Robert Charlesworth, a retired American Telephone and Telegraph Company account manager, said: "We were all sorry. But you can't play emotions; that wasn't the question here. We knew why [Humphrey] did it, but that doesn't excuse it in any way." Charlesworth didn't mention Truong.

Whatever Judge Bryan's personal emotions, he agreed with Charlesworth and the other five male and six female jurors. On July 8, 1978, he sentenced Humphrey and Truong to a total of 47 years in prison for breaking six separate laws. But he directed that the six sentences run concurrently, meaning that the longest either man could stay in prison was 15 years.

The judge agreed that there were "mitigating factors" favoring Humphrey, and he said Truong "in my view [was] the more culpable of the two." He said he would have dealt more harshly with the Vietnamese defendant if he had been an American citizen betraying his country. In any case, Bryan said, Truong "has abused the hospitality of the United States."

Predictably, counsel for both defendants had said earlier they would appeal the convictions—predictably because the case raised the question about the extent of the President's authority to authorize warrantless electronic surveillance during a national security investigation. It was the first time a federal court had considered the direct introduction of criminal evidence obtained without warrants during such an investigation.

Four months later, an ironic touch was added in the Oval Office of the White House. President Carter rejected 40 years of "inherent" executive branch power to spy as it pleased by signing into law legislation requiring court approval before the government can conduct electronic surveillance in most foreign intelligence cases.

Legally too late for Ronald Humphrey and David Truong, the measure signed by the President on October 25, 1978:

• Requires a federal court order for most installations of wiretaps or bugs to obtain foreign intelligence in this country. The warrants in the future would be issued by a special, rotating panel of seven judges named by the Chief Justice of the United States, meeting in Washington under elaborate security procedures.

• Permits the electronic surveillance of American citizens and of other "U.S. persons" (such as resident aliens and corporations) only upon a judicial finding of probable cause to believe that the person is an agent of a "foreign power" and that the person is engaged in clandestine intelligence gathering that "may involve" a federal crime. Americans suspected of other clandestine intelligence activities or of terrorism may also be targeted under certain circumstances.

• Allows the government (primarily the ultrasecret National Security Agency, with the help of an FBI break-in) to continue electronic spying without a court order if it is directed solely at the premises or communications of "official" powers, such as governments, factions, or entities openly known to be directed and controlled by foreign governments. But the Attorney General must certify that there is no substantial likelihood of Americans being overheard.

• Accords the same protections to nonresident aliens as it does to Americans except under certain conditions, such as membership in an international terrorist organization or employment, during the sojourn in the United States, by a foreign power. Court orders still will be needed to undertake such surveillance, but the government need not show any indication that a federal crime is about to take place.

5

Spies for Sale

"Go and buy a package of Marlboro cigarettes. Remove the cigarettes and put the microfilm in the package. Crumple up the package and rub it with dirt and throw it on the floor of the phone booth. Then drive to the next gasoline station on the right-hand side of the highway and go into the men's room. You will find an envelope taped to the underside of the water tank cover of the toilet in the middle of three cubicles."

According to the Central Intelligence Agency, which regularly picks up odds and ends on the Soviet Union's care and feeding of its fledgling spies, a recurring theme at a training school outside Moscow is the average American's preoccupation with money. A passage from a basic lecture given to every class of undergraduates has this to say:

"Americans will do anything for money. Even rich men in America will become thieves to make themselves richer. In seeking to recruit agents within the United States, remember that the most promising prospect is the man or woman who wants to be paid for services rendered. Investigate more carefully those who say they are turning traitor for love of the Soviet Union."

Thus, it was not surprising that the Russians responded with alacrity to the proposition submitted by an American naval officer in August 1977. At the time, Lt. Comdr. Arthur Lindberg, forty-three, was a passenger on a Russian cruise ship bound from New York to Bermuda. Lindberg, a husky six-footer with closely cropped blond hair, passed a letter to a ship's officer addressed to "Soviet Ambassador."

The letter read, in part: "I am a career American naval officer due to retire in six years. I am interested in making additional money before I retire. I can provide you with information which you may be interested in." Lindberg gave the number of a telephone booth outside a diner near Asbury Park, New Jersey, where he could be contacted, and specified the date and time when the Russians should call him. He identified himself only as "Ed."

Two weeks later, Lindberg stepped into the phone booth and took a call from a man with a heavy foreign accent. "Hello, Ed," said the caller. "We were pleased to receive your note." Then the man went on to give Lindberg a shopping list for secret data the Russians wanted him to pass on to them. Lindberg said he was sure he could provide the information. The caller thanked him and arranged for a second telephone contact in a week's time; Lindberg would be called at another phone booth outside a shopping center in Woodbridge, New Jersey.

Presumably, the Russians had arranged to have Lindberg observed as he took the first call and—unless they broke all the rules of the club—had him followed when he left the phone booth. Doing so, it was easy during the intervening week to learn that their recruit was attached to an engineering unit at the Lakehurst Naval Air Station; in America, neighbors and fellow workers are friendly and talkative. So the Russians' situation was comfortable —they knew who "Ed" was, while he was acquainted only with an accented voice.

When he took the second call, therefore, Lindberg was told that the Soviets were impatient to receive the first batch of information on recent United States advances in aircraft, missiles, destroyers, and submarine warfare systems. He said he was making progress and could have some of the material in a couple of days.

Now Lindberg found himself cast in the role of a man he never knew, a stranger to himself in the occult trade of the double agent. It was a profession that was incongruous to the life he had led as a naval officer. Until his assignment was finished, he must be satisfied with only scraps of the ordinary pleasures of a personal life, on guard against every outsider, including his colleagues and his wife. He had launched himself into a dangerous, academic excursion into the mystery of human behavior; he was observing humanity with the objectivity of a surgeon performing a difficult and chancy operation. He could have none of the solace of friendships, only the cold supervision of his overseers. He was forced to submit to a discipline for which none of his naval training had prepared him.

Lindberg took a third call at a phone booth on the Garden State Parkway. He told the caller he had some microfilm copies of documents to pass on and described them in some detail.

"Very well," said the voice. "Go and buy a package of Marlboro cigarettes. Remove the cigarettes and put the microfilm in the package. Crumple up the package and rub it with dirt and throw it on the floor of the phone booth. Then drive to the next gasoline station on the right-hand side of the highway and go into the men's room. You will find an envelope taped to the underside of the water tank cover of the toilet in the middle of three cubicles. Do not loiter or in any way draw attention to yourself. It is dangerous for you if there are police."

Lindberg did as he was told. In the men's room of the gas station he retrieved the envelope and found it contained $1500 in $10 bills and instructions telling him to take a call in another parkway phone booth the next day.

On that fourth occasion, Lindberg was given point-by-point lessons on how to go about stealing classified material and passing it on undetected. He was told to conceal microfilm copies in empty milk cartons, soda cans, and cigarette packages, and to disguise the containers as trash by crushing them and then coating them with glue and sprinkling dirt on them to make them appear filthy so no one would be tempted to pick them up. Maps would be passed to him in magnetic containers hidden under shelves in public phone booths, and drop sites for information would be shown on the maps as trees, fenceposts, and telephone poles.

The caller took some pains in advising Lindberg how to handle the money he was paid. It should be spent "very carefully," he was told, and he should have "a logical explanation for its source" in case he was questioned by his wife. It went without saying, the caller noted, that Lindberg should not confide in his wife. He also was told that it was preferable in the case of large purchases to take out a bank loan, and then use the espionage money to pay it off, rather than pay for the purchases in cash. He was advised to hide the money in caches around his home, and "under no circumstances" to put the cash in a bank or invest it in any enterprise.

Seeking to lighten the relationship, Lindberg jollied his caller. "Investing your money is part of the American way of life," he said. "Don't you believe in the capitalistic system?"

"Never mind that," was the reply.

Then the voice softened. "But now that we're friends, you can call me Jim," Lindberg was told.

And so the conspiracy progressed apace. At one point, the Russians provided Lindberg with money to buy a new camera, and "Jim" used one phone call to give him a lesson in photography. "Jim" also explained the color-coded maps Lindberg was issued to lead him to drop sites. One Saturday afternoon Lindberg found an envelope containing $5000 stuffed inside an automobile radiator hose left in an empty parking lot. In December 1977, he was given a Christmas bonus of $1000 for what "Jim" called the "excellence" of the information he had passed on.

Lindberg never met or saw any of the Russian conspirators, but he wondered one day if he had stumbled onto one of them. He had shown up early to receive a prearranged telephone call at a restaurant on the Garden State Parkway, and he saw a man sitting in a phone booth who resembled one he had seen at a distance at previous rendezvous sites. Lindberg watched as the man emerged from the booth and left the restaurant. Then he went into another booth to receive his call, which directed him to the booth in which the man had been sitting. There he found a small parcel taped under the shelf whose contents identified a new drop site.

In early May, however, the Russians decided the time had come to welcome Lindberg into the club face to face, in case a security breach threatened the current voice-only relationship. Perhaps they felt it was necessary to compromise Lindberg so that he would find it personally perilous, in that event, to tell what he knew.

Whatever the motive, "Jim" told Lindberg he had made arrangements for him to meet a Soviet agent in Helsinki on the last Sunday in June 1978. Lindberg would travel to the Finnish capital at Russian expense and rendezvous with the agent in a well-known cafe.

"Your contact will be carrying a copy of *Time* magazine,"

Lindberg was told. "He will ask you where the American film, *The Deep,* is playing. You will identify yourself to the man by responding that you don't know about *The Deep,* but that *Star Wars* is playing down the street."

The rendezvous was never consummated. On May 20, 1978, FBI agents arrested three Russians as they were attempting to retrieve a cache of secret United States military documents near a New Jersey shopping center. Charged with espionage were Valdik Enger, thirty-nine, assistant to the Under Secretary General of the United Nations; Rudolf Chernyayev, forty-three, a UN personnel officer; and Vladimir Zinyakin, thirty-nine, an attaché at the Soviet Mission to the United Nations.

Presumably to their surprise, the three Russians eventually learned that good old "Ed," their conscientious and efficient American recruit, was a double agent. Comdr. Arthur Lindberg had worked for the FBI and Naval Intelligence to dupe Soviet agents into a carefully baited trap by posing as a greedy traitor with top-secret information to sell. Every syllable of "intelligence" sold to the Russians was professionally manufactured by FBI experts in the black art of the bogus.

Diplomatic protocol and exigencies delayed the trial for several weeks. First, Zinyakin won his release on the grounds of diplomatic immunity, and he was promptly transferred home, where he was unlikely to be named the Soviet Union's "Spy of the Year." Then the State Department successfully petitioned that the judicial process go into a dawdle to prevent publicity United States officials felt could jeopardize talks between Secretary of State Cyrus Vance and Soviet Foreign Minister Andrei Gromyko. There was speculation that if Enger and Chernyayev were convicted the United States would try to arrange a swap for the release of one or more political prisoners in the Soviet Union.

Meanwhile, Justice Department officials explained what Lindberg had been doing on that Soviet cruise ship several months earlier. The FBI, it was learned, had discovered through intercepted cables decoded at the code-busting National Security Agency that the Russians were using their merchant marine to provide floating bases around the world for both spies and experts in the recruitment of foreign agents. Without divulging the circumstances under which Lindberg became a double agent, the sources said it was decided to place him on the cruise ship as a tourist to test the credibility of the intercepted communications. Both Lindberg and the FBI were surprised when his bald approach was instantly successful.

The trial finally opened in Newark, New Jersey, on September 30, 1978. During the next two weeks there unfolded the tale of a clever, cunning, and thorough FBI counterintelligence investigation, employing every trick and scientific device at the command of America's spy hunters.

Lindberg, the picture of a handsome, red-blooded American patriot in his dress uniform adorned with service ribbons, was the government's first witness. Of his first contact with the Russian agents, he said he had been assured that if he followed their directions spying would be "easy as ABC," and that he could make "dozens of thousands of dollars a year." In fact, he said, he was paid $20,000 for his efforts from August 1977 to May 1978.

During his testimony, given in a matter-of-fact tone, poster-size blowups of instruction notes he said he had received were shown to the jury by United States Attorney Robert Del Tufo. One of the notes advised Lindberg: "P.S., make necessary notes and destroy the letter. Best wishes." Another closed with an apology: "Please excuse my printing. I am not a typist." The jury giggled when Lindberg described one set of instructions which, he said, sent him on "a scavenger hunt through Essex County" and wound up at a drop site outside the Bloomfield Animal Shelter.

Then, in a dramatic courtroom confrontation, Lindberg stepped down from the witness stand, walked across the room, pointed his finger at Chernyayev, and identified him as the "mystery man" he had seen during one of a series of clandestine rendezvous. "This is the man I saw," Lindberg said, on the day he observed a stranger in the phone booth from which Lindberg later took a package of instructions from his Russian supervisors.

Chernyayev, portly, balding, and given to sudden grins, smiled broadly at Lindberg and then shook his head slowly as though expressing disbelief at what he had heard. Then he turned to Enger and lifted a sardonic eyebrow. Enger, slender, his hair carefully cut short, a master of the dour countenance, merely stared straight ahead, his demeanor that of a man determinedly divorcing himself from the proceedings.

Lindberg also told the jury that the FBI borrowed his car for a few days to turn it into a "souped-up" vehicle similar to those seen in movie spy thrillers. He said experts from the Bureau's Technical Services Division outfitted the car with hidden cameras in the front and rear that were triggered by control switches on the dashboard. He described a bizarre apparatus under the trunk that would automatically puncture a rear tire to cause a blowout when he pushed a button on the steering wheel. He said FBI technicians ripped out the rear seat of his car so an agent could "crunch down" and hide on the floorboards during one of the rendezvous.

Asked if he was recompensed for the damage to his car, Lindberg replied that in all the FBI paid him only $1950, plus mileage, for his adventures as a spy and that this payment was to cover his "time, inconvenience, and damage to my car." Clearly, the Bureau was operating on a budget whose funds were used for purposes other than fat paychecks for its amateur agent. The Russians, on the other hand, believed they were getting a bargain for the $20,000 they paid Lindberg for the "secrets" he delivered to them.

Other testimony revealed that FBI agents had bugged every telephone Lindberg used during his several months as a double agent. Listening devices were set up in the basements of restaurants along the Garden State Parkway and in the bedroom of a private home in the Fords section of Woodbridge. Lindberg identified the voices on the tape recordings as his own and that of the man with the thick foreign accent he knew only as "Jim."

The Feds also disclosed that the Garden State Parkway was the locale of a miles-long stakeout in which a dozen surveillance teams of counterintelligence agents were posted along the toll road on the lookout for the Soviet agents believed en route to a clandestine drop site. The stakeout was carried out on February 18, 1978, in broad daylight as thousands of motorists sped along in both directions.

FBI agents, outfitted with telephoto and videotape cameras, positioned their cars along the Essex and Union County sections of the turnpike, using two-way radios to maintain contact with a command post. Ironically, the operation was almost blown when a telephone company cleaning crew arrived at the scene of the drop site—a telephone booth near the Essex Toll Plaza—and began cleaning the phone booths. The crew left only minutes before the suspected spies drove up to the plaza.

Under questioning by Del Tufo, agents described how, as a light snow dusted the highways, they took up their posts in mid-morning. One agent, Daniel Newman, testified that he and other agents were concealed in a construction trailer parked at the site. Other agents told how teams monitored the movements of the suspects by shadowing their car during an intricate cat-and-mouse chase through East Orange until the Russians entered the toll road. Meanwhile, other agents kept watch over Lindberg, who was scheduled to receive a telephone contact call from the Russians at the Brookdale service area, a call that would tell him where the drop site was. Later, the agents saw one of the Russians enter a phone booth at the Essex Plaza. When he left the booth, agents found under the booth's shelf a magnetic case containing printed instructions for Lindberg.

The FBI even used that favorite of fictional espionage thrillers—a comely blonde counterspy—to watch the trio of suspects. The blonde, Special Agent Cheryl Disque, testified that she flitted about, ducking behind trees and peering around corners as she kept track of her quarry at a service area on the parkway, and watched as they conferred at a drop site. At one point, she said, she was walking across a parking lot when they suddenly appeared. She said she "innocently walked past them" as they gave her six appreciative eyes.

Agent David Von Holle told the jury he did surveillance of the suspects from a small private plane while other teams stalked the trio to the site of their eventual arrest on May 20. Later, the government released aerial photographs taken by Von Holle while the arrests were being made, and identified the three men in the photographs as Chernyayev, Enger, and Zinyakin. Television footage of a man identified as Zinyakin was taken by FBI Agent William Lynch while he was concealed in the trunk of an abandoned car, using a concealed observation peephole drilled in the car's body.

But the *pièce de résistance* of the government's case was a sound film produced by FBI agents during the top-secret espionage operation, which was identified as showing one of the accused

Soviet agents in actual negotiations with Commander Lindberg. The talkie was screened first outside the presence of the jury, because defense lawyers objected to its admissibility as evidence. Later, however, Judge Frederick Lacey of the United States District Court ruled that the jury could see the film.

FBI agents testified that the 12-minute, black-and-white film, made in a snowstorm during the February stakeout, was produced by the use of a sound synchronization system by which a videotape of one of the accused spies in an outdoor phone booth at the Essex Plaza on the edge of the Garden State Parkway was matched with a wiretap of the phone conversation recorded several miles away. The result, with both pictures and sound, was seen by the jurors on two TV monitors facing their box. The defendants, attorneys, and spectators saw the movie on seven other monitors in a hall outside the courtroom.

The film clearly showed Enger getting out of his gray Dodge sedan and walking over to and into a phone booth near the Newark exit. He was wearing a turtleneck sweater and a long leather jacket as he came into the view of FBI cameramen hidden in a construction trailer nearby. The jurors looked and listened intently as they saw Enger dial his call. A few seconds later he spoke into the phone. A voice said: "Did you get the stuff?" Then the sound track heard a voice giving the party on the other end of the line—Lindberg—directions to drive to the Essex Plaza to retrieve a magnetic box containing instructions.

"Just under the shelf, you'll see this small box," the voice was heard saying. Then the voice told Lindberg to "follow the instructions completely and you'll find everything there," while Enger was shown gesturing with one arm. Moments later, Enger hung up the receiver and his hand appeared below a shelf in the glass booth. After Enger departed, the tape showed Lindberg driving up to the booth and retrieving the box.

It came as no surprise to reporters covering the trial when defense attorneys announced that neither Chernyayev nor Enger would take the witness stand. The media had been briefed, as it were, by frequent, sorrowful references to the claim that neither defendant could speak or understand more than a few simple words of English, and of course the testimony had been relayed to the defendants by interpreters. During the trial, however, one reporter claimed to have had a brief conversation with Chernyayev in English.

No matter. The attorney for the defense, James Matthew Boylan, was content to sum up his clients' predicament as the product of a massive "frameup" by the FBI and the prosecution. He pictured Commander Lindberg as a disgruntled sailor who had simmered for eleven long years as a supply officer and never got a promotion. Lindberg, he said, sought to fashion for himself the role of a hero deserving of advancement. Boylan claimed that Lindberg had been promised a "reward" if the Russians were convicted, a charge denied by both Lindberg and the prosecution. So the issue was passed on to the antagonists' peers in the jury box.

Apparently, the talking movie clinched an already strong government case, made on earlier testimony by Lindberg and by agents of the FBI's surveillance teams. In any case, both Chernyayev and Enger were found guilty a few days later by the jury of eight men and four women after more than nine hours of deliberation. In a dramatic and unusual action, Judge Lacey announced after hearing the verdict that "I have never presided at a case where the evidence was so overwhelming. . . . The evidence of what the defendants were out to do to this nation was beyond the ability of anyone to refute." He said the evidence proved that the defendants "would destroy this country if they could do so," but added, "they were outsmarted from the beginning by the brilliance of the counterintelligence arm of the Federal Bureau of Investigation."

On October 31, 1978, Judge Lacey sentenced each of the Russian defendants to 50 years in prison, branding the case "shocking in its revelations." He also rebuked the United Nations Secretariat, demanding that that body "thoroughly screen the background of each and every person employed by the UN to ensure they were not active in espionage operations." The United Nations, he said, should take steps to see that "innocuous UN workers are not in fact a reservoir of espionage agents . . . waiting to be called upon for spy duties."

At the same time, however, Lacey agreed to the urgings of officials of the State Department that Chernyayev and Enger be placed in the custody of Soviet Ambassador Anatoly Dobrynin pending appeal of their convictions. He ordered the defendants to be confined to a 10-square-block area of The Bronx, where the Soviet government maintains a high-rise residential complex for the 600 Soviet citizens employed at the UN and at the Soviet Mission to the international peace organization.

The prosecution's chief, Del Tufo, went along. He said "the highest officials in our government" had decided it would be in the best interests of American foreign policy to allow the spies to go free in Russian custody. However, Del Tufo held to a statement he had made earlier that Judge Lacey should impose "substantial" custodial sentences on the defendants, whom he described as only part of a "comprehensive espionage system operating in this country."

As to a swap of Chernyayev and Enger for any imprisoned Soviet dissidents, the State Department reiterated its previous line that talk of such a trade was purely speculative. One Foggy Bottom official, however, noted that Chernyayev and Enger "are the only ones we've got" if a swap were to be negotiated.

In Moscow, the reaction was predictable. Dmitri Morozov, a commentator for the government television network, denounced the sentences as "monstrous" and demanded that Chernyayev and Enger be repatriated immediately. Seated beside him on the news show *Vremya* (Time) was Vladimir Zinyakin, the Third Man of the espionage trio, who had been released because he had diplomatic immunity Zinyakin dismissed the FBI agents in the case as "gangsters."

Six months later came verification from Moscow that the FBI-Lindberg team had indeed made a big catch. On April 27, 1979, the Soviet swapped five of its most prominent dissidents, including human rights activist Alexander Ginzburg, in exchange for the release of Chernyayev and Enger. All five arrived at Kennedy International Airport in New York on a regularly scheduled flight of Aeroflot, the Soviet national airline. Two hours later, the same aircraft took off on its return flight to Moscow with Chernyayev and Enger as passengers.

Ginzburg, a writer, editor, and close friend of Alexander Solzhenitsyn, a Nobel Prize winner, was well known in the United States. He was a founder of a dissident group established to monitor Soviet compliance with the Helsinki human rights agreement, and had been in and out of Soviet prisons since the early 1960s.

The other four dissidents released included Mark Dymshits, a pilot sentenced to death by firing squad in 1970 for plotting with others to hijack a plane from Latvia to Sweden. His sentence was commuted to 15 years' hard labor after worldwide protests. Others freed were Edward Kuznetsov, a member of the Union for Intellectual Freedom; Valentin Moroz, a Ukrainian historian who had spent most of his life in prison since 1965; and Georgi Vins, a Baptist leader in the Ukraine, who was serving five years in a labor camp on charges of "defaming the Soviet state."

Lindberg, who retired from the Navy in November 1978, got his military reward a couple of weeks later when he received the Legion of Merit at ceremonies at Lakehurst's Navy Air Engineering Center. The medal, for "exceptionally meritorious conduct in the performance of outstanding service," is the Navy's fifth-ranking decoration. The former lieutenant commander also received a more personal expression of gratitude.

Lindberg and the dissident Moroz were honored at commencement exercises at Upsala College in East Orange, New Jersey, on May 25. Before the ceremony, Lindberg was embraced by Moroz, whose eyes filled with tears as he murmured his thanks to the man whose cloak-and-dagger efforts had effected his release from prison. Moroz, himself a former double agent, had something to say about the often deplored espionage trade. Speaking through an interpreter, he declared that "as a spy, Mr. Lindberg has one of the most important professions in the world. It is easy to criticize Marxism, but it is difficult to catch Marxist spies."

II

In early 1979, veteran Russian watchers in the FBI estimated that 40 percent of the Soviet Union's diplomatic personnel at the Soviet Embassy in Washington and at the Russian delegation to the United Nations in New York were agents of the KGB. The KGB's official name is the Soviet Committee for State Security, and at home and abroad it performs those functions delegated in the United States to the FBI and the Central Intelligence Agency.

KGB agents in America spend most of their time engaged in legal activities. They cover congressional hearings and collect government reports and published matter on a variety of subjects. On a higher level, their function is similar to that of American lobbyists—peddling the Soviet position on diplomatic and strategic issues. As many as 20 of them are regularly assigned to Capitol Hill. But they keep the cloak and dagger handy.

Using their cover as diplomats and journalists, these spies have always tried to get classified information on The Hill by bribing or compromising congressional staff members. So far as is known, they have made no efforts to suborn a senator or a member of the House. That would be too clumsy. Besides, they know that what a congressman or senator knows is also usually known to his staff.

Thus it was not surprising that the Soviet Union was let off lightly in August 1979 when a secret Senate report on foreign espionage charged that such activities included the harassment of critics in the United States, in most cases émigrés from the countries indicted in the report. The Senate study blistered intelligence agents from Iran, the Philippines, Taiwan, Chile, and Yugoslavia, but concluded that the Russians concentrated almost entirely on classic espionage efforts. Methods used by the other governments, the report said, ranged from the sending of "hit teams" from Iran and Chile to the United States to the monitoring of political discussions by students enrolled in American colleges who were nationals of the countries involved. The report cited Iran's intelligence agency, SAVAK (disbanded after the Shah's government fell in February 1979), and Taiwan's National Security Bureau as the worst offenders. Both spy shops were accused of setting up case officers with diplomatic covers who ran "hundreds" of agents under instructions to infiltrate campus life and student organizations across the country. Yugoslav agents were suspected of complicity in the unsolved murder of a Serbian émigré in Chicago. But Moscow continued to concentrate its espionage efforts on recruiting people inside the American government, especially from the ranks of ingenuous youth with an innocent curiosity about the Russian way of life.

James Kappus was interested in learning all he could about the Soviet Union when he joined the staff of Representative Alvin

O'Konski of Wisconsin in 1967. A raw twenty-year-old just out of Eau Claire, Wisconsin, Kappus enrolled as a night student at George Washington University, concentrating in the area of Russian studies. To his delight, he soon found himself invited with other students to parties at the Soviet Embassy. He saw such socializing as an excellent opportunity to develop friendly relationships with Russian diplomats and thus further his studies.

At one of those parties, Kappus met a man of considerable charm and a good command of the English language named Boris Sedov, Second Secretary of the Embassy. He found that he and Sedov had much in common and that the Russian seemed genuinely interested in helping him learn more about the Soviet Union. They began to see a lot of each other, and eventually Sedov engaged Kappus to research and write articles about United States policies and military equipment for *Novosti,* an internal Russian news agency, on a paid basis. Kappus jumped at the assignment; as a very junior member of O'Konski's staff, he was making little more than walking-around money. His first article was about the presidential candidates for the 1968 election, for which he was paid $20. But Sedov told him future payments would be much bigger.

FBI agents can't be everywhere, but it sometimes seems their tipsters are. So it was not surprising that the Bureau should learn of Kappus's friendship with Sedov. The FBI was alarmed; it knew Sedov as an experienced and aggressive KGB agent specializing in political intelligence matters.

A couple of agents went up to The Hill for a little chat with O'Konski. The Congressman, after recovering his cool, vouched for Kappus's patriotism and loyalty. "Jim is a fine young man," he said. But O'Konski was a member of the House Armed Services Committee and of two subcommittees overseeing operations of the CIA and American development of nuclear submarines. He admitted the situation was sensitive.

The agents had a solution: Did O'Konski think Kappus would be willing to continue his relationship with Sedov in the role of an FBI double agent? O'Konski was sure he would. "He's a bright kid, and an honest kid," the Congressman told his interviewers.

So the agents interviewed Kappus. He told them he had no idea that Sedov was a spy. "Boris is so charming, it's hard to believe," he said. No doubt, said the agents, but they had information that Sedov had boasted to his colleagues about recruiting one of O'Konski's aides. That was enough for Kappus. He signed on then and there to lend a hand to the Bureau in a controlled operation against Sedov. Any information he gave to Sedov would be carefully prepared by the Bureau; it would be phony information, but not so phony as to arouse Sedov's suspicions.

Kappus continued his meetings with Sedov. The meetings were always on an informal basis, in the context of two friends talking, but as time passed Sedov made it clear to Kappus that he was to include "inside" information in his articles, using his access to committee documents.

Sedov wanted Kappus to write articles about the development of the General Dynamics F16 fighter plane for which four NATO countries had placed orders. He wanted information on the production of the United States Multiple Independently Targeted Reentry Vehicle (MIRV), a nuclear missile capable of hitting several targets with one firing. The FBI provided Kappus with carefully misleading material on both subjects. Similar information was used by Kappus to write pieces on the progress being made toward an all-volunteer United States Army, and the government's policies toward Vietnam, China, and Berlin.

The FBI was interested in knowing what subjects Sedov and the KGB were trying to learn more about, what his attitudes were at given times, and what his movements in Washington might mean when considered in light of other KGB activities.

Meanwhile, as the months passed, Sedov became more demanding. He kept asking Kappus about his opportunities to inspect Armed Services Committee documents. Could he steal those documents? Could he photocopy them? Kappus stalled Sedov as best he could while continuing to feed him FBI pablum for which he was paid from $100 to $600 an article.

The $600 payment was passed to Kappus by Sedov under a stairwell of the Old Senate Office Building in November 1969. When Sedov set the meeting place, both the FBI and Kappus realized the Russian was seeking to compromise Kappus beyond rescue. After all, a payoff from a Russian agent in a government building, probably photographed, was strong stuff. But Kappus went through with it, as a couple of FBI men lurked nearby.

Sedov didn't talk about the compromising incident, and neither did Kappus. But Sedov applied more pressure to the young man from Eau Claire. He wanted to know where O'Konski kept classified documents. Why couldn't Kappus get at them? When Kappus stalled, Sedov told him: "You know, I helped you out when things were tough. You don't want O'Konski to learn about that, do you?"

By that time, although Kappus didn't know it, he was about to be relieved of his double-agent assignment. In mid-1970, after three years of kidding Sedov along, Kappus was called up by the Army. He and Sedov had one last meeting, at which Sedov said he would arrange an elaborate system whereby another Soviet agent could contact Kappus whenever he was on leave from the military. But Sedov himself returned to the Soviet Union shortly after Kappus left his Capitol Hill job, and no further contacts were made.

Kappus felt as though someone had saved his life. Throughout his association with Sedov, he had feared that his name might be publicly linked to Soviet espionage activities, and because of the ongoing nature of FBI counterintelligence operations, he would not be in a position to defend himself. He had nightmares that public disclosures had destroyed O'Konski's reputation. To Kappus, that would have been the ball game. But he had done his job. Thanks to him, a Soviet agent had been neutralized without the exposure—by criminal trial or otherwise—that would have told Sedov's bosses that the Kappus stuff was cleverly disguised fiction.

O'Konski retired in 1973 and wound up as owner of a television station in Rhinelander, Wisconsin. But the Kappus-Sedov case was classified until the summer of 1975, when it became one of the subjects of discussion at closed congressional hearings.

Those hearings finally produced a furor in the fall of 1975, when Senator Barry Goldwater, Republican of Arizona, claimed that the Rockefeller Commission charged with investigating the CIA had information that Congress had been infiltrated by Soviet agents. The commission denied Goldwater's allegations, but 52 members of Congress signed a letter to Democratic Senator Frank Church of Idaho, Chairman of the Senate Select Committee on Intelligence Activities, to look into the charges.

Preoccupied with his own investigation of American intelligence operations, Church passed the buck to the FBI. Two days after FBI Director Clarence Kelley received Church's request, he issued a report confirming that the KGB had indeed tried to reach people who could provide sensitive information, but that there was no information that "Soviet KGB officers have infiltrated any congressional staffs." However, Kelley did tell Church about cases in which the FBI had converted into double agents some KGB congressional contacts.

Church ignored the contradiction in Kelley's report. He was content to announce that the allegations about Soviet spying had been "put to rest." His committee never even got around to discussing the Russian electronic bug that fell out of the stuffing of a chair in the House Foreign Affairs Committee room in 1973.

By that time, James Kappus—whose credentials as a double agent were impeccable—was working as a consultant to a printing firm, a tense three years of his life happily behind him.

THE
UNFRIENDLY
SKIES

6

A Bomb for Mrs. Cook

The young boy helping his father in an Arizona rock salt mine dreamt not of Thermopylae, nor of the embattled rebels at Concord's rude bridge, but of the day when he could arrange the dynamite and the detonating caps and set off his own explosion.

As usual, the crowds at Chicago's O'Hare International Airport moved with the seemingly aimless bustle of ants on that crisp morning of November 12, 1967. The man had driven his slender, attractive wife to the airport from their home in Naperville, Illinois. Now he checked in her luggage and returned to give her the baggage claim checks on her ticket. He remained with her, arm around her waist, then kissed her goodbye when her flight was called.

Later, as the American Airlines plane, bound for San Diego, was over Lamar, Colorado, the pilot heard a muffled report and felt a slight jolt. The noise was different from anything Capt. Dwain C. Duncan had heard in his 24 years of experience. He noticed a slight change in the temperature and pressure of the baggage compartment. However, the big jetliner continued its smooth flight. Duncan decided that a shift in the baggage had caused a suitcase or two to become dislodged and bang against the bulkhead. That would account for the jolt and probably explain the slight change in temperature and pressurization.

Duncan and other members of the flight crew checked the controls. Everything was in order. Duncan got on the intercom and assured the 76 passengers that "everything is all right. Apparently we encountered a bump in the air." ("Always explain in simple, nontechnical language," said the book.)

The jetliner flew on to San Diego. But when an airline crew opened the door of the baggage compartment the men smelled what seemed to be gunpowder fumes and found scattered debris and damaged luggage. Obviously, there had been a small explosion.

The unloading was delayed while a call was put in to the San Diego field office of the FBI. Special Agent Robert Sundquist was first on the scene. Among the debris he found a six-volt battery of the type used in large camping lanterns, four exploded detonator caps, two sticks of dynamite, two alarm clocks with wiring attached, the remains of a white vinyl suitcase, and three loose baggage claim straps.

A gaggle of FBI agents now arrived at the airport. While the evidence was being collected and boxed for shipment to the FBI laboratory in Washington, they interviewed each of the passengers and six members of the crew. The bombing, it seemed clear, had been an attempt at either suicide or murder.

Sundquist checked the three loose baggage claim straps. He found that two of them belonged to the luggage of a passenger, a Mrs. Cook. The number on the third claim strap was one above the number on one of Mrs. Cook's bags. Moreover, that claim strap had been checked in on Mrs. Cook's ticket.

A chat with Mrs. Cook was clearly indicated. One of the passengers said she had told him she was going to San Diego en route to her parents' home in El Cajon, a suburb, to recuperate after a long illness. Agents found her chatting in the living room with her mother and father, Mr. and Mrs. W. J. Warfield.

Jeanne Elizabeth Cook, thirty-five, seemed fatigued but in control of herself. She told them the Cooks had two sons and said she had just talked to them and her husband by telephone to assure them that "I'm safe and sound."

The agents got to the point after some soothing niceties. What, they asked, did she know about a white vinyl suitcase?

"Why, nothing," she replied, surprised by the question. "I don't own such a suitcase, just two tan bags. I have them here."

But the white suitcase was checked in on her ticket, she was told.

"Impossible," she said, her eyes wide. "My husband checked in my luggage, just the two tan bags. It took him the longest time. Thank God he only had two pieces, or it would have taken him forever.''

Of course, the white suitcase might have been checked in without her knowledge, her questioners suggested.

The agents pushed on.

"And is your marriage a happy one?'' she was asked.

"Earle and I love each other very much,'' she replied.

Conciliating the moment, an agent told her the question was just routine.

Earle Theodore Cook, a stocky, aggressive man with a crew cut and horn-rimmed glasses, was interviewed the next day in Naperville. He identified himself, rather proudly, as the manager of a Coca-Cola bottling plant in St. Charles, Illinois.

This time, agents from the Chicago field office wasted no time on niceties. They hit Cook almost at once with a question about the white suitcase.

"A white suitcase?'' asked Cook. "What's this about a white suitcase? I don't know anything about any old beat-up white suitcase. I checked in two bags for my wife. Period.''

"It took you a long time,'' he was told. "And the claim strap shows the suitcase was checked in on your wife's ticket. Don't you want to talk to us about it?''

"No I don't,'' Cook replied. "Ask my wife. She'll tell you I checked in only two bags.''

"Yes,'' he was told, "but perhaps you hadn't told your wife about the third piece of luggage.''

Cook was red-faced with anger. "I don't know where you got your crazy information,'' he said, not shouting. "I'm a respectable and well-to-do businessman. I love my wife to distraction. I'd die if anything happened to her.'' He took out a handkerchief and wiped his eyes.

Again the conciliators, the agents assured him it was their duty to talk to a lot of people in investigating a case of attempted murder, and that they had no intention of accusing him of any crime. Cook seemed mollified; he invited his inquisitors to "drop in and see my plant. It's a marvel of technology and production know-how.''

The agents thanked him and departed to look into the background of this "respectable and well-to-do businessman.''

In Washington, meanwhile, pieces of the crudely made time bomb found aboard the airliner were examined by Charles L. Killion, an FBI explosives and tool expert. Killion worked with the two small alarm clocks and found that when one of them went off, the hammer hitting the bell completed a circuit, causing the four electric blasting caps to detonate. The second alarm clock, he concluded, was used as a backstop should the first clock fail. He reassembled the bomb, connecting the wiring to the various components to form a complete electrical circuit.

The four expended blasting caps showed that the device worked, but only partially. The dynamite hadn't been detonated because the blasting caps had been clumsily imbedded in the dynamite and had become detached. Score one, thought Killion, for those airport handlers who knock baggage around; their rough stuff probably saved 80 lives.

Killion was positive about those endangered 80 lives. Because fuel lines and control wiring were immediately above the baggage compartment, the larger explosion almost surely would have started a fire and caused the jetliner to crash. "There would have been extensive damage caused to the baggage compartment and to any equipment that might be in the area," Killion wrote in his report. Thank God, he thought, that the bomb was the work of a clumsy amateur.

In the Chicago area and elsewhere, FBI men continued their investigation of the Cooks' background. The couple had previously lived in Houston. So the Houston office was ordered to look into its files, just in case. Houston hit paydirt.

In 1964, it was found, one George Cliff, a professional gambler in Hot Springs, Arkansas, had reported to the FBI that Cook had offered him $5000 to murder Mrs. Cook. Cliff gave the tip to Agent Robert Hickam, who had done business with Cliff as a paid informant on several previous occasions. Hickam remembered that he gave Cliff $200 for the information. "He's pretty reliable," Hickam reported. "I've never known him to sell me phony merchandise." But the tip officially was none of the FBI's business, so it was routinely passed on to the Houston Police Department. That department had been unable to come up with any hard evidence to verify a piece of hearsay.

Now, however, changed circumstances had put Cliff's information in the context of a federal crime. They cried out for another look-see at the gambler's allegation that Earle Cook, four years before, had been a would-be murderer by proxy.

Agent Hickam flew to Hot Springs that night and located his man the next morning in a gambling club. George Cliff, then seventy-two, was a frail and wizened man who had "worked around" gambling houses in Hot Springs, Reno, and Las Vegas since 1935. He was also loquacious, virtually bursting with information.

"Sure, as I told you before, I met Cook in the Citizens Club right here in Hot Springs in November of 1963," he told Hickam. "I was posing at the time as a private dick. We got to talking and Cook told me he was looking for some jasper like me to go to Houston and get some evidence on his wife. He said his wife was making the rounds with other men and he wanted a divorce.

"Well, what the hell, I was a working man so I told him okay, I'd do the job for him. Well, after we talked a while he gave me $250 in cash to go to Houston. I met him again in Houston five days later and he told me he'd changed his mind, he didn't want a divorce after all because his company wouldn't approve. So he said he wanted somebody to kill his wife."

Cliff paused to cough self-consciously. "Well hell," he told the agent, "I didn't never kill anybody. I might take a little advantage of a mark, but killing's out of my line. So I told him I'd send to St. Louis for a man and get the job done. Cook, he told me he wanted me to make it look like an auto accident. I told him it would take money to get the St. Louis man, and he gave me $1250. That appeared to me to be kind of cheap for a killing."

"What did you do with the money?" Hickam asked.

"I put it in my pocket—what else?"

"Then what happened?"

"Cook, he promised me half of his wife's $10,000 life insurance after she was gone."

"Then what happened?"

"Well, there was nothing I could do but stall Cook, while I tried to figure out what to do," Cliff replied.

"And what did you do?"

"You know, I went to the FBI in January nineteen-and-sixty-four. I got in touch with them right here in Hot Springs and told them all about it. I don't go for killing. I even gave the FBI a picture of Cook's wife that he had given me. He gave me the picture so no mistake would be made in the assassination. He wanted to make sure the right woman would be killed.

"I guess the FBI tipped off the Houston police all right, because a couple of months later Cook came back to Hot Springs and told me the Houston cops pulled him in to ask him about wanting to kill his wife. He said he laughed at them. Said the cops didn't have any evidence except for what somebody had told the FBI, so they had to let him go. Anyway, he said, his wife was still alive."

Cliff said he figured that ended it. "I'd have given up after a scare like that," he said. "But by God he was back in Hot Springs in the summertime. Flew here in his own plane. Well, he wanted me to go to El Cajon, California, and kill his wife with a rifle while she was staying with her folks there."

By this time, Cliff apparently feared he'd be next on Cook's hit list if he had anything more to do with the plot. Anyway, he said, "I told him I'd go. A couple of days later I called him and told him I'd gone out there but the neighborhood was too lousy with cops. I never left town, of course."

Cliff said that a few weeks later Cook showed up in Hot Springs again and suggested that perhaps Cliff could arrange "to get his wife drowned." And at a subsequent meeting, Cliff said Cook told him he had rigged up a bomb with a flashlight battery, and all he needed was some dynamite.

"Cook, he said he'd fix it so his wife would take a plane from Chicago to San Diego and he wanted me to carry the bomb in a suitcase and get on the plane at Chicago and have the suitcase put with the luggage and then I'd get off in Phoenix and the bomb would go off on the way to San Diego and kill his wife.

"Hell, I told him the plane would be loaded with people, but that didn't faze him. He told me, 'That's their trouble, not mine.' "

Cliff said he asked Cook again why he didn't get a divorce. "That's safer, I told him. But he said no, he wanted his wife dead. He said he was a big shot for Coca-Cola and the company would fire him if he got a divorce. He said an accident would be better. Well, I said I'd try to find him some dynamite, but I didn't. Screw that, with all those people on some goddam plane."

But Cliff didn't let go of a good thing. He admitted he saw Cook a few times after that, perhaps as many as eight times, and "got some dough out of him every time." He said during his last conversation with Cook, "I told him I had a couple of men just out of the Mississippi pen, but they needed expense money to get to Illinois. He wired me $150."

"Did you get in touch with the men?" he was asked.

Cliff laughed. "There wasn't any such men," he replied.

En route back to Houston, the talk was about Cliff's credibility. The agents agreed that Cliff's story had a ring of truth. It sounded good. But, as somebody remarked, it sounded *too* good. After all, Cliff was not a candidate for Scoutmaster of the Year.

Back in the Chicago suburbs, other FBI agents interviewed neighbors of the Cooks in Naperville. They found that the Cooks kept pretty much to themselves and seemed devoted to their two sons; no one seemed aware of any family discord.

"It's funny, though," said one housewife. "Their house isn't really much and they have a beat-up old car, but Mr. Cook has a lovely airplane, a four-seater. I hear it cost $18,000. And Mrs. Cook used to teach at elementary school until she went into the hospital in August. She had some kind of an intestinal operation and didn't come home until the last week of October. She was flying to California to recuperate with her parents. Her father's a retired lieutenant colonel in the Air Force. She's a nice woman, and he's very polite but he doesn't mix much. Quiet. Always thinking, kind of."

At the Coca-Cola plant in St. Charles, employes described Cook as pleasant but standoffish. One worker told the agents: "Cook is polite. He never said anything out of the way to me. Some of us gave blood to his wife when she was in the hospital, although we'd never met her. I think Cook is one of those men who has a really big future."

Meanwhile, other investigators were occupied in checking on the Cooks' insurance programs. They checked and found that Cook would have collected $117,500 if his wife had been killed in an airplane accident. And insurance companies told the FBI that $77,500 of the insurance on Mrs. Cook's life had been bought or renewed since September 1966. A $40,000 Shell Oil policy went into effect on November 1, less than two weeks before the attempted bombing.

The same day, a visit by FBI agents to the airport where Cook kept his Mooney four-seated plane caused the investigators to wonder whether what they called a "love triangle" figured in the alleged bombing plot. A supervisor at the airport had told them that "an attractive woman," not Mrs. Cook, frequently accompanied Cook on his holiday flights to various cities.

No one was found who could identify the mystery woman. "Cook didn't introduce her around," the supervisor said with a man-of-the-world wink. But other airport employes and pilots, as if to explain Cook's alleged philandering, said Cook frequently complained about his wife's poor health and the financial burden of her medical bills. The reaction of neighbors was that Cook was too nice a man to cheat on his wife. At Washington FBI headquarters, Assistant Director Catha B. ("Deke") Deloach commented: "I've known an awful lot of nice guys who cheated on their wives."

In any case, a second interview with Cook was strongly indicated. Cross-country interviews had produced at least two possible motives that could have caused Cook to try to murder his wife: (1) He didn't get along with her. (2) He was the beneficiary of hefty insurance policies on her life. And as agents were discussing the "mystery woman," two skycaps at Chicago's O'Hare Airport reported that they had checked in three pieces of luggage on the day of the bombing for a man they identified from a photograph as Earle Cook. One of the pieces was the white vinyl suitcase Earle Cook had earlier denied knowing anything about.

Cook arrived for the interview in an impatient, ill-natured mood. "Why don't you find out who tried to kill all those people, instead of bothering me again?" he asked Agent Thomas W. Parrish. "I've told you all I know. You should be quizzing people with criminal records."

"We've found out you didn't tell us all you know," Parrish replied. "For instance, you didn't tell us about a man named George Cliff."

"Cliff?" Cook said. "What about Cliff? The only George Cliff I know is a senile old gambler in Hot Springs, Arkansas. He's a sleazy old confidence man."

"That's the Cliff I mean," Parrish said. "You didn't tell us you asked him to murder your wife back in 1963 and '64."

"Murder my wife! You must be off your rocker," said Cook, his jaw jutting, his crew cut seeming to bristle. "That guy—well, I may as well admit I asked him to check up on my wife because I thought she was cheating on me. He was doing some detective work at the time."

"You told us you and your wife got along fine," said Parrish.

"Yeah, sure I did. I wasn't going to wash any dirty linen in public. That didn't have anything to do with anything. Besides, I paid him in advance and he didn't give me a syllable of evidence."

"We found out that you tried to get Cliff to arrange an accident to kill your wife."

"That's a goddam lie!" Cook's face was red now. "George Cliff is a goddam liar if he says that. And to think I gave him $800 to help start a floating crap game in Houston! The bastard."

"You gave Cliff money to kill your wife because you were tired of her and you were playing around with other women, and your wife was heavily insured," Parrish told him.

"I did like hell," said Cook. "All I wanted was a divorce. We had what you might call marital difficulties, mostly over how to discipline our fifteen-year-old son, because I'm a hardheaded German." He paused. Then, "You guys certainly did your homework."

"Thanks," Parrish said. "Part of that homework was having a little talk with a friend of yours, Anthony Chronis."

"Chronis?" said Cook. "He was an acquaintance. Not a very nice guy."

"But you asked Chronis to put up $10,000 to find someone to kill your wife and told him he'd make a profit of $15,000 out of her $25,000 insurance policy which names you as beneficiary," Parrish told him.

"Goddammit, that's another lie." Now Cook was shouting. "I never did any such thing. What happened was that we were both having trouble at home, and Chronis told me he'd like to do away with his wife. I told him that was a bad joke in very poor taste. I never told anybody I wanted my wife killed."

"Well, two people said you asked them to kill your wife," Parrish said.

"Well, two people are goddam liars! They're both liars by trade!" Cook shouted.

Parrish asked quietly: "Did you ever handle a stick of dynamite?"

"What's that got to do with anything?" asked Cook. "Oh well, sure I did, when I was a boy helping my father in his rock salt mine. As a boy I was always fascinated by dynamite—but not to kill anybody with. You're barking up the wrong tree. I love my wife."

That was on November 17, 1967. A few hours later, an Assistant United States Attorney in Chicago authorized prosecution of Earle Theodore Cook. Cook was arrested and a warrant was obtained for a search of his residence.

While Cook spent two days in the Cook County Jail awaiting arraignment on a charge of placing a bomb aboard an airplane, "with intent to damage, destroy, disable, or wreck" it, FBI agents spent long hours searching the Cook ranch house. Among other items, they collected a vise and wiring found in Cook's basement workshop. These and other tools, equipment, and materials were flown to the FBI laboratory in Washington.

Agents Charles Killion and John F. Gallagher were waiting in the lab. They went to work comparing what Killion called "the goodies from Naperville" with those parts of the bomb salvaged from the airliner.

Killion, the explosives and tool expert, used painstaking microscopic examinations to discover that the bell on an alarm clock used to trigger blasting caps that were supposed to set off the bomb bore markings made by the steel jaws of Cook's vise.

Gallagher checked and rechecked spectographic analyses of wiring found among the debris in the battered baggage compartment of the plane. He concluded that the wiring found in the baggage compartment was identical to the wiring taken from the Cook home.

Later, Killion found that letters and numerals found on clamps around wires in the bomb had been made by the same die as letters and numerals found on clamps in Cook's basement.

Finally, there was a key found by Agent Robert Rosin on a ring in the company car driven by Cook. The key bore the trademark "Cheney, England," the same marking found on the lock of the damaged white suitcase in which the bomb had been carried. "Naturally," as Gallagher put it, "the key fitted the lock."

On the opening day of Cook's trial, in late January 1968, spectators, jury, judge, and the prosecutor were surprised to see Earle and Jeanne Elizabeth Cook embracing in the courtroom. Assistant United States Attorney Richard Schultz complained to Judge Richard B. Austin of "these ridiculous scenes" between the couple. Judge Austin agreed that the conduct was improper in that it would influence the jurors, but the issue became moot when the wife was excluded from the courtroom on the legal ground that she would be a witness for the defense.

Throughout the trial, however, Mrs. Cook sat knitting in the corridor outside and telling anyone who would listen that she loved her husband and that she was convinced of his innocence. "You love your husband very much, don't you?" asked Schultz in one exchange after a court session. "Of course I do," Mrs. Cook replied. "I have every reason to." And, with Cook free on $100,000 bond, the couple left for home every night, arm in arm.

Mrs. Cook's appearance in the witness chair was easily the sensation of the trial. Although one prosecution witness after another had testified that on several occasions her husband had plotted to murder her, she steadfastly maintained that he was innocent—a loving husband persecuted because people had lied about him.

Her eyes brimming with tears, she told the court Earle Cook "has always been a good and kind man. He has always been a wonderful husband." She testified that she and Cook were separated only once during 17 years of marriage and that "during this separation he helped set up a family budget because he was concerned that I would be unable to care for myself and my two boys."

She recalled that she had suffered from a "serious disease that was completely cured due to my husband's persistence in getting the best medical advice he could for me."

"Did your husband ever abuse or manhandle you?" asked the defense counsel, Ralph Brown.

"No," she replied, "he has always been good and kind to me."

"Did he ever threaten you?"

"No, he never did. I knew he wouldn't."

"Did he ever commit any acts that would lead you to believe he would threaten your life?"

"No, he wouldn't. I know he never would."

But Jeanne Elizabeth Cook's loyalty to and affection for her husband didn't save him. On February 5, 1968, after deliberating only three and a half hours, the jury of seven men and five women found Earle T. Cook guilty of trying to blow up a jetliner on which his wife was a passenger.

Judge Austin immediately sentenced Cook to two concurrent prison sentences of 20 years each, without the usual presentencing investigation. He revoked Cook's bond and remanded him to jail. "I do this not only for his wife's protection, but for all the people of the community," the judge explained. "He has sacrificed the right to remain at large. The only reason he wasn't a mass murderer was due to something over which he had no control."

Austin noted that there had been evidence of malice for four years before the crime. He explained that an element of murder, as defined by Blackstone, the celebrated legal authority, "is that it is committed with a wicked, depraved, and abandoned heart."

Mrs. Cook stood by her husband to the end. As he was addressing the court, she left her seat and joined him in front of the bench. She listened as Cook said he'd been tried under a system he believed in. Then, as he added, "The only thing I feel sorry about is that I am innocent," the woman who almost died in a bomb-caused airplane crash put a hand on his shoulder. No one could hear what she said, but her manner was that of a mother soothing a child.

7

Family Man on a 727

As the plane zigzagged, he jettisoned the chutes one by one to confound FBI agents hoping to track him through electronic beeper devices they had concealed in the lining of the chutes' bags. He rigged the suitcases containing the ransom to a special cargo harness. Then he donned his own sport chute and walked down the stairway into the sky.

Shortly after nine o'clock on the morning of August 10, 1974, the situation was normal at the Lewisburg Federal Penitentiary in Lewisburg, Pennsylvania. Several hundred prisoners were taking the hot and humid air in an outdoor recreation area, which was in fact a huge cage. Outside the gate, a guard and an inmate chatted in the cab of a trash truck the inmate had just driven into the security area.

Then occurred the impossible that prison wardens have learned can be achieved when chance is seized by the forelock and fate fashions it into good luck. Suddenly, in plain sight of dozens of guards and assorted other prison overseers, four men scaled a chain link fence eight feet high and dropped into the security stockade. They held knives on the guard and inmate in the truck, ordered them out as unwilling shields, then jumped into the truck and crashed through a fence to the outside.

There was a fusillade of fire from guards everywhere, but not a bullet struck the truck as it roared onto an access road and disappeared.

Forty-five minutes later, the four men abandoned the truck in the small town of Forest Hill, 10 miles from the penitentiary, and broke into a private home. They tied up a visiting Philadelphia couple and two other women. The fugitives then stole a 1970 blue-and-green Ford sedan and drove off into the central Pennsylvania hill country.

Three of the men—Joseph Havel, sixty; Larry Bagley, thirty-six; and Melvin Walker, thirty-five—were relative nonentities serving prison terms for bank robbery. But the fourth was a celebrity in the secret places of crime. His name was Richard F. McCoy, Jr., thirty-one, who on April 7, 1972, had skyjacked a United Airlines 727 jetliner en route from Denver to Los Angeles and then bailed out over Utah with $500,000 in ransom money. Apprehended two days later in the Utah city of Provo, McCoy was eventually sentenced to 45 years in prison for air piracy. Now he was on the loose, carrying the fugitives' only firearm.

Back in the spring of 1972, Richard McCoy was hardly the skyjacker type. He was a devout Mormon, a quiet family man, father of a young daughter and son, and a sport parachutist. He was a Sunday school teacher who had served two hitches in Vietnam as a pilot and demolition expert, and had won both the Army Commendation Medal and the Distinguished Flying Cross. He was a conscientious warrant officer in the Utah National Guard.

But McCoy had tasted dangerous high adventure with the Green Berets in Vietnam, and within his private self he wanted more of the same. Sport parachuting was fun, but it was too tame; it had no grand objective. He wanted to do something sensational, something that would show "them" that he could do something really big. A classmate at Brigham Young University, where McCoy had studied law enforcement, called him "an organized crime freak who wanted to make his dent on the world."

McCoy was fascinated by the story of D. B. Cooper, most notorious of the wild blue yonder highwaymen. Cooper had skyjacked a Northwest Airlines 727 to Seattle in November 1971, collected a $200,000 ransom, then parachuted out of the plane somewhere over Nevada and disappeared. It was the sort of coup that appealed to the skydiver in McCoy.

He found himself planning how to get away with a D. B. Cooper—only it would be called "The McCoy." (People who called it "The *Real* McCoy" always irritated the precisionist in him.) Like Cooper, he would reject jetliners equipped with only side doors; a jumper who bailed out of one of them would be swept into the wing or part of the tail assembly. Like Cooper, McCoy would take over a 727, which had a rear exit with a stairway that dropped from the afterbelly, allowing the skyjacker to fall free of the rear-mounted engines and the tail.

Thus, on that day in April 1972 McCoy boarded the United Airlines 727 in Denver, ticketed as "T. Johnson." He was wearing dark spectacles, a black wig, and a false mustache. In his flight bag were his highly maneuverable sport parachute, a pistol, and a hand grenade.

A few minutes out of Denver, McCoy took over the jetliner with its 94 other passengers, crew, and three stewardesses without ever leaving his seat. He notified the pilot of the skyjacking by passing him a note carried to the cockpit by a stewardess. Using a series of notes, he forced the pilot to fly to San Francisco. A passenger, Joseph Zaleski, felt his heart jumping when he saw McCoy open his flight bag, take out a hand grenade, and put it in his jacket pocket. Again, McCoy summoned a stewardess and this time dispatched her to Capt. Jerry Hearn with an envelope containing the pin from the grenade.

The jetliner was on the ground in San Francisco for three and a half hours, during which McCoy sent his demands for the $500,000 ransom in bills of $5, $10, $20, and $100 denominations and four parachutes. When the money and the parachutes were brought to the runway, McCoy handed a note to a convict who was being transferred to San Quentin Prison, one William Coggin, twenty-one. The note read: "Go see the captain." Coggin went. Hearn told him to bring aboard two black suitcases containing 40 pounds of money and the chutes. With all those bodies aboard, Hearn was not inclined to heroism; in one of his notes, McCoy had informed the captain that he was armed with plastic explosives, hand grenades, and two handguns.

Diane Surdam, the stewardess McCoy used as a messenger, spoke for herself and the other two stewardesses, D. K. Sugimoto and M. N. Yewby. "We're scared," she told Hearn. Hearn agreed that he and his crewmates, First Officer Ken Bradley and Second Officer K. W. Owen, were apprehensive that some passenger might try to subdue McCoy. "Tell everybody to stay calm—and still," he ordered.

But McCoy never threatened the passengers. He just sat

silently, the cool organization man. Mickey Luckoff, sales manager of KGO radio station in San Francisco, was impressed with McCoy's organizing expertise. To Luckoff, everything went so smoothly that he wondered whether there was more than one skyjacker.

Finally, McCoy released the passengers and the 727 took off. Expertly, McCoy directed the pilot on a wandering eastward course toward Utah. As the plane zigzagged, he jettisoned the chutes one by one to confound FBI agents hoping to track him through electronic beeper devices they had concealed in the lining of the chutes' bags. He rigged the suitcases containing the ransom to a special cargo harness. Then he donned his own sport chute and walked down the stairway into the sky.

That was McCoy's only mistake. In effect, he was hitchhiking home. When a radio signal from one of the jettisoned chutes was spotted in mudflats between Utah Lake and Provo Airport, something clicked in the head of a Utah highway patrolman named Robert Van Ieperen, one of McCoy's close friends. He told FBI agents McCoy had talked about skyjacking a plane in D. B. Cooper style. "But I can't believe it was Dick," he said. "He's a fine man."

Possibly. But the FBI, like all law enforcement agencies, had had some unfortunate experiences with "fine" men. A picture of McCoy was located and a passenger identified it as that of a man closely resembling the skyjacker. McCoy's military record yielded handwriting that matched that on the notes he had passed to the pilot. McCoy was arrested at his Provo home less than 48 hours after the skyjacking, and all but $30 of the ransom was recovered hidden in the house and buried in the backyard.

McCoy's mother couldn't understand what had happened to her son. "He's been very devoted to his church," she said. "He's a model husband and father." Fighting back tears, his wife asked: "How could he?" Neighbors said he was a man who wanted to turn his back on the violence of Vietnam, to wipe it from his memory.

II

Now, 27 months later, McCoy had turned again, not away from violence, but back to it. The rangy war hero with the clean-cut features and low-key manner, like so many first-time offenders, obviously had learned a new philosophy during his stay in the maximum-security Lewisburg Penitentiary. It was now, violently, him against "them" for the devout Mormon who had broken out of prison and fled law and order, gun in hand.

Whatever his inner feelings, McCoy accepted the inevitable along with his fellow fugitives. They needed money to assure their continuing freedom, and the only way they could get money was to steal it. Experts at their grim trade, Havel, Bagley, and Walker proposed the obvious—a bank robbery.

So, after three days of furtive driving—in a succession of stolen cars—through three states, the four men found themselves in Pollocksville, North Carolina, a small dot on the map. There they stole another car, pilfered four ski masks in a dry-goods store, and headed for a Bank of North Carolina branch. Somewhere they had acquired three more pistols, providing them with both an arsenal and new self-confidence.

Wearing the ski masks and brandishing the guns, three of the fugitives walked into the bank. They herded four bank employes into the bank's vault as the afternoon sun streamed into the little building, and then walked out with about $16,000 in cash and escaped in a getaway car driven by the fourth member of the gang. They abandoned the car just outside town and transferred to another car with Pennsylvania license tags.

For two hours, they seemed to have dropped out of sight. Then a police highway patrol cruiser spotted the second car on an unpaved logging road in the Great Dover Swamp near Cove City, North Carolina. A helicopter with FBI agents aboard flew low to check out the car. All four men jumped out of the vehicle, and four pistols fired a barrage at the chopper. Then they dashed into a stand of almost impenetrable woods.

There the gunfight continued, FBI men firing from the helicopter and police on foot from cover in the woods and nearby swamp. Suddenly, after about 30 minutes of intermittent firing, one of the men walked out of the woods and surrendered. He was Joseph Havel. A few minutes later, Larry Bagley threw up his hands and gave himself up in the swamp.

But McCoy and Walker remained at large, and Edward J. Krupinski, agent in charge of the Charlotte FBI office, warned residents in the so-called Sandhills region to be on a careful lookout for them. "These individuals are armed and should be considered extremely dangerous, and no unnecessary risk should be taken," Krupinski announced on the local radio station.

In October, Melvin Dale Walker was added to the FBI's list of the "Ten Most Wanted Fugitives." The Bureau warned that Walker had "fired on police to avoid arrest in the past," and had been described by a former crony as a man "who would kill at the drop of a hat." McCoy was mentioned in a police report only as a former skyjacker "believed to be in Walker's company."

As the hunt for the two men continued it was enlivened by assorted horse's-mouth tips from volunteer informants. One told the FBI that McCoy and Walker had been seen by a friend of his in Las Vegas. Police in that gambling capital wasted a month checking on that one without success. Another tipster said he had heard the men were in Brussels. Another was "sure" he had seen them in Kansas City. From Rome came a report McCoy and Walker were working as bodyguards for a Saudi Arabian prince on an Italian holiday. At FBI headquarters in Washington, they were betting that both men were still somewhere on the East Coast of the United States. And they were right.

In late October 1974, an FBI agent working undercover talked with an informant on the Bureau's payroll whose identity was kept secret because he was still only twenty-two and had a long future ahead of him as a highly credible tipster. The young man had been in southeastern Virginia on assignment and reported that several sources had told him of seeing two men who resembled McCoy and Walker in Norfolk and Virginia Beach.

"How sure are you of those sources?" Agent Nick O'Hara asked.

"As sure as I've got a right arm," was the reply. "They've never given me a bum steer yet. You could look it up."

O'Hara didn't have to look it up. The informant was batting better than .600 percent in his little gossip league. So headquarters ordered a "ransacking" of the area where Cape Henry bumps out at the point at which Chesapeake Bay and the Atlantic Ocean meet.

A couple of dozen agents were put on the job looking, asking, and checking every scrap of information they could gather, not only in Norfolk and Virginia Beach, but in the small towns and crossroads that dotted the surrounding territory. Summer and early fall had gone, and it was now coming up to the third monthly anniversary of the prison breakout. Wherever McCoy and Walker might be, they were a threat to the common peace.

Wherever they might be, they had to have a roof over their heads, so one potential source of leads checked was the real estate rental trade in Virginia Beach. Agents on that beat made a surprising finding. Six furnished houses had been rented through six agencies by two men who looked like McCoy and Walker. In each case, the men had used credit cards as references. An FBI request set the computers whirring in the offices of various credit card establishments, and within 24 hours the computers reported the cards had been stolen.

"What the hell," Agent Richard Rafferty commented. "Did these guys rent six houses just because they liked to sit in different surroundings six nights a week?"

It did seem crazy, but something *that* crazy cried for investigation. The unrelenting commandment governing fugitives decrees that they must be careful not to settle down; even if they do establish a base, they must travel as much as possible to avoid the danger of too many people growing accustomed to seeing them in one place—or even three or four. So all six houses were placed under surveillance. Four days passed, and it was as if no one lived in any of them. Then a talkative neighbor gossiping with Rafferty told him about a "nice" man next door on North Great Neck Road. She said he always greeted her friendly-like when she encountered him while he was jogging around the neighborhood. The "nice" man she described had McCoy's looks and flavor.

Eight agents were staked out in the empty house on the afternoon of November 9, 1974. They ate a picnic supper of cold chicken and coleslaw. Tables of three took turns playing pinochle until the house got too dark. Then they all simply sat, occasionally stretching their legs. It was the usual boring assignment, made more tedious by the knowledge that, as on previous stakeouts, they could be wasting their time.

Then, just before midnight, a car drove up to the house. A man got out and headed for the front door, and the car was driven off.

"That's McCoy or I'm Queen Elizabeth," said Agent Joseph

Smith in a stage whisper. Smith was not Queen Elizabeth. The man *was* Richard Floyd McCoy. He opened the door.

"This is the FBI!" yelled Nick O'Hara. "Hold it, then come in real slow."

There passed what seemed to be a split second. Then McCoy drew a pistol and fired. As the bullet from his gun slammed into a wall, Agents O'Hara, Kevin McPartland, and Gerald Houlihan returned the fire as if a single entity. McCoy was blasted three feet onto the front lawn. He was dead when he hit the ground.

The second man drove up to the house again just as the firing started, then sped off, followed by two cars full of agents. Minutes later the lawmen's cars pulled the fugitive's car over, guns leveled through open windows. The second man was Melvin Dale Walker, and he surrendered to Rafferty and Henry Bolin without a fuss. Unused on the passenger-side seat were two loaded pistols.

"Where did you go?" Bolin asked Walker.

"Go to hell!" Walker snapped. Then, "Oh shit, I was just having a look around to see if any creeps like you were playing cops and robbers."

A search led by Gerald Coakley, agent in charge of the Norfolk office, discovered an arsenal the fugitives would have found handy had they planned to launch a small civil war. Two caches were found, one in the house and one in the prisoners' car. Their contents revealed that the one-time antiviolent McCoy had been recruited to the philosophy of the violent Walker. They included several pistols and shotguns, a crossbow killers employ to deal out sudden death silently, a slingshot used for the same purpose, a quantity of ammunition, three submachine guns, a dozen hand grenades, several bullet-proof vests, and a gorilla-head disguise.

In December 1974, Walker, Bagley, and Havel pleaded guilty in United States District Court in New Bern, North Carolina, to the Pollocksville bank robbery and to escaping from Lewisburg Penitentiary. They were sentenced the same day.

Walker and Bagley were hit with the book. Each drew 20-year prison terms on the bank robbery charge, to run consecutively with the sentence he was serving at the time of his escape—55 years in Walker's case, 20 years in Bagley's. Each also was sentenced to five years' incarceration on the escape charge, the sentences to run concurrently with those imposed for the bank robbery. Havel got 15 years tacked onto the 10 years he was serving when he escaped, and a five-year term to run concurrently with the Pollocksville sentence.

Richard Floyd McCoy, described by a Provo neighbor as "a real kind person who would help push our car out of the snow when nobody else would," wound up deep in the soil from which he believed he had sprung. He had, as he had hoped back in Utah, made his "dent on the world." But he died a man nobody really knew.

8

The Wandering Skyjacker

To Captain Berkebile, the skyjacker didn't seem nervous at all. Through Berkebile, the man dispatched a cucumber-cool message to the authorities. "He wants another 727," Berkebile radioed the tower. "He says if the transfer to the new plane isn't on the up and up something bad is going to happen. He wants that plane."

Barbara Bailey, a young nurse at Barnes Hospital in St. Louis, was startled when the 727 American Airlines jetliner bound from St. Louis to Tulsa made a sweeping turn about 15 minutes out of Tulsa.

"What's happening?" she asked a stewardess.

"There's a man back there with a gun," was the reply.

It was just after three o'clock on the afternoon of June 23, 1972. Flight 119, which had originated in New York, had taken off from St. Louis at 2:40 P.M. with 94 passengers, three crew members, and four stewardesses. Moments after the stewardess explained to Barbara Bailey what was going on, the plane's intercom system was switched on and the pilot announced: "There's a guest on board who asked us to return to St. Louis." Capt. Ted Kovalenko had learned well the first commandment of a skyjacking age: Play it cool.

A few minutes later, six passengers who were seated near the skyjacker in the rear of the plane were asked to move up to the first-class section. Just before passengers noticed that they were returning to St. Louis's Lambert Field, Captain Kovalenko ordered them not to look around, to "just look straight ahead."

Kovalenko himself was doing just that. He had not seen the skyjacker, but he had it in writing that the snatch was on. Stuck in the pocket of his shirt was a note passed him by another stewardess, Jane Furlong, which told him: "Do not panic. This is a ransom hijacking. If the following demands are met, no one will get hurt." The note was typed in red ink, and the skyjacker had given it to Miss Furlong when she obeyed his summons to "step back here, Miss." A machine gun was held across his chest, and he was wearing rubber surgical gloves. The note demanded a ransom of $502,400, five parachutes, three parachute harnesses, an army-type collapsible shovel, goggles, and a right-hand glove.

Tod Nelson of Tulsa had taken a good look at the skyjacker, sitting calmly three seats away, a submachine gun in the crook of his elbow. He recognized him as a man who had boarded the plane at Lambert carrying what appeared to be a trombone case. The man looked between twenty-five and thirty, with dark bushy hair—another passenger, James Price of St. Louis, decided it was a wig—and a dark complexion marred by pockmarks and open sores. The man had gone to the men's room shortly after the plane took off for Tulsa—probably to put the weapon together, Price told himself.

When the jetliner landed at Lambert, the skyjacker released 81 passengers, including all women and children; the passengers left the plane by emergency exit chutes—sliding down from the plane to the ground. The plane took off again at 5:16 P.M., and as it circled the St. Louis area at about 11,000 feet the skyjacker relayed his demands through the pilot, who kept radio contact with Lambert's control tower, where FBI agents had joined the control crew.

"That's an odd number of dollars," an air controller remarked.

"Well, he also wants a shovel," said an FBI agent. "My guess is that he plans to bury the $500,000 somewhere and use the remaining $2400 to finance his plans to escape."

In any case, the plane flew off in the direction of Fort Worth, with the 13 remaining passengers and crew, plus the four stewardesses. The skyjacker obviously had decided he was not going to wait around at the airport while the ransom and equipment were being rounded up. Approaching Fort Worth, the plane turned and headed back to St. Louis.

During the flight, a stewardess poked the shoulder of one of the passengers, Aubrey Mallory, forty-seven, of Norman, Oklahoma. She told Mallory the skyjacker had selected him to pick up the ransom and the paraphernalia he had asked for when the plane made its first return to St. Louis. Why me? Mallory asked himself. Those red slacks I'm wearing must be damned conspicuous. Whatever, the stewardess told him the skyjacker had promised that if he went out and "got the stuff" and carried it into the plane he would be released.

"What about the others?" Mallory asked.

"If everything goes the way the man wants it, they can leave, too," was the reply.

Mallory thought about it and discussed it with another passenger, T. W. Webster of Tulsa. They talked about Mallory running away. No, Mallory told himself, he couldn't be responsible for the skyjacker shooting everybody on the plane.

So when the plane landed, Mallory made four trips to bring the stuff aboard. Each time, he dumped his load in the front of the aircraft, and when it was all aboard he made four trips down the aisle to stow it in the rear of the plane near the skyjacker's seat. Then the man ordered the tower to send an expert aboard to show him how to put on the parachutes. The skyjacker was a hard learner. Twenty minutes passed before he said he had "everything right" and dismissed the expert. Mallory was allowed to leave. Then, surrounded by questioning FBI agents, he sweated out exactly 55 minutes by his watch before the other passengers left the plane.

The next two hours were taut with suspense. First the jetliner was refueled. The skyjacker seemed lost in thought. For a time he fingered the ransom notes, frowning. Then more thinking. Then he demanded an altimeter, a device that measures height above ground. It was delivered to him by an airlines official. More thinking. Then two stewardesses were released and the skyjacker demanded a new crew. When the crew came aboard, led by Capt. L. F. Berkebile, the skyjacker told the original crewmen they could leave.

Captain Berkebile radioed the tower that the skyjacker was not satisfied with the denominations of the bills in the ransom packages. There was some discussion about the man's demand that smaller notes be located. Airlines officials were just about to send for some new money from the First National Bank of St. Louis when the man changed his mind and told the pilot the original currency was satisfactory.

Finally, at about 12:30 A.M., the jetliner began its roaring dash down the runway. As it gained speed, a black Cadillac convertible crashed through a wire fence and sped toward the plane. The car smashed into its target, grazing the plane's nose, then spun around and plunged into the left landing gear.

The impact demolished the car and disabled the plane. The driver, later identified as one David J. Hanley of a St. Louis suburb, was critically injured. Police cars and emergency vehicles converged on the scene, their lights blazing. Rescuers were unable to pull Hanley out of the car from the driver's side, but they finally got him out from the passenger side. A uniformed policeman prayed: "Hail Mary, don't let anything explode."

Hanley, unconscious, his face streaming blood, was hustled into an ambulance while firemen began spraying the wrecked car and plane with fire-extinguishing foam. A St. Louis policeman was telling spectators at the fence he had tried to intercept the car. "My God, he must have been going 80 miles an hour," the policeman said. "He hit the fence once, but it didn't give, so he backed up and then hit it again and the fence collapsed just as I was running toward it."

Three FBI agents armed with rifles moved toward the jetliner under the direction of William A. Sullivan, special agent in charge of the St. Louis field office. From Captain Berkebile came a radio message to the tower: "Don't open any doors. Don't attempt to board. He thinks we're pulling some shenanigans. He may be getting a little nervous."

Flight Engineer Art Koester was busy trying to keep the skyjacker talking. He was thinking: God, I can't let him shoot somebody. The skyjacker had pulled a grenade out of his pocket and held it in one hand while he cradled the machine gun with his other arm. "It's not the FBI or the airlines trying to pull something," Koester told him. "The tower says it was just some kook."

To Captain Berkebile, the skyjacker didn't seem nervous at all. Through Berkebile, the man dispatched a cucumber-cool message to the authorities. "He wants another 727," Berkebile radioed the tower. "He says if the transfer to the new plane isn't on the up and up something bad is going to happen. He wants that plane."

The skyjacker got it, too. Nobody was about to argue with a man who obviously was equipped to give the Red Cross a pint of ice water. Ten minutes later, as the second plane rolled up to the runway, Berkebile told the tower: "He says he doesn't want another goddam car ramming into us."

At 1:35 A.M., the skyjacker, crew, and two stewardesses transferred to the fresh 727. The three FBI agents with their rifles watched helplessly as the skyjacker used two stewardesses as shields to make his way safely to the aircraft, after the ransom money, parachutes, and other items had been hoisted onto the plane. Agent Sullivan was frustrated. He had hoped his men could get a safe shot at the skyjacker, but the man was crouched down low behind the stewardesses. Sullivan never considered giving the order to fire.

The jetliner took off thirteen minutes later. "He wants us to head for Toronto," Captain Berkebile radioed his tense official audience on the ground.

And at 2:53 A.M., the skyjacker parachuted from the plane through a rear door as the plane flew over an area the captain's calculations pinpointed as in the neighborhood of Peru, Indiana. The jetliner flew on and landed at O'Hare Airport in Chicago. During an ordeal that lasted twelve and a half hours, the only casualty was David J. Hanley, whose bloodstained driver's license said he was thirty years old. Hanley was in the operation room at St. John's Mercy Hospital under armed police guard.

There was a mixed bag of developments as the investigation got under way. The FBI learned that the only passenger unaccounted for was a man who had boarded Flight 119 in St. Louis under the name of Robert Wilson, and assumed he was the skyjacker. The Bureau in Washington issued a memo describing the man as about five feet eleven inches tall, weighing about 175 pounds, and wearing a brown wig over dark black hair. The skyjacker's lip was said to be "shaped like a trumpet player's."

There was a brouhaha about security at Lambert Field. The media noted that only four days before, United States Attorney

Daniel Bartlett had called security arrangements at the airport "absolutely appalling." Whether or not Bartlett had indulged himself in a spot of hyperbole, the fact was that Robert Wilson was not among nine passengers whom security people had picked as potential skyjackers. The nine who were designated as possible suspects had been questioned, searched, or run through a metal-detecting magnetometer before being allowed to board the aircraft.

And the FBI's Sullivan announced that the skyjacker had given two of the stewardesses $1400 of the ransom money. Admirably, the stewardesses turned over the $1400 to the FBI, and it was returned to American Airlines, which—not so admirably—kept it.

Up north in Indiana, more than 200 lawmen mounted an air-and-land search in the area of Peru. Two helicopters hovered over the dense foliage and rolling terrain. Police and FBI agents sought to cover every foot of ground by "straight-line" walking. James F. Martin, the FBI agent in charge of the search, commented: "All we have is a lot of geography." Reports that bloodstains had been found were never verified.

An assortment of experts expressed the opinion that the skyjacker had jumped to his death. Captain Berkebile told Agent Sullivan he had maneuvered the plane to increase the risk to the skyjacker. Considering the speed at which the plane was flying, Berkebile said, "the extreme tumbling he was subjected to would have put him out of commission. The centrifugal force would have taken the blood right from his brain." Art Koester, the flight engineer and copilot, agreed. "Very few people can jump out of a jet and live," he told the FBI. "And this guy had no knowledge of jumping at all." Koester said the crew showed the skyjacker an instrument which registered 250 miles per hour, although the actual speed had been 320 miles an hour. "The guy was very nervous at that point," Koester said. "He didn't want to die. Can you imagine jumping out of a jetliner, carrying this huge bag, a machine gun, and a case that's supposed to have a grenade? The engines are pointing straight at you and as soon as you leave the plane you start tumbling so quickly the blood just leaves your brain. The bag is almost sure to split and the money's going to scatter."

In any case, the bag of money and a submachine gun did succeed in landing on terra firma. On the afternoon of June 27, two farmers found them in fields about five miles apart, both just outside the perimeter of the lawmen's search. Only one of the ransom envelopes was found in the bag, still containing the $500,000 with which the skyjacker had flown off. Apparently, the fugitive had carried the "spending money" on his person. Agent Martin concluded that the skyjacker and the bag of money "separated" because of the shock of leaving the airplane at more than 300 miles an hour.

Admiringly, Martin asked Art Koester how the crew knew the skyjacker jumped in the vicinity of Peru. "The cabin pressure gauges told us," Koester explained. "When the skyjacker went through the door it was like popping a cork from a bottle, and the cabin pressure gauges immediately showed the change in pressure. Captain Berkebile instantly made a radar fix on the location."

Martin pressed the search. He refused to assume that the skyjacker was dead; he wanted evidence. "The only thing that would stop this investigation is to establish that the man is dead and identify him," he told a news conference. "Or, if he's not dead, we've got to find him and prosecute."

The FBI search chief was encouraged when a pair of greenish gold slacks was found in another field near Peru, and a few hours later a tractor turned up a matching jacket on a farm four miles away. Martin theorized that the slacks and jacket had been thrown out of the jetliner before the skyjacker bailed out. They were found too far apart, he concluded, to have been discarded after the man jumped. Meanwhile, two stewardesses brought to the search headquarters said the slacks and jacket resembled those worn by the skyjacker.

Still, all that was known about the skyjacker was that he had jumped out of the airliner. Authorities now had to accept the possibility that he had survived the jump and somehow made his escape from the drop area. The search had to be expanded to urban areas. FBI men turned their attention north to South Bend and Fort Wayne in Indiana, and northeast to Detroit. A city was still the best place for a fugitive to hide.

It was in Detroit that the FBI hit paydirt. By sleuthing

methods never made public, but probably through the use of an undercover agent or informant, its investigators were put in touch with an individual who was rumored to be a friend of the skyjacker's. The man talked freely. He identified the fugitive as Martin J. McNally, who lived in the Detroit suburb of Wyandotte, Michigan. He said he had been with McNally prior to the skyjacking and that McNally had talked of commandeering a jetliner—preferably a 727 because it had a rear door from which to parachute.

The informant also claimed that he met McNally after the skyjacking and that McNally had said he was "sorry" that he had lost the $500,000 ransom money. FBI Agent Lawrence Bonney asked if McNally had told him any details of the skyjacking. He "sure did," the informant replied. He went on to say McNally had told him that the bag containing the money had been strapped to the skyjacker's body and that McNally had worn two sets of clothing and had discarded a jacket and a pair of slacks during his jump.

Agents James R. McCance and Richard A. Marquise arrested McNally on a street corner in Wyandotte about midnight on June 28, five days after the skyjacking. McNally, twenty-eight, a slender man with a longish face marred by a fresh bruise on one cheek, didn't resist arrest, but he was alternately surly and boisterous before calming down and going quietly with the agents. En route to his arraignment, he donned an occasional smile, and his voice was low-toned.

Two days later, FBI agents arrested a man they charged with being an accomplice to the skyjacking. He was Walter J. Petlikowski, thirty-one, of Ecorse, Michigan, who walked into the police station at River Rouge, Michigan, and said he had information about the case. After making an oral statement, Petlikowski was arrested on charges that he drove McNally to St. Louis before the skyjacking and then picked him up in Peru after the jump and drove him to Wyandotte.

On that same day, Police Chief Richard Blair of Peru admitted ruefully that McNally was the man he and his wife picked up on a road three miles south of Peru five hours after McNally bailed out of the jetliner. Blair said McNally showed him a Michigan driver's license issued to a Patrick Clarence McNally of

Wyandotte. But Blair insisted that the hitchhiker didn't match the first description issued by the FBI. He said he drove McNally to Peru and "believed" that the skyjacker planned to check into the Peru Motor Lodge.

That McNally did. Mrs. Faye Dutton, the lodge's manager, told the FBI that a man identifying himself as Patrick McNally checked in that Saturday night and stayed three days. She described him as "having a scraped face." Miss Amy Martin, the desk clerk, who knew the area was swarming with lawmen searching for the fugitive, asked McNally a facetious question:

"You aren't the skyjacker, are you?"

McNally said no, he wasn't, that in fact he was an FBI agent who had just come off search duty.

Miss Martin said McNally was dressed in blue jeans and a long-sleeved blue sweatshirt. He carried a pair of dark glasses in his hand and had no luggage. He told her, she said, that "he had got into a fight with his brother."

Martin Joseph McNally was one of eight children. He had bought a two-story, gray-shingled house in a quiet middle-class neighborhood in 1969, shortly after he was married, and remained there after he was divorced. His father, Walter McNally, wondered whether one cause of the divorce could have been that Martin "just refused to work."

The father told reporters Martin had been in and out of scrapes since high school, and was "always making big plans and talking big—quiet, but always thinking big." Martin McNally received a general discharge, a step below honorable, from the Navy in December 1964, after serving three years. No reason was given for the lower-grade discharge. His neighbors called him clean-cut and well mannered, although a touch eccentric. One reported that Martin used to mow his lawn in the middle of the night. "But we never complained," she said. "It was an electric mower and it didn't make much noise."

When his father spoke to the suspect after his arrest he asked, "What should I tell your mother and your brothers and sisters?" and the son replied, "Just tell them to forget me."

The father was bewildered by the turn of events. "I've got seven other children and most of them are honor students," he said. "I don't understand this at all."

Meanwhile, FBI agents were busy collecting physical evidence against McNally. Agent Richard G. Stilling of Chicago had found two small pieces of paper typed in red stuck between steps of the jetliner when he searched it after the plane landed at O'Hare Airport. The pieces obviously were parts of the ransom note McNally had dispatched to Capt. Ted Kovalenko on the aborted flight from St. Louis to Tulsa. In Washington, a specialist in the FBI's fingerprint laboratory named Carl E. Collins found that one print on the note matched a print of McNally's right ring finger taken after his arrest. And an assortment of aeronautical charts and maps were found in the trunk of McNally's car.

In July, both McNally and Petlikowski were indicted by a federal grand jury in St. Louis on two counts each of air piracy. But Petlikowski later pleaded guilty to a reduced charge of being an accessory to the skyjacking and was sentenced to 10 years in prison. That cleared the way for McNally's trial in December, also in St. Louis.

McNally, described by neighbors in Wyandotte as a friendly, quiet man, who nevertheless occasionally would break his reserve to talk about making a big score, didn't have much going for him. Mostly, he had only the efforts of his two court-appointed lawyers, because he didn't take the witness stand to tell his side of the story. Indeed, there were only two defense witnesses, both of whom testified merely that they couldn't identify McNally absolutely as the skyjacker.

By contrast, the state produced physical evidence and the testimony of FBI agents and scientists, and American Airlines employes, to construct its highly professional case. Jennifer Dumanois, one of the jetliner's stewardesses, identified a piece of the ransom note—the piece with McNally's fingerprint—as part of the note she had passed to the aircraft's crew. The FBI's Carl Collins explained how he concluded that the fingerprint was McNally's. No surprises there. But two other government witnesses added more colorful testimony during their identification of McNally as the skyjacker.

Art Koester, the flight engineer of the captive aircraft, testified that McNally threatened to kill him when he accidentally knocked off the skyjacker's sunglasses in the flight from St. Louis toward Toronto. Koester said he had walked past McNally in the cabin section of the plane and then turned to close the curtain separating the two sections of the cabin. As he did so, he bumped McNally and McNally's sunglasses fell to the cabin floor.

"He told me, 'You're about to die,' " Koester said of Mc-Nally's reaction. "I said it was an accident and a short time later he told me to go back to the cockpit."

Koester's testimony was telling because it punched a hole in the argument by defense attorneys that the skyjacker was difficult to identify because he wore the sunglasses and a wig. So did that of FBI Agent Robert Meredith, whose identification of McNally resulted from another close encounter.

Earlier, the parachute expert who showed McNally how to put on a chute had been identified as an American Airlines employe. In fact, the jury was told, the expert was Meredith, who was dressed in American Airlines coveralls.

Meredith testified he got a good look at the skyjacker when he boarded the plane and saw him holding a machine gun pointed "in the general direction of myself and two stewardesses." Meredith said he was told by the skyjacker to turn around and then turn back and put on a parachute and harness. He said he did so, with the help of a stewardess, all the while sneaking more looks at the skyjacker. Meredith also testified that he had identified McNally in a Detroit police lineup.

First of the two defense witnesses was Aubrey Mallory, the passenger from Norman, Oklahoma, who had been selected to bring the bag of ransom money and assorted equipment aboard the 727. Mallory said he could not positively identify McNally because he stayed away from the suspect after being told not to look at him.

The second witness was David Spellman of Tulsa, an American Airlines auditor, and one of the hostages. Spellman said he was too worried "about having a machine gun pointed at me" to get a good description of the fugitive. Under cross-examination, Spellman conceded he had identified an FBI agent as the skyjacker at the Detroit police lineup, but he claimed he had narrowed his choice to McNally and the FBI man from six persons in the lineup.

In his closing argument, one defense counsel, Frederick H. Mayer, argued that the state had not proved McNally was the skyjacker, citing discrepancies in testimony by eight passengers on the two skyjacked planes who had identified the defendant. He commented that "with the intense publicity about this case . . . it is easy for the people who were there to imagine things and project things in their minds." Some witnesses in the case were grossly mistaken, he declared.

Mayer also contemptuously dismissed the statements of Hester Faye Harris, Petlikowski's common-law wife, who had testified against McNally. "She did it to help Petlikowski," he said. And although he admitted that McNally was in the Peru area where the skyjacker had bailed out, he charged that McNally's arrest was the result of the "desire" of federal authorities to find someone in that neighborhood to link to the case.

Nonsense, replied Assistant United States Attorney Robert B. Schneider, the chief prosecutor. He reminded the jurors that one of McNally's fingerprints matched a print on the ransom note. "Maybe McNally didn't think very clearly, and put the print on when he typed the note," Schneider said. "He may have put it on in tearing up the note when he left the plane. He almost got away with it." Schneider went on to argue that the prosecution evidence during the seven-day trial was so overwhelming that "we proved our case not only beyond a reasonable doubt, but beyond any doubt."

The jury swiftly agreed, returning a verdict of guilty on two counts of air piracy after deliberating less than an hour. And eventually Judge John K. Regan sentenced McNally to two concurrent terms of life in prison. He would be eligible for parole in 15 years.

Eighteen days shy of a year after the skyjacking, federal prosecutors dropped a charge of willfully damaging a commercial aircraft against David Hanley, who had crashed his Cadillac convertible into the first captive plane. The intimation was that Hanley had suffered enough from the serious injuries he received in the crash, including damage to an arm that doctors said probably was irreparable. But the government gave Hanley no high marks for good intentions, pointing out that his attempt to thwart the skyjacking imperiled the lives of everyone on the jetliner.

II

Martin McNally and Richard McCoy before him were relative professionals in the grisly craft of skyjacking. That is to say, they approached the job of getting what they wanted from their acts of air piracy with a certain technical touch. Both were equipped with the means by which they hoped to escape with their ransom monies—parachutes. Both *did* escape, temporarily.

Then there are the amateurs who don't think through their strategy. They can be more dangerous because their amateurism places them as well as everyone else in a captive jetliner in deadly peril.

There was, in May 1978, Barbara Annette Oswald of Clayton, Missouri, an affluent suburb of St. Louis, who rented a helicopter and ordered the pilot at gunpoint to fly to the federal penitentiary at Marion, Illinois, to help her free her lover and two other prisoners. She was shot to death as the pilot struggled to take away her gun in mid-air.

Mrs. Oswald's lover at the time was Garrett Brock Trapnell, who was serving a life sentence for skyjacking an airliner in January 1972. Trapnell had demanded a ransom of $306,000; the release of a convicted crony; political asylum in Europe; and freedom for Angela Davis, the black activist then on trial in California. An FBI agent at New York City's Kennedy International Airport posed as a crew member when Trapnell allowed a change of crews, then shot Trapnell in the arm to end the ordeal for 94 passengers and seven crew members aboard the flight from Los Angeles to New York.

One of the two other prisoners Mrs. Oswald had sought to release was Martin McNally, the wandering skyjacker from Wyandotte, Michigan. The other was one James Johnson. On December 21, 1978, Trapnell was convicted in Benton, Illinois, of conspiracy in connection with the helicopter-skyjacking-escape attempt.

On that same day, a young woman, Mrs. Oswald's daughter, Robyn, sixteen years old, was aboard TWA Flight 541, en route to Kansas City from Louisville. Minutes out of Kansas City, Robyn Oswald skyjacked the jetliner. She announced she had a bomb strapped to her body and would blow up the aircraft unless Trapnell was freed. At her insistence, the pilot landed the plane at

Williamson County Airport near Marion.

There, after six hours of negotiations, FBI agents were permitted to put a telephone aboard the plane. Meanwhile, Robyn Oswald released all but 20 of the 87 passengers. Taking turns on the phone, the agents kept Robyn talking throughout the day and into the evening. Once, Robyn announced that if Trapnell was not on the plane within half an hour—it was then 6:00 P.M.—"all the people left on the plane are going to be blown from the face of the earth."

The FBI had no choice but to stall; there was a good chance Robyn was bluffing. A trained FBI negotiator flown in from Louisville got on the phone and talked soothingly to the youthful skyjacker.

Six-thirty passed, and nothing happened. Finally, as one passenger put it, Robyn "came to her senses . . . she felt concerned for the other passengers." Several FBI agents boarded the aircraft, and Robyn surrendered without a struggle. At 8:48 P.M., nine hours after the plane was seized, Washington FBI headquarters received the terse note: "We have the subject and everything is under control."

Robyn Oswald's "bomb" was a phony. She had described it to stewardesses as consisting of three sticks of dynamite. One stewardess saw something under Robyn's blouse that looked like dynamite sticks, wiring, and a button. The device turned out to be three railroad flares attached by wires and a doorbell button. "It would not have exploded any more than Robyn could have walked on water," said FBI Agent Ed Hagerty. Robyn was found to be a juvenile delinquent at a hearing in a federal court in Illinois and was placed in a foster home.

Then there was Irene McKinney, a forty-nine-year-old divorcee from Cypress, a tiny community in the urban sprawl of Los Angeles near Anaheim. Mrs. McKinney, mother of two children, seized a United Airlines 747 jet en route from Los Angeles to New York as it soared over Prescott, Arizona, on January 27, 1979. She handed a note to a stewardess and told her: "Take this to the captain. No questions asked, please." Captain Thomas C. Cook didn't like what the note said: "I have enough nitroglycerine with me to blow this plane up . . . I have some demands. . . ."

The demands actually were one. Mrs. McKinney ordered that

one of three actors—Charlton Heston, Jack Lemmon, and the "Bionic Woman," Lindsay Wagner—read a note over television. She said the note could be found in a phone booth at Los Angeles International Airport. Heston and Lemmon were promptly taken to the airport to await Mrs. McKinney's order to read the note.

Among the 119 passengers and 12 crew members, someone opened a bottle of wine shortly after the jetliner touched down at Kennedy International Airport, and the word was passed that the plane had been skyjacked. Meanwhile, nobody could find the note at the Los Angeles Airport.

Mrs. McKinney watched the in-flight movie, *Going South,* starring Jack Nicholson, but she refused lunch. Celebrities among the passengers included actors Theodore Bikel, Sam Jaffe, and Dean Martin's son, Dino. Bikel picked up his guitar and played and sang for two and a half hours. Jaffe sucked on a lollipop, explaining that it was his "pacifier." One passenger found that "nobody was petrified. None of us applauded Bikel because we didn't want the skyjacker to think we were having too good a time."

FBI Agent Walter F. Yoos, in charge of the Bureau's operations at Kennedy, drove to the airport from his home in Levittown, Long Island. He set up an emergency unit with police from the Port Authority of New York and New Jersey and the New York Police Department, and airport officials.

The plane had taxied up to the United terminal at 7:29 P.M. At 9:00 P.M. the passengers were still sitting in the jet. They were told the captain was not to be disturbed. Half an hour later, Mrs. McKinney asked for a telephone line so she could communicate with Heston and Lemmon. Yoos asked her through an open door if he could come inside the plane, unarmed. She agreed, and Yoos entered through a rear door. Yoos took off his brown plaid sports jacket to show her he carried no gun.

"I'm trying to help you resolve the problem," he told Mrs. McKinney.

"All right," Mrs. McKinney said, still tightly clutching the flight bag she said contained the nitroglycerine.

She looks nervous, Yoos told himself. A few minutes later, he persuaded Mrs. McKinney to let 25 passengers, mostly women and children, leave the plane.

"I have my demands," Mrs. McKinney told Yoos. She opened her purse and took out a typewritten document.

"There are 25 pages here," Yoos said. "Instead of wasting time and reading this here, I'll take it to my people outside." Mrs. McKinney agreed, but warned him that she did indeed have "that glycerine."

Yoos returned to her side about 10 minutes later. He perched on the arm of a seat across the aisle from where she was sitting and leaned over to talk to her, his beefy 220-pound frame looming over her. They talked, and talked, as the hours passed. "People won't listen to me," Mrs. McKinney told Yoos. "I can't get published. I'm a good writer."

They talked some more. Mrs. McKinney quoted from the Bible. She said: "You have to have faith. We all have to have faith."

"Then you must believe me. I want to help you resolve this," Yoos replied.

By then it was 2:10 A.M. They had been talking for four and a half hours. It's just about time to take her, Yoos told himself. If I'm tired, she's tired. He looked up at Lyn Collins, the flight supervisor, standing at his side. Just then, distracted, Mrs. McKinney lowered her flight bag onto the floor. Had it contained nitroglycerine, that would have been the big bang.

"Okay, Mister Collins," Yoos said. Then he lunged at Mrs. McKinney, pinning her down with his body while Collins grabbed the bag. After 11 hours, the ordeal of United Airlines Flight 8 had come to an end.

And as Yoos had suspected—but until then had dared not test his suspicion—Mrs. McKinney was carrying no explosive but a bluff. The flight bag contained only her cosmetics, some prescription pills, and her airline ticket.

"Yeah," he said later. "Maybe I should have moved sooner. But there were human beings on that plane, and you never can tell with amateurs."

Yoos, of course, knew his trade well. He was a graduate of the FBI's course in how to talk to skyjackers and other terrorists holding hostages—a course that has trained several score agents in the various psychological approaches designed to soothe the complex psyches of a relatively new kind of lawbreaker. And FBI

Director Webster had established a special Crisis Control Center in Washington that can go into action within minutes after a hostage situation develops.

A prime example of how the FBI reacts to such a crisis was what went on after a militant Serbian nationalist named Nikola Kavaja skyjacked an American Airlines Boeing 727 bound from New York to Washington on June 20, 1979. Kavaja, forty-five, had been free on $350,000 bond and was on his way back to Chicago to be sentenced for his part in a 1975 bombing of the suburban Chicago home of the Yugoslav Consul to the United States in which there were no casualties. The aircraft was carrying 136 persons, including a crew of three and five flight attendants.

Seventeen minutes after Kavaja, then merely a nameless passenger, informed the plane's pilot that he was carrying a briefcase full of dynamite and was taking control of the plane, a red telephone rang at FBI headquarters in Washington. The call was from the Federal Aviation Administration, and its message was crisp and to the point: another skyjacking.

W. Douglas Gow, chief of the FBI's section dealing with crimes against persons at the Crisis Control Center, called in Bruce Brotman, a former member of the FBI's bank robbery squad in New York, and J. D. Carey, a specialist in the section charged with responsibility for handling kidnappings, hijackings, and civil disturbances.

Gow informed the chain of command that the FBI had two choices. It could use force to capture the skyjacker when the plane landed in Chicago, or it could meet his demands that authorities release a Serbian Orthodox priest, also held in the 1975 bombing, and make arrangements for flying the two men to Peru.

Webster's reply was terse: "Force is the last resort. Remember that."

At that point, Kavaja was still nameless. But the airline supplied the Bureau's New York office with a passenger manifest. The list was checked through FBI files, and Kavaja was identified as one of the passengers. The files showed that no other passenger had any reason to seek the release of the priest, Stojilko Kajevic, forty-three, serving a 12-year sentence. Knowing the man they were dealing with, the Control Center took certain steps. A bomb expert was called in, and an agent from the Bureau's counterintelligence section who was an expert in the militant politics of the Yugoslav dissident community in the United States. Shortly, an FBI agent who spoke Serbian joined the team.

Meanwhile, viewing machines were giving the team TV-like pictures of the interior of a 727 so that Washington could identify escape routes and appraise the maneuvering room in the aircraft. Expert advice was provided by members of the Bureau's Hostage Negotiations Center in nearby Quantico, Virginia.

"We've got a lot of work to do," Gow remarked calmly. "There are all sorts of complications."

Gow was right. Before there could be any talk about permitting Kavaja and Kajevic to fly to Peru, the Peruvian government had to be consulted. Would it allow such a flight? Would it allow the hostage plane to land? The State Department was asked to handle that ticklish business. If the FBI let the two men go, arrangements would have to be made with Chicago authorities to release Kajevic from the Chicago Metropolitan Correctional Center where he was awaiting sentencing. Douglas Moore, an Assistant FBI Director and Chief of the General Crimes Division, ordered the FBI Chicago office to get that OK so the priest could be driven to the airport.

But Kajevic didn't want to go anywhere with Kavaja. Chicago agents finally persuaded him to come to the FBI field office, then had to get official permission from a federal judge to move the priest, and arrange for an escort by members of the United States Marshal's office. The skyjacked plane was not equipped for intercontinental flight. American Airlines agreed to provide another plane, but couldn't guarantee that another crew could be found to climb aboard a plane carrying an armed skyjacker.

Meanwhile, the priest was on a special telephone hookup to the plane, trying to talk Kavaja into surrendering. He kept turning to the FBI agents around him and saying: "It's no use. The man is mad." He was told to keep trying.

In New York, Kavaja's lawyer asked American Airlines to fly him to Chicago so he could talk to Kavaja. The lawyer, Deyan R. Brashich, described himself as "the only person Kavaja trusts." He was flown to Chicago's O'Hare International Airport and got on the special telephone hookup to the plane. He was joined from time to time by a Serbian-speaking Chicago police officer, the pilot who kept his cool throughout, and the priest.

Finally, Kavaja released the passengers and the five flight attendants, but he spent another hour demanding that he be flown out of the country. So to save the lives of the crew, the FBI had to give in a little. After checking with the Irish Embassy, agents worked out an agreement by which Kavaja would be flown to Ireland. There he surrendered to Irish police.

Ireland had no extradition treaty with the United States. But Kavaja was informed, perhaps with a twinkle in Irish eyes, that since he had not passed through Customs he was not officially in Ireland. So Kavaja was shipped back to the country of his crime and in due time was convicted and sentenced to 20 years in prison.

In New York, FBI Agent John Otto told a news conference that Kavaja was carrying a "number of sticks of dynamite." He described the explosive as "a device with a hand grenade simulator used in military training that could have detonated the dynamite." Until the bitter end, Nikola Kavaja had meant business.

MURDER
SHRIEKS
OUT

9

Death of a Family

"Drove to select area and killed husband & baby. Now the mother and daughter were all mine. Then tied and gagged, led to her place of execution and hanged her."

Carroll Vernon Jackson, Jr., was twenty-nine, a quiet, good-natured, 212-pound worker in a feedstore in Louisa County, Virginia. He lived in a neat frame bungalow near Apple Grove, a few miles from his job, with his wife, Mildred, twenty-seven, and their two daughters, Susan Anne, five, and Janet Carroll, eighteen months.

The Jacksons were a happy family and regular churchgoers. There were no domestic problems, no financial burdens. Neighbors spoke affectionately of their daughters as "laughing and dancing" and of the Jackson marriage as "a perfect match." Jackson was looking forward to a new job in a bank that offered him opportunities for advancement.

This, then, was the family that on Sunday, January 11, 1959, drove to Buckner, Virginia, to visit Mrs. Jackson's parents, Mr. and Mrs. B. L. Hill. As the evening drew on to night, they decided it was time to leave and drive the 15 miles back to their home. The baby was sleepy and a bit fussy. Grandfather Hill announced as they were leaving that it was "exactly 9:40—no wonder Jan is sleepy."

On the way home, the Jackson family disappeared.

"It wasn't like" Carroll Jackson not to show up for work, so his employer phoned the Jackson home about mid-morning of the next day. There was no answer. He figured he'd hear from his dependable employe, and didn't think of checking further.

Late that Monday afternoon, Mrs. Hill called the feedstore office for a chat with her son-in-law and learned that he hadn't reported to work. She called the Jackson home. No answer. An aunt of Carroll Jackson's remarked offhand that she'd seen a car that looked like the Jacksons' as she was driving to Richmond on State Route 609.

To the Hills, that was funny. Scary funny. Mr. Hill and Mrs. Jackson's brother, George Hill, drove down State Route 618 and turned onto State Route 609.

They found the Jacksons' car, a 1958 Chevrolet sedan. There was nobody in it. The car evidently had been left in some haste. Ignition keys were in the switch. Mrs. Jackson's purse, containing a dollar bill and some change, lay on the dashboard shelf. Two pillows were on the back seat, along with the girls' identical dolls, dressed, as were their mistresses, in red-and-white pinafores. There was also a soiled diaper and a baby's bottle containing a few last drops of milk.

The left rear wheel of the Chevrolet was on the hard surface of narrow Route 609. Its front wheels were cut inward slightly onto the muddy shoulder. A few feet ahead was a half-moon skid mark about 20 inches long—as though made by an auto that had cut suddenly in front of the Jackson car. George Hill called the state police at 7:20 P.M., a little less than 20 hours after the Jackson family had left the Hill home.

Virginia police checked the neighborhood. A family that lived about 100 yards away had heard car doors slam several times, saw lights flash onto their windows, and heard one car drive off—at about 10:00 P.M. A young man driving down Route 609 Sunday night, taking his girl home from a movie, saw a car parked where the Jackson car had been abandoned. The parked car looked like a Chevrolet. He and his girl friend also saw another car's taillights a short distance away. It was about 10:00 P.M.

A housewife nearer to Route 618, from which the Jacksons would have turned off on their way home, remembered that two cars had passed at about 9:55 P.M. She said one of the cars had a noisy muffler. Later, two couples with children in their cars said someone, probably a man, in a light-colored Ford, a 1951 or 1954 model, had forced their cars to stop on back-country roads about 20 miles from the spot where the Jacksons' car had been found.

Both families had managed to elude their tormentor. One couple said the car had a noisy muffler. Both incidents occurred about 7:30 P.M. or 8:00 P.M.

That Monday night, 200 civilian volunteers joined with police in a ground search. The next day, FBI agents appeared from Richmond, looking for a possible federal offense—abduction. They were there to help, they told G. S. Cooper, head of the state police investigative team, and his partner, R. L. Bumgardner.

"Looks like we can use it," said Cooper soberly. "Welcome to a job of work."

More volunteers showed up the next day, and the ground search was expanded. A state police plane flew low over the fields and scrub pine of Louisa County. The aerial search was joined a day later by two Marine Corps helicopters, manned by FBI men and state police. Police asked residents to search their own land and buildings. Abandoned mines, sawmills, and abandoned buildings in a 50-square-mile area were searched. So were well-known lovers' lanes. Ponds, rivers, and creeks were dragged. An anonymous friend of the Jacksons offered a $5000 reward for information leading to the recovery of the family, or their bodies.

But the search was still on almost two months later, on March 4, when two men from Fredericksburg, Virginia, drove to an abandoned sawmill site in a broken and brush-tangled area off State Route 631. The men, James Beach, a foreman for the American Viscose Corporation in Fredericksburg, and a barber, John Scott, had gone to the site to dig up some sawdust Beach wanted for his rosebushes.

Their pickup truck became mired in the mud and sawdust, and Beach and Scott gathered brush to pile under the wheels. As Beach was tugging a large branch from a pile, he saw a man's leg sticking out.

"Scott," yelled Beach, "there's a man in there."

As Scott moved toward him, Beach said: "Let's not touch anything. We better get the cops."

Beach walked two miles to a pay phone and called Game Warden Francis Boggs, who in turn summoned the police. Lifting the pile of brush carefully, the police uncovered the bodies of a tall, husky man and a little girl. The man's body was lying face-down, his hands tied in front of him. The girl's body was partly under the man's left side, as though the man had been cuddling her to keep her warm. The man had been shot in the left temple, and there were bruises on his head. A minor bruise was found on the top of the child's head, but she had apparently suffocated.

The man's body was tentatively identified as that of Carroll Vernon Jackson from personal cards in the pockets of his blue pin-stripe suit. Both bodies later were identified by Curtis Jackson, an uncle of the dead man, as Jackson's and that of his daughter, eighteen-month-old Janet Carroll. The child's body was clad in a blue coat and the red-and-white pinafore she had worn to her grandparents' house.

"When the law got here and I saw the kid, that was—that was something," Beach said, his eyes wet and his mouth working. "It just got to me. I felt funny all over. You know, I've got a grandchild just her age. The man, God, he was trying to protect that little girl."

There was little physical evidence found at the scene that could be developed into a clue until William R. Smith, a member of the Fredericksburg, Virginia, Rescue Squad, started poking at the fallen leaves several yards from the grave. He spotted something that was a little lighter than the brown leaves. Stooping, he found that there were two somethings, made of plastic. An FBI agent identified the somethings as a pair of pistol grips.

"Is that so?" said Smith. "Looks like they might fit a fairly big handgun, maybe a .38."

A few hours later, in the FBI's Washington laboratory, George Berley agreed with Smith. Berley, a precise, monosyllabic gun expert, took microscopic pictures of the grips and then enlarged them. He found markings on the right grip that looked as though it had been torn from the handgun by what he called, carefully, "a sudden force."

With characteristic caution, Berley "allowed" that the markings could have been caused by someone using the gun as a club. It figured. The bodies of both father and child bore bruises that could have resulted from a pistol-whipping. "Of course, we've got to find that particular gun if we're going to get anywhere," Berley said. "I don't believe anyone's going to turn it in," he added, permitting his voice a sardonic tone.

Besides, there was the possibility, a slight one, that Jackson had wielded the gun against the assailant in a futile attempt to protect his little girl and himself.

But there had been no protection for the Jackson family from the someone who had violently intruded into their quiet lives on the night of January 11, 1959. Seventeen days after discovery of the bodies of father and child, two boys named Johnny, both thirteen, found the remains of the mother and the other child— 100 miles away from the grave of the father and youngest child.

Johnny Paddy had finished the chores, piling the wood up straight behind the shed and stacking the trash cans, and he hurried over to Johnny Bolin's house, a few fields away in the bucolic setting of Gambrills, Maryland, not far from the state capital of Annapolis. The two boys flew a kite for a while, so high the string broke. Then they took their BB gun, which they had chipped in to buy for $1.50, and went off to take target practice at tin cans in a patch of woods.

Johnny Bolin saw something that looked like a rat's nest. Each boy took a couple of shots at the low mound of sand and brush, and then walked over to get a closer look. Johnny Bolin scraped away some of the sand and suddenly saw the back of a human head.

"That's a real person, not a doll or anything!" the Bolin boy yelled, and the youngsters bolted for the Bolin house. Ralph Bolin, sixteen, was polishing the family car in the backyard.

"Mommy, Mommy, I found a dead body," Johnny Bolin screamed.

"If you're kidding me I'm going to smack you," warned his big brother.

Johnny Bolin was in tears now. "If I'm wrong I won't mind if you smack me," he cried.

Ralph Bolin dug into the mound of sand and brush with the stock of the BB gun. When he saw the bodies of a woman and a little girl, he ran back to tell his mother and she called the police.

The bodies were those of Mrs. Mildred Jackson, twenty-seven, and the Jacksons' elder daughter, Susan Anne, five. The mother was lying face-up, with the little girl on top of her, her feet pointing toward the mother's head. Mother and child both had been savagely beaten. Mrs. Jackson's head was a mass of bruises and lacerations, and there were bruises on her knees. A silk stocking was knotted around her neck, apparently to finish the ghastly work. Susan Anne had died of a fractured skull. Neither mother nor child had been sexually assaulted. As for the weapon, it was described, apologetically, by Dr. Russell E. Fisher, Maryland's Chief Medical Examiner, as, "I'm sorry to have to report, only the usual blunt instrument." Mrs. Jackson's blue kid shoes were missing and she was barefoot. A second stocking, presumably hers, was found in the brush near the shallow grave.

It seemed clear that the murders of father and child and mother and child had taken place within a period of a few hours. Food was found in the stomachs of Carroll Jackson and Janet, but not in the stomachs of the other two victims. Police officials and the FBI thereby concluded that father and child had been killed first and that the murderer buried their bodies before slaying mother and child some time later and dumping their remains nearly 100 miles away from the scene of the first killings.

In any case, the killer knew exactly where he was going when he drove away from that first grave. It was a deserted house on a long unused lane—a frame building with a caved-in roof, rotting floors, and a collapsed porch, which had been abandoned years before when its owner died without heirs.

The house was only about 100 yards from the grave in which the two Johnnys found mother and child. Investigators knew the killer had taken Mrs. Jackson into that house, because a button from her coat was found there by FBI Agent John C. Bonner. They also discovered tire marks in the dirt driveway circling the house, as if the killer had braked at that point.

There was no way of knowing whether Mrs. Jackson and Susan Anne were killed in the house or outside; bloodstains were found in both the house and on its grounds. One theory was that the child was already dead when the killer's car arrived at the house. In any event, there was the possibility that the killer showed uncommon audacity—or massive confidence—in getting to the house.

Time, of course, was of the essence once father and child had been slain. And the most direct route from the scene of the first murders is north via U.S. Route 301 over the toll bridge spanning the Potomac River in Dahlgren, Virginia. Did the killer really dare to stop and pay the toll with his victims in the car? "He was in a hurry," an FBI agent remarked dryly. "And murderers have huge egos. They think they can get away with anything, and everything so far had gone right."

In any event, there was a good chance the killer had been at the ramshackle house before and had been impressed by its isolation. That explained the sloppily arranged grave; the killer believed it unlikely that anyone would venture on a lane so overhung with branches and cluttered with brush that it would intimidate even the most curious hiker.

Moreover, something else had happened in that neighborhood, less than a mile from the deserted house and its tragic grave. Two years before, the driver of a green Chrysler or De Soto accosted a couple parked on a little-used road and shot Mrs. Margaret V. Harold to death. Police found evidence, including a small stock of food, in the basement of an unoccupied cinder-block dwelling on the other side of a stretch of woods from the Jacksons' grave site. Someone had used that cinder-block shack as a hideout shortly after the murder of the woman in the parked car. It had to be someone who knew the territory. Thus, the search for the Jacksons' killer could be concentrated for the most part in Virginia and Maryland, within a 50-mile radius of Washington, D.C. The rest of the country could not be entirely neglected, but the signs pointed to what Detective Capt. Elmer Hagner of Maryland's Anne Arundel County called "hometown talent."

By then, the FBI had moved in on the case in full force with 75 agents, backed up by its laboratory and other crime-solving scientists. Until the bodies of the mother and child were found in Maryland, there had been no clear federal violation. Now the mass murder fell under the federal kidnapping statute; state lines had been crossed.

Working with task forces of police from Virginia, Maryland, and the District of Columbia, the FBI looked for a common denominator to the family tragedy that took place in different states. Agents were looking for a perverted, "career" killer-rapist whose *modus operandi* was to cruise about in a wide area of countryside in the search for victims. They believed there had to be people who knew what the killer looked like from personal experience. And they found such people, in official files, and from patient, often door-to-door canvases.

The agents talked to Keith Waldrop of Montpelier, Virginia,

who told them that on the night the Jacksons' car was abandoned he was driving along a road with his wife about 12 miles from the scene of the Jacksons' abduction. He fixed the time at about half an hour before that frightful incident. He said "a wild-eyed man" driving a light blue or green Ford—a 1952 to 1954 model—tried to shunt their car off the road.

"We were scared," Waldrop said. "He looked like a maniac. But when the man slid across the seat of his car as if to get out, my wife yelled to me to step on the gas and we got away."

In August 1958, a Ford of the same description was used to block a married couple driving along a back road near Laurel, Maryland. The husband was slugged at gunpoint by the assailant and then forced into the trunk of the attacker's car. During the next half hour the wife was raped as the attacker alternately drove around and pulled up at roadside. Then the couple was released.

Earlier, in June 1957, a man drove up to the car of an engaged couple parked at Lake Waterford, 12 miles north of where Mrs. Jackson and her daughter would be buried. As in the Laurel and Jackson cases, the man's hands were tied. But when the intruder tried to force the man into the car trunk, his victim grappled with him and he took off in a green Chrysler or De Soto.

Twelve hours later, the driver of the same car attacked a parked couple in the incident that ended in the shooting murder of the woman.

Meanwhile, the two Johnnys—Paddy and Bolin—were interviewed again about their discovery of the bodies of Mrs. Jackson and Susan Anne. They had nothing to add to what they had told police about their grim discovery. But, making casual conversation, the two FBI men asked if the neighborhood was popular with "loving couples."

The boys didn't know. They hadn't seen any cars around on the day they found the Jacksons' grave. "Last car we seen," said Johnny Bolin, "was a Ford we saw parked on a side road the day before when we were in the school bus." A nice car? Not bad, they said. "It was pretty new," added Johnny Paddy. "About a 1956. Light green."

Summing up what had been learned, the FBI circulated a question addressed to the readers of newspapers in Virginia, Maryland, and the District of Columbia. It read:

"Do you know a man who used a 1946–1948 green Chrysler or De Soto on June 26, 1957, acquired a 1952–1954 dull-colored light blue or green Ford before August 24, 1958, and had the Ford on January 11, 1959?"

At the same time, the FBI set out to locate owners of all late-model Fords registered in Maryland, Virginia, and the District of Columbia, and to determine from their owners where their cars were on January 11, 1959.

From information furnished by the witnesses interviewed, the FBI and local police got together and had a composite drawing made of the murder suspect. The description accompanying the drawing was amazing in its detail. Its subject was pictured as "White, about six feet tall, weighing 175 pounds, between 25 and 30 years old, dark brown or black hair, dark brown eyes, very fair complexion, hair parted on the left and combed back, a large shock of hair over the right side of the forehead which the man frequently brushes back with his hand. The man is neat and clean, with a better than average vocabulary, known to be a sex pervert and exhibitionist. He is carrying a snub-nosed .32- or .38-caliber pistol and should be considered extremely dangerous."

Copies of the drawing were made at FBI headquarters and distributed not only in Virginia, Maryland, and the District of Columbia but across the country through the FBI's network of 55 field offices. Bill Gunn of the FBI's Public Affairs Office explained this bit of Bureau thoroughness.

"Actually, nobody knows where the guy is," he said. "He could be across the street from us, having a cup of coffee, or trying to pick a winner at the Pimlico track in Baltimore. But he also could be in San Francisco or Denver. My personal guess is he's put a helluva distance between himself and the Washington area."

The drawing, made by Cpl. Vyrl Couperthwaite and Detective Walter Evanoff of the Washington Police Department, apparently faithfully reproduced the prime suspect's features and other physical specifications. Three days after it was circulated, a woman called the FBI from Montpelier, Virginia. "It's him," she said excitedly. She reported that she, her husband, and their two children were driving home from visiting relatives a few weeks before when a car "whipped in front of us and made us stop."

She said the car was driven by a young white man with long dark hair. "It was a Ford," she said. "He'd been following us bumper-to-bumper for about three or four minutes. When he started out the right door our car lights hit him and I got a good look at his face." Her husband, she said, "managed somehow to get around him and we took off."

Other citizens wrote or phoned to say the suspect had been seen in Washington, D.C., Kansas City, Memphis, Dallas, Los Angeles, Chicago, and Miami, as well as in a score or so of small towns. FBI agents followed up each lead from the Bureau's field offices without success.

Then began the year of the long months. Most of the investigation centered in the Virginia–Maryland–District of Columbia area, but agents from FBI field offices fanned out into all of the 50 states, asking their quiet, careful questions, and listening quietly and carefully to even the most far-fetched answers.

Wherever they went, the agents asked one final, desperate question: "Do you know of any couple accosted in a parked car or abducted, or of an attempted abduction for perverted sex purposes which was not reported to police?"

Routinely, FBI agents questioned routine suspects—criminals with a history of sex offenses and acts of violence, former inmates of mental institutions, street people who knew their way around in the demi-underground of various far-out cultures. By July 1959, they had interviewed more than 1400 suspects. And that month they got their first solid lead.

A letter was delivered to the police department in Prince George's County, Maryland, which adjoins Washington. The informant wrote that he suspected a former acquaintance of involvement in the murder of Mrs. Margaret V. Harold, thirty-six, a clerical worker at Fort Meade, Maryland.

Mrs. Harold's name rang an instant bell. It was *the* Mrs. Harold who had been shot to death in June 1957 as she sat in a car with an army sergeant near Gambrills, Maryland, not far from the spot where the bodies of Mrs. Jackson and her daughter had been found less than two years later.

The informant identified the suspect as Melvin Davis Rees, Jr., about twenty-nine, a musician and piano teacher who had lived in Hyattsville and Washington and had played in small clubs in the Capital. The letter was turned over to the FBI by the Prince George's police, and agents interviewed the informant. But all they could get out of him was his suspicion that Rees was a killer. Nor did he know where Rees was living; he could only surmise that his one-time acquaintance was working at his profession.

The FBI went looking for Rees, and discovered that he was hard to find. No one who knew him, including his parents, had any idea of even where the FBI might start its search for him. Meanwhile, agents went to work on Rees's past and sought evidence linking him with other crimes.

They learned that on March 12, 1955, Rees had been charged with assault on the complaint of a thirty-six-year-old woman he had accosted near a bus stop, pulling her into his car when she refused his invitation to go for a ride. Later, however, the woman refused to prosecute.

The FBI also learned that Rees had used or owned automobiles that matched descriptions of those seen near the site of Mrs. Harold's murder and the neighborhood where the Jackson family had been abducted. For example, shortly after the shooting of Mrs. Harold as she sat in a car with an army sergeant, a truck driver had told police he helped a man in a 1948 green Chrysler get his car out of a ditch not far from the murder scene. Separate investigations indicated that Rees might have been the driver of other cars used by the assailant who intercepted other couples and, in at least one case, raped a woman occupant of a parked car.

On the day that the important letter was delivered to the FBI, the Bureau had eliminated 1331 suspects. One hundred and forty-six others remained on the "possible list." Now Rees's name was added to that list. Within hours, he became the most wanted man when agents interviewed the sergeant who had been with Mrs. Harold when she was murdered but who had managed to escape. The GI was shown several photographs and identified Rees's as that of Mrs. Harold's killer.

It took time—perhaps too much time. But the FBI's dogged routine, with its time-wasting but vital nit-picking, paid off. An agent working undercover in Little Rock, Arkansas, was shooting a game of pool for nickels and dimes in a sleazy neighborhood of mostly empty storefronts. His opponent kept chattering about a "big score" he was going to make, but not around the pool table.

"How can you be sure?" the agent asked with the accustomed derisiveness of the scene. "Hell, the way you talk you don't seem to know where it's coming from, any more than I do."

"I'm sure," said the other man. "I know where it's coming from. I did some work for the big man and he's gonna cut me in on the profits. Some dude in Memphis is running away from a murder rap back East, and the big man found out who he is from one of them FBI posters and he's gonna hold him up for regular bread, like the guy was making weekly payments on a new car."

"The big man had better be careful," said the agent. "A killer like that, he won't worry about blowing somebody else away."

"No way, no way at all," his opponent told him, chalking his cue. "The dude is a musician, a scared guy. He's livin' scared, workin' for a music store days and hidin' nights. Name of Melvin. Melvin something. The name ain't even a killer's name. Melvin, that's a name for a pussycat."

The agent asked a few more questions, but the other player clammed up. "I told enough," he said finally. "All you had to know was that I know where the bread is coming from."

As it turned out, the agent had learned enough. He drove out into the countryside, found a pay phone, and relayed his information to the FBI office in Memphis. Agents launched a series of visits to music stores, spending a dollar here, a couple of dollars there. And on June 25, 1960—more than 17 months after the Jackson family was murdered—Rees was arrested outside a music store in West Memphis, where he was working as a piano salesman and teacher.

The army sergeant was flown to Memphis and identified Rees in a police lineup as Mrs. Harold's slayer. The initial charge against the fugitive was unlawful flight to avoid prosecution for the Harold murder. Later, he was arraigned for two of the Jackson murders. Under the so-called Lindbergh Law, the FBI charged him with kidnapping Mrs. Jackson and her daughter, Susan Anne, transporting them across a state line, and killing them.

The next day, Virginia authorities lodged charges against Rees for the kidnapping and murder of the Jackson father and eighteen-month-old Janet. Because the father and daughter had not been carried across a state line, the Commonwealth of Virginia had jurisdiction in that case.

Meanwhile, FBI Agent Francis X. Jhan of the Hyattsville field office led a team of six other agents to the Hyattsville home of Rees's parents and got written consent to search the premises. During the search, Agent Gene S. Weimer climbed to the attic and noticed a section cut out of the wall in a closet. Behind the wall, deep under the eaves, Weimer found an accordion case containing a .38-caliber Cobra revolver and an obscene, handwritten document. Attached to the document were newspaper photographs of Mrs. Jackson and Susan Anne.

"Here's a motive for you," Weimer told Jhan. "This is a kind of diary; the creep is telling why he killed that family."

One passage of the writings, on unlined white paper, read:

"Caught on lonely road—after pulling them over with leveled pistol and ordered them out and into car. Trunk was open for husband and both bound. Drove to select area and killed husband & baby. Now the mother and daughter were all mine." Underscoring emphasized the "all mine."

There followed an obscenely worded account of perversion, with the conclusion: "Then tied and gagged, led to her place of execution and hanged her."

An FBI expert studied the document for less than 30 minutes before concluding that the handwriting matched that of samples in Rees's hand. It was, he said, "a piece of cake. Nobody but Rees could have written that garbage. He writes a perfect, forgery-proof hand, with a unique formation of letters that couldn't be duplicated."

In any case, the indictment of Rees by a federal grand jury a couple of days later cited "sexual gratification" as one of the motives for the kidnap-murder of mother and child. The document said Mrs. Jackson was held for that purpose "upon her body and for the further purpose of killing her." Rees was not charged with having sexually molested five-year-old Susan Anne.

Rees, a slender six feet three inches with thick black hair, looked younger than his thirty-two years. His demeanor at his arraignment fit the frequently ill-used adjective, "impassive," and his voice was firm and strong when he pleaded not guilty. A bailiff described him as "very gentlemanly."

A guitarist at the West Memphis Piano Company, where Rees

had been working, told reporters Rees was "a very neat, very quiet, reserved, well-mannered gentleman. It came as a complete shock to us when we heard he'd been arrested. It was as if you had just learned your mother was involved in something. We never heard him say a profane word, or an obscene one. He was an excellent musician at the piano and on a lot of other instruments, including the clarinet, and a very fine teacher. His pupils came along beautifully."

Rees's parents in Hyattsville were inconsolable. Neighbors described them as "fine people . . . religious people . . . perfect neighbors." Rees's father, a telephone repair man, was active in civic affairs and a devoted gardener who built a big greenhouse in the rear of his two-story brick home. The Rees couple had two married daughters, both older than the son.

Elaine Rees, who had obtained an absolute divorce from the suspect in March 1959, told the press Rees was never violent to her or their son, Phillip, six. "Once he merely winced when Phillip hit him with a hammer," she said.

Rees had been sharing a garage apartment in Memphis for about five months with a tiny blonde professional singer, who had played in various cities, including Washington. She said she was Rees's wife and claimed that the man who had informed on Rees was jealous of Rees's musical talent and blamed Rees for "blackballing" him when he tried to get a job.

Rees did not go on trial in federal court in Baltimore for the murder of mother and daughter until January 25, 1961—seven months to the day after his arrest in Tennessee. The government asked the jury of 10 men and 2 women to find him guilty and to recommend the death penalty.

Halfway through the trial, the prosecution was dealt a setback when Judge Roszel Thomsen excluded the obscene document, purported to be an account of the crime in the defendant's handwriting, found in his Hyattsville home along with the .38-caliber Cobra revolver. After a day and a half of argument, Thomsen barred the prosecution from introducing the writings, but said it could use the revolver as evidence against Rees.

Thomsen did not say so, but court attachés let it be understood that the judge had ruled under the Fifth Amendment provision "that no person shall be compelled in any criminal case to be a witness against himself."

It didn't matter. The essence of the prosecution's case was the gun and the plastic pistol grips found at the scene of the father-daughter slaying.

William Bage, a Hyattsville insurance agent, testified that he had sold the gun through an ad in a Washington newspaper to a man who paid for it with a check signed "Melvin D. Rees Jr." The pistol was equipped with bone grips when he sold it, Bage said, but he threw in a pair of plastic grips and a box of shells. The check bounced, the witness said, but he finally got his money from Rees in cash.

Then the FBI linked the grips with the gun agents had taken from Rees's Hyattsville home. It was the grips that brought George Berley, the FBI gun expert, to the stand.

With his usual precision, Berley told of examining the gun grips at the FBI laboratory, then showed the jury enlarged pictures taken through comparison microscopes of Rees's .38 Cobra and the right gun grip. Rees frowned as Berley testified that a large photograph showed "a series of markings in agreement" between the right grip and metal on the right side of the gun butt. "The right grip at one time had been attached to the Colt Cobra revolver," Berley said evenly. He explained that the similar markings were made when the plastic grip "moved under pressure against the metal of the butt." Those markings, he said, could have been made by "using the gun as a club."

That was the ball game. The FBI evidence was circumstantial, but strong. It had managed to tell the jurors that Rees must have been at the scene of the first murders if his gun was there, and that the grips fit his gun. Jackson had been beaten before he was shot to death. Berley gave the jury to understand that the gun probably was the weapon used by Rees to beat Jackson. There was no evidence by either side suggesting any other weapon. And although the obscene "diary" found in the attic of Rees's Hyattsville home was excluded as evidence in court, portions of it had been published by both Memphis newspapers as part of the FBI's evidence in seeking indictment. The contents of the "diary" became common knowledge long before a jury of his peers was selected to try Melvin Davis Rees, Jr., for murder.

It came as no surprise, then, when Rees was found guilty on February 23, 1961, of the kidnap-murder of Mildred Jackson, twenty-seven, and her daughter Susan Anne, five years old.

Sixteen days later, Judge Thomsen sentenced Rees to life imprisonment, a sentence that would make him eligible for parole in 15 years.

But the law was not through with Rees. In his first public words during a trial at which he refused to take the stand, Rees said simply, "My attorneys spoke for me." They would have to speak for him again in Virginia, which was prepared to try him for the murder of Carroll Vernon Jackson, twenty-nine, and his daughter Janet Carroll, eighteen months.

As it turned out, Virginia tried Rees only for the murder of the father. After evidence by 60 witnesses during a nine-day court session in Spotsylvania, it took a jury less than an hour to reach a verdict and condemn Rees to the electric chair.

Circuit Judge John D. Butzner set April 6, 1961, as the date for Rees's execution. Rees had not taken the witness stand during that trial, either, but when asked by the court if he had anything to say he replied, "Yes, Your Honor, I wish to reaffirm my innocence."

As it turned out, there was no need for Rees to say any more. He did not die in the chair because psychiatrists ruled that he was mentally incompetent to participate in an appeal. Because he couldn't appeal, he couldn't be executed.

But the government won out in the end. His conviction in Virginia rendered him ineligible for parole from a federal judge's imposition of a life term in the Maryland case, so he was remanded to federal authorities to remain in custody until death set him free.

10

Massacre in Washington

"Put it in the sink! The kid is only a few days old. The sink is big enough to drown it in."

Warily, FBI officials refer to it as the Black Mafia. In Washington, no public servant wants to risk seeming to denigrate a religious denomination. But it is, in fact, the Black Muslim Mob that has muscled into the original Mafia's rackets in many of the country's big cities.

The Black Muslims date from 1930, when Elijah Muhammad (then Elijah Poole) announced he had met the human form of Allah in the person of an Arab immigrant named W. D. Fard, who appointed Elijah his special prophet. The Black Muslims emphasize black supremacy, capitalism, and a belief that whites are "devils." No fool, but a shrewd businessman, Elijah established an empire of black farms, ghetto real estate, newspapers, department stores, and co-ops valued at more than $100 million. To provide the necessary cash flow, Elijah levied a cash quota on each local mosque. His organization eventually sought donations, or "loans," from street blacks.

The Black Muslims accept all blacks, regardless of their criminal records. Their duty, they say, is to rehabilitate criminals and make them responsible members of the community. As a result, the organization was infiltrated by hardened felons who used the Black Muslim religion as a cover to weld disorganized black dope pushers, pimps, loan sharks, protection peddlers, and petty hoodlums into a powerful and effective criminal source. The "converts" wouldn't know the sacred teachings of the Koran from a centerfold in *Playboy,* but they recognized a respectable base of operations when they saw it.

Two of those opportunists who tarnished the escutcheon of a respectable and deeply moralistic sect were Ronald Harvey and Sam Christian, hulking six-foot bullies with IQs that would shame a third-grader. Harvey and Christian joined the Philadelphia Black Muslims in 1959, and within a year had taken over the loosely organized original Black Mafia of mostly small-time hoodlums to weld a syndicate whose discipline was enforced by a continuing reign of terror.

Shortly, Harvey became a lieutenant, or assistant to the minister, of the Philadelphia Mosque. Christian slugged his way to the leadership of a paramilitary youth group called the Fruit of Islam. In their new surroundings, both men learned valuable lessons about organization and discipline.

At first, Harvey and Christian followed the teachings of their new "faith" by taking the initiative in driving dope pushers off the streets. They were hailed within the sect as raging generals in the war against an evil that was destroying their black brethren both physically and morally. But it wasn't long before they reverted to type. They began extorting "dues" from the pushers as a price for letting them alone. As the money poured in, they expanded their operations and eventually took over the heroin and other drug traffic in the black ghetto. They divided most of Philadelphia into territories, and built up an army of more than 200 "street soldiers," armed and schooled to be trigger-happy. Some new pushers were recruited; others were permitted to operate so long as they paid tribute to the Black Muslim Mob. Those who balked were executed.

One of those who didn't go along was a fat and wealthy heroin dealer named Tyrone ("Fat Ty") Palmer. Warnings delivered by the mob's errand boys failed to frighten Fat Ty into cooperating. After all, Fat Ty had his own corps of bodyguards, including one Gilbert Satterwhite, a crack shot. So Harvey and Christian decided on the ultimate persuasion, down the road in Atlantic City.

Billy Paul and Flash Wilson were playing the Club Harlem's Easter Show on April 6, 1972. Fat Ty was among the 600 patrons, mostly black, in the club's spacious ballroom. There was a commotion at a couple of tables near the stage, and then a fusillade of gunfire. There were high-pitched screams, and a rush for the exits.

As the smoke began to settle, five persons lay dead or dying, three others nursed illegal bullet holes, and six had been injured by flying glass. Fat Ty was killed outright. Satterwhite was hit as he struggled to unholster his gun and died later of head wounds. Both Harvey and Christian were seen in the ballroom. Later, Christian was seen having a drink in a saloon across the street.

But police found nobody who would identify the mob's two warlords in a court of law. Eventually, one of the wounded men, Larry Starks, identified by the FBI and Philadelphia police as a twenty-six-year-old professional hit man, was charged with Satterwhite's murder. He never went to trial. The state's prime witness suffered a sudden lapse of memory after a visit from a couple of the mob's goons.

By this time, straight members of Philadelphia Mosque No. 12 had become alarmed by the bad publicity creeps like Harvey and Christian were giving their sect. Philadelphia police came to the sect's defense. In an official department statement, the Mosque was described as a "truly religious denomination, 99 per cent of whose members are true believers and detest criminal activity." There were no demurrers from the community at large. Clergymen of other denominations expressed their respect and sympathy for the Mosque, and declared in a joint statement that "Men like Harvey and Christian no more represent the Black Muslim membership than Mafia hoodlums represent the Roman Catholic Church or Protestant criminals represent the congregations to which they belong."

In fact, however, Harvey, Christian, and their troops continued to parade themselves as Black Muslims, and in line with Muslim policy they were not barred from religious services and other Mosque activities. The sect stood fast in its belief that no human being is beyond redemption.

But Harvey and Christian were ineffable. Several black clergymen and community leaders reported to police they had been marked for assassination by the mob. One of those who said he had been targeted by the mob's errand boys was Muhammad Kenyatta, executive director of the Black Economic Development Corporation. Another was Reggie Schell, former leader of the Black Panther party and a tireless worker in the mean streets of the black ghetto.

"What has marked the activities of this mob is the wholesale disregard of human life," said an official FBI statement. "Even the Italian Mafia, if they decide to rub somebody out, hit just that person, not his family. These men kill the family, innocent bystanders, anyone. We're dealing with animals here."

The "animal" label was no outraged hyperbole. There was the case of Bo Agney, an independent dope pusher who lived dangerously. Agney wouldn't get up protection money. So Agney was murdered and his head chopped off and put in a bag. The bag was left on a doorstep in the ghetto with a note which read: "This is what happens to dudes who don't pay their dues."

One hot July night in 1971, Mrs. Philomena Molo heard a knock on the door of her home in Middletown Township, Pennsylvania. Her husband, Daniel Molo, a white who had moved from South Philadelphia and set up more luxurious housekeeping with the money from his lucrative cigarette-smuggling racket, didn't hear the knock. He was in the basement labeling the 5000 cartons of untaxed cigarettes trucked up from North Carolina.

When Mrs. Molo went to the door, a voice outside shouted: "FBI! Contraband cigarettes! Open up!" Instead, Mrs. Molo ran to call her husband. Molo came up the cellar stairs, but stopped behind the door to the kitchen and yelled to his wife not to open the front door.

So one of the callers, a tall, skinny black named Ronald Connolly, who paraded his membership in the Black Muslims, fired his gun. The bullet penetrated both doors and slammed into Molo's chest, wounding him mortally.

Then Connolly and another black broke down the front door. Mrs. Molo tried to leave by the back door, but was stopped by a voice outside. "Get back inside," yelled the voice. "The place is surrounded."

The robbers took $12,000 from the basement and roughed up Mrs. Molo. But they didn't kill the five children in the house. "We don't have time for that shit," one of the robbers told Connolly.

Arriving after neighbors reported hearing shots, Pennsylvania State Police checked the house next door. They found the occupants, Mr. and Mrs. Gerald Shoemaker, handcuffed and suspended upside down from pipes and rafters in the basement. In a blunder characteristic of the Harvey-Christian leadership, the hoods had first gone to the wrong house. Seizing the opportunity, they quickly took $700 from Shoemaker's pockets and slapped the couple around before hanging them up.

The FBI, always involved when criminals pose as federal agents, traced the handcuffs back to a South Philadelphia pawnshop. The handcuffs had been bought by Sam Christian. As usual, that mastermind was miles away. But his errand boy, Connolly, was convicted of first-degree murder, thanks to Mrs. Molo's eyewitness identification.

But Christian preferred the on-the-scene excitement of doing his own jobs whenever possible. He was fond of saying he got his kicks out of watching his victims "squirm and yell for mercy." Thus, he led a commando raid with three of his henchmen on the Adelphi Bar in a decaying Puerto Rican neighborhood of Atlantic City on September 6, 1971. Seventeen patrons were living it up in that bistro when Christian & Co. burst into the place, guns drawn.

The hoods tied up the customers with rope and adhesive tape, then robbed them of $20,000 in cash and jewelry, plus a few sacks of heroin and cocaine. Alerted by phone calls from neighboring establishments, police arrived just as the robbers had finished their work. Shots were exchanged, and the cops chased two late-model luxury sedans back toward Philadelphia. One car and its occupants disappeared into the night. The other, driven by Christian, flipped over and landed in a field.

Somehow, Sam Christian managed to extricate himself from the overturned car and escape on foot across country even as police cars roared up. But what Ron Harvey called "Sam's 100 percent luck" didn't save two other hoods, who were collared as they fled. One told police he was a respectable businessman, a partner in a sandwich shop in Philadelphia. The other owner was Ronald Harvey.

Christian continued to walk the streets in safety, but his days as a free man with no legally admissible case against him were numbered. A few weeks later, Sam and an unknown assistant traveled to New York City, where they visited an Upper East Side apartment and tried to relieve a narcotics dealer of $100,000 worth of heroin. Again, police interrupted the transaction, and one cop was wounded in a shootout. But this time they nabbed "Lucky" Sam. Fretful in the slammer, Sam coughed up a fat fee to hire an expensive mouthpiece, who arranged to have his $50,000 bail reduced to $15,000. Christian, described by an FBI agent as "meaner than a junkyard dog," promptly disappeared.

Ronald Harvey took over the store. Out in the open because the cops couldn't translate into admissible evidence the contents of their fat dossier on his criminal operations, he expanded the Black Mafia, ordered occasional executions of hoodlums who wouldn't "cooperate," and lived off the organization's swollen treasury. He also took a dim professional view of a rival religious sect, the Hanafi Mussulmans.

Harvey couldn't have cared less that the orthodox Hanafis interpreted the Koran literally and criticized the Black Muslims for excluding whites, although he was fond of claiming that the Hanafis "are as black as we are, only ignorant." What bugged him was that the Hanafi leadership had snubbed him. The organization was straight on law and order, and wanted nothing to do with converts whose profession was crime. Harvey was told to get lost when he tried to recruit "soldiers" from the Hanafi sect; he was shocked when his overtures were met by threats to inform on him to the police. To Harvey, such threats were tantamount to treason, imperiling his freedom.

So Harvey was interested to learn that the professional basketball star, Kareem Abdul-Jabbar, previously known as Lew Alcindor, had turned over an expensive three-story house in Washington to fellow black converts of the Hanafi persuasion. Beneficiary of Abdul-Jabbar's generosity was a "family" headed by Hamaas Abdul Khaalis, a man Harvey detested for moralistic views and his contempt for hoods of the Harvey stripe. It didn't bother Harvey that Khaalis had attacked Elijah Muhammad for preaching false doctrine; that was a religious difference of opinion. What mattered to Harvey was that Khaalis was a potential ally of the hated police establishment.

Harvey decided it was time to teach the apostate Hanafis a lesson. He called a meeting of seven trusted members of his organization and made an impassioned speech demanding that they "wipe out" the Khaalis "family," including Khaalis's two wives and several children. Revenge must be taken, he told his little fold, because Khaalis had written to their very own Mosque No. 12 in Philadelphia "defaming our leader, the great Elijah Muhammad, as a false prophet."

That did it. Harvey had chosen as his assistant hit men hoods who were fanatics about the Black Muslim sect, not only because the sect gave them cover, but because it provided them with a religion they could call their own. As one of the men, John Clark—Brother John, thirty-eight—told Harvey: "Those Hanafis are trying to take away our faith."

So on the morning of January 16, 1973, Harvey and six of his vicious toadies arrived in Washington by train. They registered into two rooms at the Downtown Motel in the rundown Southeast section of the Capital, using false identification documents provided by John Clark. That day and the next they reconnoitered the brick-and-fieldstone house on tree-lined Juniper Street, Northwest, in a middle-income neighborhood, where the Khaalis group was living. They did their cruising in two stolen cars, which they parked on a neighboring street at the end of the second day, and then bused back to their motel.

After stealing two more cars shortly after noon on January 18, the men again drove to the Hanafi home, listed as headquarters of the American Mussulman's Rifle and Pistol Club and as the national seat of the sect. After circling the block, they drove over to fashionable Connecticut Avenue, where one of them called the house from a pay phone.

When a woman answered, the caller said: "My name is Tony Jones. I want to buy a book by Hamaas Abdul Khaalis. It's called *Look and See*. I may buy two books. What's the best time to come round?"

There was silence and then a male voice came on the line and told the caller that two o'clock would be convenient. The caller thanked him and hung up.

At two o'clock, give or take a few minutes, the doorbell rang at the house on Juniper Street. As the door was being opened, six men headed by Ronald Harvey swarmed in, ripping off the door chain. They were armed with pistols and sawed-off shotguns, and Harvey was howling, "C'mon, c'mon, this is a stickup!"

There followed the worst mass murder in Washington history. Three of the seven victims—Abdul Nur, twenty-three; Daud Khaalis, twenty-five; and Rahman Uddein Khaalis, ten—were shot to death. Four small children were drowned, three of them—toddlers—in a bathtub. Ronald Harvey took charge of the execution of Abdul Khaalis, nine days old.

"Put it in the sink!" he yelled. "The kid is only a few days old. The sink is big enough to drown it in."

Hamaas Abdul Khaalis's younger wife, Bibi, twenty-six, and Almina, twenty-three, his daughter by his older wife, were shot in the head and left wounded. Both would live, but Bibi suffered brain damage that left her paralyzed on the right side, blind in the right eye, and a mute for life.

Khaalis was visiting in the neighborhood, and thus the killers failed in their prime objective: the execution of the family's leader. Khadyja Khaalis, his older wife, was shopping at a nearby supermarket with her son, the ill-fated Abdul Nur. As she reached the checkout counter, Mrs. Khaalis realized she had left her money at home. She sent Abdul Nur back to get it. When he didn't return, she repeatedly—"many times," she said—called home but got only busy signals.

Concerned now, Mrs. Khaalis picked up her husband and the two drove to the house. They found the front door locked and heard the voices of strangers inside. Khaalis told his wife to call police, then ran around to the back, in time to see the men fleeing on foot down an alley. Khaalis jumped into his car and gave chase onto Sixteenth Street, where one of the killers turned and fired a shot, shattering the car's windshield. Then, as Khaalis pulled to a stop, the men converged on the two cars they had parked nearby the day before and made their getaway.

Steven E. Levow, a District of Columbia policeman, arrived on the scene to find Khaalis waving hysterically in front of his car. Khaalis screamed: "My family has been shot, they are all dead."

Almina Khaalis was sitting on the back porch steps, dripping blood from her wounds, conscious but unable to respond to questions. The two men rushed through the open back door and down to the basement. There they found Bibi Khaalis lying on the floor in a pool of blood.

Hysteria overcame Khaalis. He ran up the stairs to the first floor, shrieked a curse as he saw the bodies there, then rushed up to the second floor, Levow following. As Khaalis entered the bathroom he screamed, "Oh, my God!" The three toddlers were dead in the bathtub. What looked to Levow "like a doll" was submerged in six or seven inches of water in the sink. Nine-day-old Abdul Khaalis was dead, too.

"It was ghastly," said Levow. "Those animals went to work efficiently, like a raiding squad in wartime."

But in retreat the animals turned sloppy. They left a trail of clues, including two pistols and expended shell casings dropped on a nearby lawn; a blue suitcase in the alley containing shotgun shells and two sawed-off shotguns; a brown paper bag with latent fingerprints later identified as those of Harvey and John Clark; a copy of the Philadelphia *Daily News,* and a copy of *Time* magazine's Philadelphia regional edition.

But, efficiently, the animals had disappeared. The FBI and police were reasonably sure their home lair was in the Philadelphia area, and the search was concentrated there. Meeting places, including Mosque No. 12, and hangouts of the Black Mafia were placed under heavy surveillance. Longtime informants were questioned and set to work checking underworld gossip. But Harvey, Clark, and the other executioners had dropped both out of sight and out of the underworld's shop talk. Two informants came up with a negative crumb. Sam Christian, still sought by police, had been seen by several people in Jersey City on the day of the massacre.

"It's hard to believe, but Christian apparently missed this one," commented Brian Carroll of the FBI's Philadelphia office. "The bastard must be sore as hell that they didn't count him in on it."

Christian, however, was still doing dirty business as usual on the run, and shortly he and Harvey were reunited to pursue the final solution to a problem. The problem was a man named Coxson, who wore his Christian name, Major, as a royal title. Coxson was suspected, on strong evidence, of playing footsie with Philadelphia cops and politicians, to the detriment of the Black Mafia. He had to be dealt with.

Major Coxson was a colorful black wheeler-dealer in the rackets, known on the street—half admiringly, half contemptuously—as "The Aristocrat." He lived in an elegantly overdone mansion in Cherry Hill, New Jersey, and his hands were clean, if not his conscience. Coxson was deeply involved in dope trafficking, but boasted that he "never touched the stuff, never saw it." He financed the traffic or invested in a piece of the action. He was the arranger; he knew the right people in Philadelphia and New York, and he got them together, for a fee. He hobnobbed with politicians. Police and the FBI suspected he knew where to find the best hit men and that he did the heavy thinking for Ronald Harvey and Sam Christian.

Coxson also collected entertainers and athletes, including his prize pal, heavyweight champion Muhammad Ali, and he usually got something out of all of them. For example, he persuaded Ali to let him buy the furnishings for Ali's Cherry Hill home, then told Ali they cost twice what "The Aristocrat" had paid for them, pocketing the difference.

But Coxson never joined the Black Muslim Mob. He wanted to be his own man, free to pick and choose his divertissements and investments. As a result, the Harveys and Christians never fully trusted him. He was too much the non-Muslim, and he moved too easily in the white power structure. They tolerated him because they needed his New York narcotics connections and his access to cash from respectable white banks. Then someone had a bright idea. The mob needed political power, so why not run Coxson for mayor of Camden, New Jersey, across the Delaware River from Philadelphia?

Coxson was delighted with this offer of the final jewel to his crown. He saw himself raised to equal status with his political pals. So the Coxson campaign against one Angelo Errichetti was heavily financed by the mob, and 40 soldiers were dispatched across the river to keep an eye on the investment.

Then the worst happened. Six splinter candidates entered the race. Honest blacks, notably the Black People's Unity Movement, seized the opportunity to denounce Coxson as a carpetbagger. Key black politicians joined the Errichetti bandwagon. And Errichetti trounced Coxson by 15,716 votes to 3746.

Coxson's star was fading. The mob didn't need him now. So Coxson's credentials were investigated, resulting in his denouncement in the inner councils of the mob as a stool pigeon. The leadership paid what was necessary to line up informants who testified that Coxson had been trading bodies to the law in exchange for being left alone. The charges probably were true; it didn't matter to Harvey, Christian, and their fellow conspirators. They didn't need Coxson anymore, and they wanted to get rid of him so they could share the money he was raking in.

Thus it came about that shortly before four o'clock on the morning of June 8, 1973—just a month after Coxson's defeat at the polls—four gunmen invaded the Coxson mansion. Coxson, his common-law wife, Lois Luby; Mrs. Luby's fifteen-year-old son, Toro; and her sixteen-year-old daughter, Lita, were bound and gagged and shot. Mrs. Luby's youngest child, thirteen-year-old Lex, fled the house uninjured.

Coxson apparently died instantly. His body was found kneeling against the waterbed of his second-floor bedroom. Mrs. Luby was found in the same bedroom. Lita was found in another bedroom, her nightgown pulled up over her head. Toro was found on the floor of the dining room. Mrs. Luby and the two wounded children were taken to Cherry Hill Medical Center. Lita Luby died several days later. Her mother was left blind and paralyzed; Toro lost the sight of one eye.

Harvey and Christian were prime suspects. The FBI, investigating the whereabouts of both men under the Interstate Flight to Avoid Prosecution Statute, learned through informants that a car registered by Christian under the alias Samuel Bey had been seen in Cherry Hill the night of the slayings. They found the car abandoned in a quarry outside Philadelphia. Fingerprints found on two of the car's doors were checked. They were Harvey's and Sam Christian's.

But long months passed and Harvey and Christian remained at large.

Then in the late fall of 1973, an FBI agent named Roger Schweickert in Detroit was seized by a notion. He had learned that the Sons of Africa, a paramilitary offshoot of the Black Muslims, was recruiting "soldiers" in the Pink Lady Bar on the rundown West Side. He arranged to have the bar placed under surveillance. Meanwhile, he had a chat with a "snitch"—an informant named Arthur Hadden—who told him a Philadelphia mobster was interviewing the recruits. Hadden's description of the man closely matched that of Sam Christian.

The next day, Hadden was murdered in another ghetto bar, cut down by 12 shots, obviously fired from at least two different guns. Schweickert mourned Hadden, cursed the luck, and continued his surveillance of the Pink Lady Bar.

November had been succeeded by December before Schweickert's luck changed for the better. An underground Bureau agent phoned in a tip: A man he was sure was Sam Christian would be at a house on the West Side in 15 minutes.

Twelve minutes later, Schweickert and three other agents turned into the street where the house was located, made a pass by the house, then turned around and parked on the opposite side of the street. Moments later, a woman emerged, followed by a hulking black man. Both got into the back seat of a Chevrolet sedan.

"That could be our man," Schweickert muttered. He drove past the Chevrolet; there was no one at its wheel, but now Schweickert was sure the man was Christian.

"Pull up," Schweickert told his driver. He drew his .375 Smith and Wesson revolver. Supervisor Carl Bresco was holding a Thompson submachine gun. Schweickert got out of the car and ran over to the Chevrolet.

Standing beside an open window, Schweickert barked: "Get out, Christian, and put your hands where I can see them." The man got out of the car, protesting. "What's this all about?" he growled. "What's going on?" He was wearing a full-length mink coat and a mink hat.

"This is what it's all about, Christian," Schweickert snapped. He bent the man over the roof of the car and frisked him while Bresco held the submachine gun at ready. Schweickert examined one side of the man's head. The right scar was there, behind the right ear. The man was Sam Christian; to Schweickert the check of his fingerprints back at the field office was mere formality.

Meanwhile, the search for the Hanafi mass murderers was making progress. Six suspects had been identified. Harvey led the list, of course. The others were William Christian (no relation to Sam), John Griffin, Jerome Sinclair, James Henry Price, John Clark, and Theodore Mooney. Four were arrested in Philadelphia: Sinclair, Price, Clark, and Mooney. Now the FBI went after Harvey, William Christian, and Griffin.

An informant reported that Griffin and William Christian were hiding out in a hotel in Tampa, Florida. It was a bum steer; nobody had seen anyone even slightly resembling either of the men. But the two men had credit cards, and they used them. So did the FBI, by subpoenaing records of charges to the cards. The records said the men were living in an apartment building in West Jacksonville, Florida.

A dozen agents converged on the apartment building.

Neither Griffin nor Christian was on the premises, but neighbors identified the two men as tenants after examining photographs of them. Both were using aliases. The little army of agents staked out the neighborhood. Shortly after 5:00 P.M. on October 3, 1973, two men strolled up Edgewood Avenue West, where the apartment building stood. The order was bellowed: "FBI. Freeze!" One of the men turned as if to flee. "Stay right there," an agent yelled. "When we say 'freeze' we don't want to kiss you guys." The men admitted they were Griffin and William Christian, and within a few hours they had been arraigned, held on $500,000 bond each, and flown to Washington.

Now the FBI lusted for Ronald Harvey, number one on its list and still maddeningly at large. An agent gossiping with barflies heard about a man resembling Harvey who worked at a Tampa shipyard and lived in a boardinghouse. There was no Harvey registered there, but the owner's description of one of his tenants was almost as accurate as a mug shot of the fugitive.

Teams of agents loitered about the boardinghouse and shipyard for the next four days. No Harvey. But they did learn that William Christian and Griffin had palled around with a man who resembled Harvey. The man turned out to be one Robert Anderson, who looked only a little like Harvey. But the agents scooped him up when Washington notified them that Anderson was a federal parole violator, with a murder warrant out for him in Philadelphia. Anderson, it turned out, had been a cellmate of Griffin's in prison a few years before.

The pursuit moved north and west to Chicago, and agents maintained a stakeout of three Black Muslim neighborhoods for more than a month without results. Still, a man resembling Harvey had been reported in all three neighborhoods, so the stakeouts were continued. And patience paid off late in the afternoon of March 27, 1974. One of the many extensive interviews with people who had seen Harvey in Chicago led agents to a South Side apartment where Harvey was said to be living.

There were two late-model sedans parked outside the address, a Cougar and a Plymouth. Shortly, the surveilling agents under Merrill C. Sherer were interested to see six well-dressed dudes, clean-cut types in well-pressed suits and wearing ties with their shirts, carrying clothing and other personal effects from the apartment building to the two cars.

"Somebody's moving," remarked Sherer. "If we're lucky for a change, it's that upstanding citizen, Ronald Harvey."

Shortly, a man and a woman and two little boys came out of the building and got into the Cougar, the man in the driver's seat. "Goddam," Sherer muttered, stirring excitedly in the unmarked FBI car. "If that isn't Harvey I'll jump in Lake Michigan. But we can't take him with the woman and the two kids in the car. Everybody play it cool."

The Cougar drove off and went several blocks, the FBI car trailing discreetly. When the Cougar stopped outside another apartment building, the woman and the two little boys got out and went into the building.

"Now!" snapped Sherer as the Cougar pulled away from the curb. The FBI car lurched off, caught up with the Cougar, and pulled in front of it. The Cougar stopped and Sherer walked over to it, .38 revolver in hand.

"Get out!" he ordered the man. "FBI." The man got out. "Harvey, you're under arrest," Sherer said matter-of-factly.

"Harvey?—who's that?" asked the man. His face with its black mustache was that of an honest citizen mistaken for a wrongdoer.

"It's you," Sherer told him.

Manacled in the FBI car, the man continued to deny he was Harvey. But when Sherer asked him if he was glad the chase was over, he sighed resignedly. "Yeah," said Ronald Harvey. "Running is a bitch."

Harvey's longtime partner, Sam Christian, was charged with the murder of Major Coxson and Lita Luby, daughter of his common-law wife, but the case was dismissed because of "lack of evidence." A witness who said he would testify against Christian died of an "accidental" overdose of heroin. Other witnesses forthwith announced they couldn't remember anything about the killings, including who might have done them. So Christian was turned over to New York City authorities and eventually was convicted of the 1971 shootout-wounding of a city policeman and sentenced to 15 years to life in prison.

Harvey was also charged with the Coxson murders, but New Jersey's law enforcement establishment waived prosecution so Harvey could be tried for the Hanafi massacre in Washington. Given his druthers, Harvey undoubtedly would have opted to be tried on the New Jersey charges, but to the FBI and Washington lawmen a conviction on the Hanafi mass murders seemed to be in the bag.

First, however, six other defendants in that case went on trial in a Washington courtroom converted into a virtual fortress by extraordinary security measures. Windows were covered with steel plates, and the windows of the jury room with plywood. A metal-detecting device was installed to scan persons entering the courtroom, and special battery-powered lights were available for emergency use should the electricity fail. Extra United States marshals and District of Columbia guards were on hand, and defense and prosecution witnesses were held in separate rooms instead of one room, as was normal procedure.

Immediately, it was announced that one of the defendants, James Price, would testify for the government, and his case was severed from the others. That left in the dock John Clark, Theodore Mooney, William Christian, and Jerome Sinclair and John Griffin. Later, Price astounded everybody by refusing to play a role as a member of the government's witness team and was held in civil contempt by Judge Leonard Braman.

But it didn't matter. The government did indeed have the trial well in hand, with its eyewitnesses from the Hanafi house and its collection of physical evidence, including fingerprints of all the accused taken from a variety of places and items involved in the massacre. The five Black Muslims were convicted by a jury after only two days of deliberations. Two months later, on July 9, 1974, Judge Braman sentenced three of the defendants to life sentences totaling a minimum of 140 years in prison for each man.

Then the judge contributed *his* little surprise to the proceedings. He ordered a new trial for John Griffin, one of the convicted five, explaining that as a judge and "thirteenth juror," he could not fairly say that there was enough evidence against Griffin to support his conviction. But two months later, on October 19, a three-judge appeals court ruled that Braman was wrong in ordering a new trial for Griffin and ordered him to proceed with sentencing him. Once sentenced, the panel said, Griffin then would have the option of appealing his conviction.

Ronald Harvey went on trial for the Hanafi massacre on October 20, 1974. The trial lasted a month, but the government might well have rested its case on the testimony of two women—Khadyja Khaalis, one of Hamaas Abdul Khaalis's two wives, and Almina Khaalis, daughter of the Hanafi leader, and one of the survivors of the murder rampage.

Both women in turn walked calmly over to the defense table and pointed to Harvey as one of the band of men who committed the mass murders more than a year and a half before. "That is the man," each witness said in turn, and then walked calmly back to her seat. Harvey, who had lost 40 pounds from his six-foot-one-inch frame, looked down at the floor, his eyes blinking, as he heard the damning words.

"He's had two heart attacks since he was arrested, you know," a United States marshal whispered to a reporter behind the guard rail. "Being Ronald Harvey is enough to make any man sick."

Anyway, the jury deliberated for four hours and 15 minutes and then found Harvey guilty of 14 counts of murder. In due course, he sat in the same courtroom and heard Assistant United States Attorney Henry F. Schuelke describe him as "Mister Enforcer, who gave the orders to kill the victims of the massacre." Then he stood up, hands clasped behind his back, and heard Judge Braman sentence him to an absolute minimum of 140 years in prison.

"There's a man who's gonna have plenty of time to be sick," the marshal told his reporter friend. "He can set a new sick record."

Even so, Harvey fared better than James Price, who was and then wasn't the government's little helper in the first Hanafi trial. While awaiting his turn in the dock for the Washington massacre, Price was incarcerated in the federal prison in Holmesburg, Pennsylvania. In the same stir were the men against whom he had testified before a grand jury; indeed, Price shared a cell with one of them, Theodore Mooney, although there were 37 vacant cells at the time.

It was inevitable. Price's no longer quick body was found hanging from a bedsheet in a cell six cells away from his own on December 29, 1974. He had been beaten about the head, then strangled with a pair of shoelaces before his remains were hung like a picture as a warning to other would-be snitches.

John Griffin, for whom the judge had ordered a new trial, first was dispatched to Philadelphia, where he was convicted in 1975 for robbing the Continental Bank and sentenced to 40 years in prison. Two years later, Griffin was acquitted of taking part in the Hanafi murders. "That's why we gave Philadelphia the first shot at him," explained Prosecutor Schuelke of the government's Hanafi team. "They had an airtight case against the creep."

11

The Globe-Trotting Killer

There spoke the dreamer whose dream he believed was about to come true. And it is, after all, common for a human being to believe fondly that he is in command of his own destiny . . . there is something almost grand in a Harvey Rosenzweig, faceless to the outside world, certain that he was destined to become a rich man.

Lucky politicians who have been exposed to a few books are fond of explaining their success by quoting a Frenchman named Chamfort, who said that chance was a nickname for Providence. Possibly. Such an explanation, however, begs the question of why a Higher Authority permits chance to visit ill fortune on so many harmless and even beneficent people.

Consider the chance that caused Harvey Rosenzweig, a Chicago accountant, to be vacationing in Montreal in July 1958. Rosenzweig was forty years old, a citizen who would be described by the elitists as one of the "little people." He was indeed physically little, standing only five feet three inches and weighing a fragile 130 pounds. Rosenzweig lived in a "ranch-style" bungalow on the city's North Side with his mother, Tillie, and his sisters, Celia and Edith. His associates found him a quiet but friendly man, easy to get along with. Harvey Rosenzweig did not stand out in a crowd. But he did have a dream; he wanted to score a coup and become a millionaire. Not a shady coup. He often told his mother and sisters that an honest man could get rich with a break or two.

It was not surprising, then, that Rosenzweig should have answered a classified advertisement in a Montreal newspaper for an enterprising partner who was interested in becoming a wealthy real estate tycoon. Shortly, he was interviewed by a man named Warren Reddock, an easygoing Texan of forty-two with crew-cut hair and a collection of warm "you-alls." After two days of discussions, Reddock offered Rosenzweig the job and Rosenzweig snapped it up. He would be Reddock's equal associate in something called the European Arms Corporation, with offices in Canada, Italy, and France. Reddock told him the firm planned to set up real estate developments in the United States and wanted Rosenzweig to become president of the American subsidiary. Rosenzweig also would oversee sales of arms to legitimate sporting goods outlets in the United States.

"Once we get the contracts drawn up, we'll make a quick visit to Europe so you can meet the big bosses," Reddock told Rosenzweig. "They've got a swell place in Monaco—you know, the place with all those glamorous gambling casinos."

Impressed, and confident that he was about to launch his career in the field of Big Money, Rosenzweig returned to Chicago in early August and sought out a lawyer friend, Richard L. Kahn. He asked Kahn to draw up an employment contract for him to present to Reddock, who would be in Chicago in a week or so.

Kahn was suspicious. He had known and liked Rosenzweig for more than 10 years, and he had always regarded his friend as a gullible sort. "You don't really know anything about this man," he told Rosenzweig. "He could be a crook, a confidence man."

Rosenzweig smiled, his face eager and beaming. "I know enough about him," he said. "He impresses me as a man who knows what he's talking about, and he talks big. He's been all over the world and he knows a lot of important people. Besides, I don't have to put up a red cent of my own money."

There spoke the dreamer whose dream he believed was about to come true. And it is, after all, common for a human being to believe fondly that he is in command of his own destiny. Most people, of course, direct their destiny toward more modest goals; they are the practical ones. But there is something almost grand in a Harvey Rosenzweig, faceless to the outside world, certain that he was destined to become a rich man. He didn't stoop to trifling with the thought that he might be just another bit of sport for circumstances beyond his control.

So Kahn drew up the contract. He made it outrageously favorable to his friend, hoping that Reddock would back out of the deal. Rosenzweig must have had some doubts about it, too, but big dreams do not admit to doubts. And when Reddock arrived in Chicago, he signed on the dotted line. There, Rosenzweig probably told himself, I was right: Warren Reddock is too important to quibble when the stakes are high.

Rosenzweig promptly quit his job, and on August 14 he accompanied Reddock to a real estate office in Grayslake in northern Lake County, Illinois. Reddock wanted to buy 1050 acres of virgin land and turn it into a recreation center. He didn't balk at the asking price of $1500 an acre, or $1,525,000 for the entire tract. Perhaps Rosenzweig thought of advising his new friend and partner to do a little bargaining. More than likely, he remained silent. A man who had spoken of dealing in millions of dollars must have known what he was doing.

Back home, Rosenzweig told his mother and sisters of the great opportunity Reddock had granted him. "He says there's no limit to how much money we can make," Rosenzweig boasted. "He says all he needed was an expert accountant and that he found one in me. We're going to Monaco—think of it!—day after tomorrow. I'm going to mingle with really important financiers and enjoy the gay life."

Two days later, Rosenzweig packed his bags and left to join Reddock for another look at the Grayslake tract before they took off for Monaco.

Two weeks later, his sisters called the Chicago office of the FBI and reported that their brother had disappeared, and that a number of his personal checks, which they believed to be forgeries, had been cashed in New York City. The office went looking for Rosenzweig—and for Warren Reddock as the man with whom Rosenzweig had left town.

There were no leads in Monaco. Neither Rosenzweig nor Reddock had registered at any of the little principality's hotels. FBI agents and Monaco police interviewed scores of businessmen and people on the streets; nobody had seen or heard of either of the two men. A check of records in the United States and European cities developed no trace of the European Arms Corporation. But agents discovered that Rosenzweig and Reddock had registered at a Waukegan, Illinois, motel on August 16 and had departed the following day.

Meanwhile, Rosenzweig's family got a phone call from a representative of Carte Blanche, the credit card firm. They were told that bills amounting to $1165.25 had been charged to Rosenzweig's card in New York City. This was some comfort to his mother and sisters, since Rosenzweig had planned to stop over in New York with Reddock, and perhaps had dallied in other European cities before going on to Monaco. But Monaco still knew nothing about the two men.

So far, there was no evidence that suggested anything more serious than check forging and, perhaps, illegal use of a credit card. For all Lake County authorities and the FBI knew, Rosenzweig and Reddock had decided to disappear so they could live it up for a few weeks in foreign pleasure domes. The suspected checks were examined at the FBI laboratory in Washington, but they were so covered with fingerprints that they told the scientists nothing. Rosenzweig's family could only suspect that someone else had signed the son's and brother's name to the checks.

Then on September 26, 41 days after Rosenzweig dropped out of sight, two off-duty policemen training a hunting dog found a decomposed body in a woodland near Round Lake in Lake County. The body was in such poor shape that it took the FBI three days to identify the badly beaten remains through a check of dental records. The body was that of Harvey Rosenzweig, dumped in a corner of the land he and Reddock had inspected as a possible recreation center development.

"Thank God he had that special bridgework done," Rosenzweig's mother said. "He didn't want to, but I made him. And now at least I know what happened to him."

What had happened to Harvey Rosenzweig confirmed the FBI's belief that Reddock was the key to his new partner's disappearance. If Reddock had murdered Rosenzweig, the motive could not have been to acquire big cash money—Rosenzweig was carrying only about $200 when he disappeared. But he had carried his checkbook, passport, and six credit cards. And, as the American Express and Diner's Club would put it, such cards are as good as, and safer than, cash.

The Bureau's laboratory had no samples of Reddock's handwriting to compare with the signatures on checks and credit cards. Nevertheless, the lab experts continued to examine newly received canceled checks and credit card slips for fingerprints. At last they got results in the form of three latent prints on one check. The prints were not Rosenzweig's, so a painstaking search had to be made of FBI files in Washington. The searchers finally located a record for Warren D. Reddock, born in Cherokee, Texas, who had been arrested 15 times on confidence man and bad check charges and convicted five times. The record showed that Reddock had been sentenced to a five-year prison term on November 7, 1963, and paroled on May 18, 1967. Other scientists found that the latent fingerprints on one Rosenzweig check were those of Warren D. Reddock.

The FBI turned over the results of its investigation to the Lake County authorities, who formally charged Reddock on October 10, 1968, with the murder of Harvey Rosenzweig. But the Bureau stayed on the job of locating Reddock under provisions of the Fugitive Felon Act, and a warrant was issued in Chicago charging him with unlawful flight to avoid prosecution for murder. The Bureau also added Reddock to its list of "Ten Most Wanted Fugitives."

Celia Rosenzweig told agents she had seen Reddock with her brother a couple of days before Harvey Rosenzweig disappeared. Her description checked with that in FBI files, which said Reddock stood about five feet eight inches, weighed about 150 pounds, wore his hair in a crew cut, and was a neat dresser.

A confidential police report on Reddock described him as "a known liar," but lacking in the finesse required of a professional confidence man. "He always overplays his hand or forgets what he told the victim the first time they met," the report said. But none of the lawmen who had encountered Reddock in the line of duty saw Reddock as a man who would commit a violent crime. An underground FBI agent in Kansas City quoted one of Reddock's victims as saying the fugitive "was never mean . . . I thought he was a nice guy."

Speed of course is important in tracing a credit card thief, and the 41-day delay between Rosenzweig's death and the discovery of his body gave his killer a long head start on the relatively cumbersome process of discovering that such cards are being misused. As a result, credit card charges and forged checks continued to pour in unchallenged until they reached the end of the line and stop payments were issued.

Meanwhile, FBI agents across the country developed details of Reddock's life style and habits before and after the murder. They learned that Reddock rented a car in Peekskill, New York, in May 1968—three months before Rosenzweig was beaten to death—and abandoned it two months later in Plattsburg, New York. On July 22, 1968, Reddock rented another car in Burlington, Vermont, and drove it to Montreal. More FBI digging placed Reddock in Montreal as late as August 6, 10 days before Rosenzweig disappeared.

By now, "wanted" notices had gone out to police in cities all over the world—from Springfield, Illinois, to Singapore. FBI attachés at American embassies were ordered to check recent arrivals of Americans on both holiday and on business. And as the picture of the fugitive emerged, it was that of a man desperately trying to find a safe place to hide. For more than a year, Reddock traveled to what must have been the point of exhaustion.

About three weeks after the murder, the FBI learned that a man answering to Reddock's description had stayed in a seedy hotel on the Left Bank in Paris. He paid for his lodgings with a check bearing the signature "Harvey Rosenzweig." But he had flown from Chicago to New York to Paris on one of Rosenzweig's credit cards. Again with a credit card, he bought air passage to New Delhi. When police went to pick him up at a hotel, they discovered he had flown to Hong Kong on September 6, two days after Rosenzweig's family had reported him missing. He forged Rosenzweig's name to a $500 check in Hong Kong, but again he eluded his pursuers by flying to Mexico City. He had used Rosenzweig's credit cards extensively, but the lag between their use and the time it took the FBI to go after him enabled Reddock to fly to Los Angeles, arriving there on September 19.

And so it went as the FBI expended time, money, and manpower in its pursuit. The day after Reddock arrived in Los Angeles he rented a car in Montreal, and during the following six days he rented and abandoned three more cars, using the cars and commercial airlines to continue his flight through Niagara Falls;

Erie, Pennsylvania; Cleveland, and Denver. He returned to Los Angeles on September 26 and boarded a plane for Mexico. From Mexico he flew to Kingston, Jamaica, and then to Miami.

Miami police and FBI agents were on his trail when Reddock rented another car and drove to California and then back to Denver. Another of his rented cars was found abandoned in Los Angeles on November 4. Credit card charges showed he then flew out for a second visit to Hong Kong. Reddock returned to California in early 1969 and rented a room in Berkeley, near the University of California campus. He used a Rosenzweig credit card to pay for dinner at a Berkeley restaurant on March 11, 1969. Then he abandoned the credit card route and dropped out of surveillance's knowledge for more than a year.

It was not until late 1970 that an underground FBI agent picked up what seemed to be a hot tip. A paid informant working on another case reported that a man answering to Reddock's description had told a barfly he was "getting healthy" by working on a farm somewhere in northern California. That covered a lot of territory, and the tipster could only quote the barfly as saying the man had told him the farm was "up in the hills." If the man was Reddock, he had not let a couple of drinks loosen his tongue too much.

"But he sounds like your man," the informant told the agent. "He mouthed off a lot about pulling a confidence game on a guy who wanted to get rich quick."

The agent sent the informant back to the saloon and told him to hang around the neighborhood and see if he could pick up more intelligence from street gossip. While waiting for a report, the agent did some firsthand investigating by visiting several ranches, looking for a job. None of the workers he chatted with resembled Reddock, and no foreman reported hiring or even seeing a man whose appearance was anything like Reddock's.

Back came the informant. "I heard what the swindle was," he said. "At least what a couple of grifters said it was. The guy let it get out that he got the mark to quit his job and go into partnership with him in a gun-running outfit, only the mark thought it was strictly legit. He bragged that he was a pal of Huey Newton, the Black Panther boss, and Angela Davis, and was going to buy guns in Europe and sell them to militant gangs. Only the mark thought they were gonna sell to sporting goods stores.

But the mark wouldn't come up with any bread, so your man said he told him to get lost."

Back went the agent for another tour of area ranches. In a bar in a small town outside Berkeley he had a couple of drinks with a man who said he'd been working on a ranch for a few months and when he quit his job he hitchhiked a ride to Berkeley with a man who looked like Reddock and who said he was working on a ranch, too.

"Where is this ranch where the guy was working?" the agent asked.

"Geez, I don't know," he was told. "I got drunk and stayed drunk for almost a week. He told me where it was, but when I woke up everything was blacked out. For all I know he might've been working in Oregon."

The agent departed, cursing the curse of drink. A thin, gaunt man who talked out of the side of his mouth and lived with a queasy stomach, he went furiously back to his underground life, wearing the accustomed expression he had trained to be entirely uncommunicative. He called again on his reserves of patience, tinged with bitterness and controlled anger at the elusive, ghostly murderer. Once again he could expect long, fruitless hours of searching, pursued by all kinds of weather, waiting for somebody who *might* know something and who might never come, or who might come and go before he could be interviewed. It was a life spent in beastly fast-food joints, untidy saloons, and sleazy pool halls, a life spent at the mercy of personalities—and, unavoidably, made always uneasy by the impatience of his superiors—harassed by the knowledge that weeks or even months of patient, mind-numbing work could go for naught and add the inevitable question mark to his record.

But finally the FBI got a break. *Life* magazine published a story on the Bureau's list of the "Ten Most Wanted Fugitives" in early April 1971. The FBI's San Francisco field office got an anonymous phone call from a citizen who said he recognized Reddock's picture as being that of a man who worked from April 1969 through July 1970 on a ranch in the San Francisco area. Pressed, the caller said he was sure that Reddock now was working as a general hired hand, and said the ranch was located in Pacifica, California.

Warren Reddock's worldwide travels came to an end on April

11, 1971. Three agents visited the ranch and arrested him on a fugitive warrant. Almost three years had passed since Harvey Rosenzweig left his home in August 1968 to fly to Monaco with the entrepreneur he had met in Montreal. Reddock was turned over to Illinois authorities and indicted for murder.

Reddock, who had grown his hair long and donned eyeglasses, waived his right to a jury and was tried before Lake County Circuit Judge Fred A. Geiger. Forty-three witnesses, including 15 FBI agents and laboratory experts, testified against Reddock. Celia Rosenzweig identified him as the man she had seen with her brother shortly before the murder. FBI fingerprint experts said the prints on the forged checks were Reddock's. Other FBI agents placed him in the Waukegan motel with Rosenzweig on the night of August 16 and the morning of August 17, 1968.

But although the evidence against Reddock was solid, a key prosecution witness managed to throw the trial into confusion and redden the state's face. The witness, William Thompson, former manager of the motel, was asked if he could identify the man he saw leaving the motel with Harvey Rosenzweig on the last day Rosenzweig was seen alive.

Thompson got up from the witness chair and walked across the courtroom. He passed Reddock, then placed his hand on the shoulder of Deputy Sheriff Lee Hollis Austin, who was guarding the defendant. Reddock was still five feet eight inches tall but was wearing glasses, and his hair was longer than it had been three years before. Austin, who was wearing civilian clothes, was six feet two, had curly hair, and also wore glasses.

Judge Geiger, an eyebrow raised, excused Thompson from the courtroom while Assistant State's Attorney Kenneth Clark and Chief Public Defender Robert Wills, Jr., argued about the situation. After a two-hour recess, Thompson returned to the witness stand. He was shown front and side shots of Reddock, a portrait of Rosenzweig, and a picture of a third person. From these three, Thompson selected Reddock.

Clark must have wished he could quit while he was ahead. But he had to ask Thompson again: "Do you see Reddock in the courtroom?"

"Yes," Thompson said.

"Has the man changed any since you last saw him?"

"Yes, he has grown stouter," Thompson said.

And then, for the second time, Thompson got up and identified Deputy Austin as Reddock.

While the spectators first tittered, then roared with laughter, Judge Geiger pounded his gavel. When the room was quiet again, Wills asked for a directed verdict of not guilty, contending that the prosecution had not presented a proper case. Judge Geiger sighed, then denied the motion and told the state to get on with its case.

On the next day, Judge Geiger returned a bench verdict of guilty. In announcing that verdict he admitted, "I had doubts in this case. It is one of the hardest cases I have had to try." Then he added: "But the doubts did not comprise grounds enough to warrant acquittal and I have an abiding conviction that you are guilty." He called Reddock beyond rehabilitation, but said the "circumstances of conviction did not merit the death penalty."

Reddock showed no emotion then or a month later when Judge Geiger sentenced him to 30 to 50 years in prison for the murder of a quiet and friendly Chicago accountant who had a dream made impossible by a man he met in Montreal.

CRIME
AND
POLITICS

12

Martyrdom of a Prophet

He stepped into the bathtub and opened a small window. Then, peering through a telescopic sight, he trained the rifle on the Lorraine Motel's balcony, 206 feet away. He fired only once, but that was enough.

The John Willard who registered in at Bessie Brewer's rooming-house in Memphis between three and three-thirty on the afternoon of April 4, 1968, was a white male, described by Mrs. Brewer as about thirty-five, five feet eleven, weighing about 180 pounds. She said he was of medium build and looked "neat and clean." Mrs. Brewer directed him to room 8 on the second floor, which had a stove and refrigerator. "No, I just want a sleeping room," he told her. So she rented him room 5-B in the rear of the house. When the man glanced out the window his view took in the balcony of the Lorraine Motel across the street.

Later that afternoon, another roomer named Charles Stephens heard footsteps between room 5-B and the common bathroom. The footsteps were repeated several times, and on one occasion Stephens found the bathroom occupied when he sought to use it.

Shortly before six o'clock, someone in that bathroom took from the folds of a blanket a rifle loaded with dumdum bullets, whose power can tear a four-inch hole in a human body. He stepped into the bathtub and opened a small window. Then, peering through a telescopic sight, he trained the rifle on the Lorraine Motel's balcony, 206 feet away. He fired only once, but that was enough.

Taking the air on the balcony, the Reverend Martin Luther King, Jr., had walked into the cross hairs of the gunsight. As the shot rang out, he collapsed, his body bouncing on the balcony's concrete floor. A screaming ambulance carried him to St. Joseph's Hospital, where he was pronounced dead at 7:05 P.M. The bullet had torn the major red blood vessels and severed the spinal cord at the root of the neck.

On the scene, Memphis police telephoned the FBI Memphis field office headed by Special Agent in Charge Robert G. Jensen. Jensen relayed the information to FBI headquarters in Washington, which in turn notified Attorney General Ramsey Clark and FBI Director J. Edgar Hoover, who ordered an investigation aimed at uncovering a possible violation of the civil rights conspiracy statute.

Charles Stephens told investigating FBI agents and police that when he heard the shot he opened his door to the hallway and saw a man running down the hall carrying a large bundle wrapped in "cloth." Stephens remembered seeing the man earlier with Mrs. Brewer. He described the man as of average build, in his thirties, about five ten or five eleven, weighing about 165 pounds, and wearing a "neat" dark suit.

Another roomer, William C. Anchutz, said he was watching television in his room at the time of the shooting. When he opened his door, he saw a man running toward him. The man, he said, was carrying "a big bundle," and covered his face with one hand as he ran.

"I thought I heard a shot," Anchutz said.

"Yeah, it was a shot," the man replied.

A few minutes later, there was a "thud" outside the Canipe Amusement Company, a few doors from the Brewer rooming-house. The owner, Guy W. Canipe, and two customers went to see what had happened. They found a blanket-wrapped bundle in the recessed entrance to the store. At the same time, they saw a man dressed in a dark suit walking south down the street. Shortly, they said, a white compact car, possibly a Mustang, sped past them in the opposite direction.

FBI agents found that the bundle contained a Model 760 Remington Gamemaster rifle, 30-06 Springfield caliber (the "high-powered" rifle of fictional lore), a telescopic sight, and a blue zipper bag. The bag contained various toilet articles, a pair of men's undershorts with laundry tags, a pair of binoculars, two cans of beer, a paper bag labeled York Arms Company, Memphis, Tennessee, and a York Arms cash sales receipt dated April 4, 1968. SAC Jensen had the bundle flown to Washington for laboratory examination.

Meanwhile, all FBI field offices were ordered by teletype to conduct a top-priority investigation of the King murder. This meant that all leads were to receive immediate and thorough attention and all possibilities from such leads exhausted within 24 hours. In Washington, the machinery was set in motion for contacts with all informant sources—racial, security, and criminal. The Ku Klux Klan and other hate groups would be checked. Name checks were ordered on Selective Service records, city and telephone directories, driver's license bureaus, motor vehicle divisions, financial institutions, credit records, criminal and civil court records, marriage licenses, public utility rolls, labor unions, and common carrier passenger lists.

Within a few days, the FBI had traced the rifle, scope, binoculars, and even the beer cans. Agents found the rifle and scope had been purchased at the Aero Marine Supply Company in Birmingham, Alabama. The scope and a rifle were purchased on March 29, only six days before the murder, by a man who gave his name as "Harvey Lowmyer." However, on the following day, "Lowmyer" returned to the store and exchanged the rifle for the one found wrapped in the blanket. The salesman said "Lowmyer" explained that he had talked to his brother, who told him that a more powerful rifle was needed for deer hunting in Wisconsin. His description of "Lowmyer" matched those the FBI already had gotten of the suspect.

The paper bag and sales receipt from York Arms Company led agents to the Memphis store where the binoculars had been purchased. A salesman said he sold the binoculars at about 4:00 P.M. on the day of King's slaying to a man whose description also matched those previously obtained. By checking the manufacturer's can codes and distribution records, the two beer cans were traced to the Southhaven Minnow Shop, Southhaven, Mississippi.

"Great," cracked SAC Jensen. "Now we know the guy was once thirsty in Mississippi."

But since the rifle and scope had been bought in Birmingham, agents checked Memphis hotels and motels for a registration carrying a Birmingham address. They speculated that the man who had registered as "John Willard" at the Brewer rooming-house could have arrived in Memphis earlier. The only registration found with a Birmingham address was that of one Eric Starvo Galt at the Rebel Motel. Galt registered on April 3 for one night and drove a Mustang with Alabama license plates.

In Birmingham, agents learned that Galt bought a 1966 white Mustang on August 29, 1967, and that in October of the same year a motor vehicle operator's license was issued to Eric Starvo Galt, 2608 Highland Avenue, Birmingham. The physical description on the license read like that of John Willard.

Galt also bought a .38-caliber revolver. He took dancing lessons at the Continental Dance Club Studios, whose manager said his new pupil was "enthusiastic, eager to learn." He drove to Mexico on holiday.

Then the FBI got a big break. A housewife in Atlanta learned from a neighbor that the Bureau was looking for a white Mustang. "I've seen a car like that!" she exclaimed. "It's been parked down the block from here ever since the morning after Dr. King was shot."

Sure enough, it was the Mustang bought by and registered to Eric Starvo Galt—and its discovery led the FBI to California. Service station stickers pasted inside the door showed the car had been serviced twice in the Los Angeles area. And on a scrap of cardboard torn from a Kleenex box agents found the Los Angeles addresses of Anita Katzwinkel and Ginger Nance. A couple of days later, Special Agent Bill Gunn at Washington headquarters commented that "our cup runneth over" when investigators traced the laundry markings from the underwear found in the zippered bag left outside the Canipe Amusement Company to the Home Service Laundry and Dry Cleaning Company in Hollywood.

Three hundred agents were concentrated for a saturation search of the Los Angeles area. Galt may have pursued his enthusiasm for dancing there, so dancing schools were checked—with eventual success. His name was found in the records of the National Dance Studio in Los Angeles. When agents interviewed the manager, they learned that Galt also had expressed an interest in going to bartending school. Another check located the International School of Bartending—and Galt's graduation photograph. The picture might have been that of Willard or Lowmyer. Copies were made and circulated among the news media.

Still, the investigation moved no closer to locating Galt. The FBI knew a few things about him—that he liked to travel and enjoyed dancing, that he had bought a .38 revolver, and that he looked like the suspect. But its cup did not run over after all. Los Angeles was a dead end.

So was Atlanta, where the abandoned white Mustang was found. Plodding along, agents did find evidence of Galt's presence in the city. They discovered he had lived for a time at Jimmy Dalton Gardner's roominghouse late in March 1968, and in the room he occupied the manager had found and tossed into a drawer a couple of interesting items. One was a booklet, *Your Opportunities in Locksmithing,* and a collection of maps. One of the maps was of the city of Atlanta with the residence of Martin Luther King, Jr., and the headquarters of King's Southern Christian Leadership Conference circled. Laundry tickets showed he picked up laundry on April 5, the day after the murder. But Galt's trail was cold. There was no sign of where he had fled from Atlanta.

Routinely, scientists at the FBI fingerprint laboratory pored over the maps found in Galt's room, looking for a set of fingerprints. They found only a single print of a single finger.

That made things tough. At the time, FBI files contained the fingerprints of 82 million people. That meant there were 820 million prints of single fingers, five to each hand. It would take forever to check that Galt print against each of those 820 million prints. So the order was given to the identification experts to limit their search to cards bearing only the fingerprints of fugitives. That shrank the number to 53,000 cards. The search was narrowed to the cards of white male fugitives between twenty-five and fifty years old. Now the experts went to work on a pile of less than 2000 cards.

It was a tedious, brain-numbing task, pursued by teams working 24 hours a day. But the job didn't take as long as expected. The experts found what they wanted on FBI Record Card No. 405,942G, the 702d card examined. Eight of them looked hard and long at the print, with its enlarged ridges and whorls, and decided it matched that of the print taken from the map left in Galt's room.

The name on the card rang no bells in that long room. It was: "James Earl Ray, born 10 March 1928, Alton, Illinois." Yet the FBI had 10 separate cards on Ray. A further check showed he was an escaped convict caught and imprisoned often for a variety of crimes, from forgery to armed robbery. Now the investigation of the murder of Martin Luther King, Jr., was redirected to a search of Ray's whereabouts since he escaped from the Missouri State Penitentiary on April 23, 1967.

Ray had served seven years of a 20-year sentence for armed robbery when he escaped from the prison at Jefferson City by hiding inside a huge breadbox he knew would be loaded on a truck for delivery to a nearby prison farm. Somewhere en route to the farm, Ray climbed out of the box and disappeared.

It was one of the few clever things Ray managed to do in a lifetime of crime. He dropped his bankbook as he was fleeing with a stolen typewriter in Los Angeles, stopped to pick it up, and was nabbed. Fleeing a deputy sheriff in St. Louis, he sought refuge in an elevator but neglected to close the door, and was nabbed. He fell out of a speeding car after robbing a grocery store, when the car made a sharp turn. Twice he had been caught trying to escape from the Missouri pen.

These and other incidents in the life of an apparent born loser poured into FBI headquarters in reports wired from more than 500 agents across the country looking into Ray's past. Ray's family was identified, located, surveilled, and questioned time after time. His father and seven brothers and sisters said they knew nothing, and had not heard from or been in contact with Ray for years. Agents quizzed former teachers and schoolmates, fellow convicts, and prison officials. They learned only that James Earl Ray had had a wretched upbringing and adulthood.

He lived with his family in several Mississippi River towns, always knowing poverty firsthand. Sometimes the family lived in shacks with dirt floors. He was a school truant and somewhat of a bully. He dropped out of school at fifteen. In 1946 he joined the Army and spent 30 months in postwar Germany, but his life style didn't change. He drew three months at hard labor for drunkenness and resisting arrest, then was discharged as an undesirable.

He lost a factory job in Chicago and turned to crime. His dossier showed he had an IQ of 105.

Frustrated by the Ray family's silence, J. Edgar Hoover asked Attorney General Clark for authorization to surveil the family by telephone and microphone; the request lay moldering on Clark's desk.

But eventually the FBI was able to account for Ray's whereabouts almost continuously since his escape.

Early in May 1967, Ray worked as a dishwasher and cook's helper in Winnetka, Illinois, and lived in Chicago under the name John L. Rayns. In June he bought a 1959 Chrysler sedan for $200. He failed a driver's test on June 5 but passed it on June 12. He quit his job a week later. He bought a 1962 Plymouth sedan in East St. Louis, Illinois, on July 14. He drove to Montreal the next day. There, he first used the name Eric Starvo Galt to lease an apartment for six months. He tried to get a Canadian passport but was turned down.

Ray spent two and a half months in Canada as Galt. During that time, he told several people he had met in bars that he was well acquainted with a powerful underworld figure named "Raoul." He met a couple of girls and spent several nights with them, trying to persuade them to vouch for him on a passport application. From Canada, he drove to Birmingham and registered at the Economy Rooms as Eric S. Galt. He paid $1995 in cash for the white 1966 Mustang to one William D. Paisley. He went on to Mexico and then to Los Angeles, where he began a series of visits to Dr. Mark O. Freeman, a clinical sociologist. He told Dr. Freeman he wanted to overcome his shyness, gain social confidence, and learn self-hypnosis so he could relax, sleep better, and improve his memory.

By December, Ray, as Galt, was telling barflies he wanted to emigrate to a white-ruled country in Africa. He wrote a letter of inquiry to the American-Southern African Council in Washington and signed it Eric S. Galt. He sent his photograph and his address to a woman calling herself "The Local Swinger," whose address he obtained for a dollar.

On March 17, 1968, Ray left Los Angeles to drive to New Orleans. From there he went on to Selma, Alabama, on March 22 for an overnight stay. Then he drove to Montgomery and finally to Atlanta on March 24. Ray stayed until March 28 at Jimmy

Dalton Gardner's roominghouse. While there, he bought a United States postal money order payable to the Locksmithing Institute; the order was signed Eric S. Galt.

Using the alias Harvey Lowmyer, Ray bought the rifle and telescopic sight in Birmingham. Back in Atlanta on April 1, he left his laundry and dry cleaning at the Piedmont Laundry pickup station at 1168 Peachtree Avenue; the ticket said the items were the property of Eric S. Galt. Then he drove to Memphis, stayed overnight at the Rebel Motor Hotel, and moved the next day to Bessie Brewer's sleazy caravansary. He bought the binoculars at the York Arms Company and returned to room 5-B about five o'clock on the afternoon of the King murder.

As detailed in an official discussion of the course of the FBI's investigation, the assassin could have cleared and undoubtedly did clear the corridor and the stairs to the street within 45 seconds after firing the shot that killed Dr. King. In another 15 seconds at the outside, he could have reached and undoubtedly did reach the white Mustang after dropping the blanket-wrapped bundle at the door of the Canipe Amusement Company. Thus, witnesses in the roominghouse and outside had had time to get a good look at him.

So far, so good. But as spring waned and summer approached, James Earl Ray was still at large. The FBI learned that he had picked up his laundry at Atlanta the day after the murder. Where he went from there was anybody's guess.

The FBI's high command agreed on a collective guess. Ray had tried once to get his hands on a Canadian passport. After the murder, had the fugitive managed to pick up a United States passport under an alias other than Galt? Or, using another name, had he tried again in Canada? Hoover & Co. decided either was a pretty good possibility: Ray had to be thinking that America was too hot for him.

Some 1.5 million passports had been issued since Ray broke out of prison. Checking them all seemed a hopeless task, but it had to be done. Several teams of 30 agents each were assigned to inspect the passport files one by one; they were looking for an application bearing Ray's photograph. They worked at the Passport Office across from the White House, and they worked only at night to keep the operation secret.

Meanwhile, the FBI's legal attaché at the American Embassy in Canada requested that a similar search be launched by the

Royal Canadian Mounted Police. A few hours later, the Bureau was notified that Mexican police were going through the passport files in Mexico City on their own.

"My God!" exclaimed "Deke" DeLoach, one of Hoover's top-level assistants. "If this works out there's no reason why we can't make a stab at walking on water."

For two weeks it looked as if no one would be asked to perform another miracle. Then, on Saturday, June 1, at 3:00 A.M., a Canadian constable found himself staring at a photograph of an application submitted by one Ramon George Sneyd.

"I believe this could be it," he told his fellow searchers. They agreed with him.

Two RCMP detectives drove to the listed address, a rooming-house in Toronto that had seen better days. "Sneyd" had been in Toronto for four weeks. The passport was filed by the Kennedy Travel Agency in that city. The agency's manager reported that on May 2 "Sneyd" had paid $345 in Canadian currency for a round-trip ticket to London. She gave them a hand-printed note from the applicant concerning his passport. A latent palm print was found on the note. Both passport photo and note were flown to Washington for examination in the FBI laboratory.

Only an hour after the evidence was delivered to the lab, the word was rushed to Hoover: "Sneyd" and James Earl Ray were the same person.

Ray, traveling as Sneyd, had been booked on a flight leaving for London on May 6. But in London, New Scotland Yard discovered that Ray-Sneyd had turned in the return portion of the ticket in exchange for a May 7 flight from London to Lisbon, plus a $14.60 voucher. In the Portuguese capital, immigration officials found that Ray-Sneyd had entered Lisbon on May 7 but had flown back to London on May 17.

New Scotland Yard issued stops for the fugitive. And shortly after eleven o'clock on the morning of Saturday, June 8, two Yard men at Victoria Cannon Row police station questioned a man traveling with a passport issued to Ramon George Sneyd, Canadian. They wanted his fingerprints, but didn't want to wait for a court order to get them. So they gave the suspect a glass of water. When he put down the glass, it was dispatched to the Yard's laboratory for examination.

In London an FBI agent telephoned Washington about 10

minutes later. "The fingerprints checked," he said. "It's Ray. They grabbed him at the airport. He was trying to get to Brussels. He was carrying a .38 revolver."

The FBI, with yeoman help from Canada and Great Britain, had wound up history's greatest manhunt. It had deployed 3014 agents, who traveled 500,000 miles and spent $1.4 million.

James Earl Ray pleaded guilty to the first-degree murder of Martin Luther King, Jr., after several plea-bargaining sessions at which he was represented by Percy Foreman, a trial lawyer from Houston. Foreman would say later that the guilty plea was Ray's idea, "because he knew that otherwise he would be executed."

Whatever, before Ray was sentenced to 99 years in prison, on March 10, 1969, he was asked a question by Judge W. Preston Battle, presiding in Criminal Court of Shelby County, Tennessee. The question was: "Are you pleading guilty to murder in the first degree because you killed Dr. Martin Luther King under such circumstances that would make you legally guilty of murder in the first degree under the law as explained to you by your lawyers?"

"Yes," Ray replied.

Ray then told Judge Battle that he was pleading guilty freely, voluntarily, and understandingly. He and Foreman initialed a copy of these questions and answers. Ray also signed a detailed stipulation confessing that he fired the fatal shot. Thus, Ray judicially confessed that he "accomplished" the murder of Dr. King with premeditation and malice aforethought—that he intended to and did kill Dr. King.

II

When James Earl Ray reached the milestone age of twenty-one, he was still uneducated, untrained for any particular job, unskilled even at making small conversation. Almost inevitably, he went to work as a journeyman criminal. As a result, he spent 14 of the next 18 years of his life in prison, until his 1967 escape from the Missouri State Penitentiary.

However, when Ray observed his fortieth birthday in March 1968, he had never been convicted of a crime in which victims or witnesses were physically harmed. The question then was why a man whose past was free of major violence would suddenly turn to assassination. Some probative facts offering a motive emerged from an analysis of Ray's prison records and interviews with prisoners who had known him.

Serving time for forgery of Post Office money orders in the federal penitentiary at Leavenworth, Kansas, in 1955, Ray declined to be transferred to the honor farm because it was racially integrated. An inmate with Ray at the Missouri prison told FBI interrogators Ray had said that all the black prisoners in the pen "should be killed." Other prisoners claimed Ray had said he would kill Dr. King if the price were right. He was suspected of participating in the murder of three blacks during a prison riot in 1966. Another of Ray's "colleagues" in confinement quoted Ray as remarking about the assassination of President John F. Kennedy: "That is one nigger-loving son-of-a-bitch that got shot."

Similar sources told investigators that during the period when Dr. King was leading civil rights demonstrations Ray became upset when he read of Dr. King's activities in newspapers, and cursed Dr. King and all blacks for "causing trouble." Ray was reported as having sworn that when he got out of prison he would "get" Dr. King.

Thus, the picture evolved of a man who was obsessed with a hatred for the black race. Known in prison as a "lone wolf," Ray nevertheless confided to other prisoners that when he got out of jail he was going to "make myself a bunch of money." The money, Ray said, was to come from a "businessmen's association," which he said had offered $100,000 for killing Dr. King.

"What's this association of businessmen?" one prisoner told the FBI he asked Ray.

"I don't know," he quoted Ray as replying, "but I'm sure going to find out."

A cellmate of Ray's and other prisoners told of having heard that a businessman had raised a million dollars as a bounty on Dr. King's head; the story apparently was common knowledge. Ray's cellmate said Ray had told him: "If I'd known there was a bounty on Kennedy's head I'd have killed him."

Some light also was shed on the question of whether Ray would turn to murder for self-importance and profit. During his stay in Puerto Vallarta, Mexico, in the fall of 1967, Ray spent considerable time with one Irma Morales, described by the FBI as

a prostitute. Irma told agents about an incident that took place on
October 29. She and Ray were sitting at a table in a bar when four
blacks came in. She said Ray kept goading the blacks, "and had
me feel a pistol in his pocket." Irma claimed Ray said he was
going to kill "all" the black customers, and when they left "he
wanted to go after them, but I told him it was time for the police
to arrive to check the bar, and he said he didn't want anything to
do with the police, so he didn't go."

Then there was Ray's psychological background. After a
psychiatric examination in 1966, Ray was described as a
sociopathic personality, an antisocial type with anxiety and de-
pressive features. In 1954 a prison sociologist found that Ray's
delinquencies seemed due to impulsive behavior, especially when
drinking. And Dr. Mark Freeman, the psychologist from whom
Ray sought help in Los Angeles, said he believed Ray was
potentially capable of assassination, was a self-motivated individual who could act alone, and most likely fantasized about being
someone important.

All this probing into Ray's psyche, of course, did not provide
a single conclusive motive for the King murder. He was, after all,
a man who liked to make big talk, and such people more often
than not don't have the guts to kill. But it was clear that Ray
hated blacks and considered the civil rights movement subversive.
Such a man could have considered it his "duty" to rid the world
of a Martin Luther King.

There remained, then, the question of where James Earl Ray
got the money for his many travels in three countries. Proponents
of the conspiracy theory insisted that Ray must have had a dark
angel who paid him a large sum to kill Dr. King, that Ray lived on
a down payment from about April or May 1967 until the King
murder in April 1968, and then paid his way with the proceeds of
the second and final installment until his capture two months after
the slaying.

In any case, the FBI tried to find out if Ray had financial
assistance and hence possible co-conspirators. All field divisions
were ordered to consider Ray as a suspect in unsolved bank
robberies, burglaries, or armed robberies occurring after April 23,
1967—the date of his escape from the Missouri pen. There were
no results. Then the field offices contacted all law enforcement

agencies which maintained unidentified latent fingerprints so they could be compared with Ray's prints. Nothing. Photographs of Ray were shown to witnesses in unsolved bank robberies and bank burglaries. Nothing.

Literally scores of alleged conspiracies were propounded in telephone calls, telegrams, and letters to FBI headquarters. As the months and years passed, it sometimes seemed to the Bureau that everybody capable of communicating in the English language had his own pet conspiracy theory. Admittedly, the FBI found itself in a difficult position. J. Edgar Hoover and his field marshals had long conducted what amounted to a vendetta against Dr. King personally and as a civil rights "agitator." Confidentially, certain FBI officials told tales of Dr. King's alleged sexual adventures. Tapes of wiretaps of Dr. King's conversations were hand-carried to President Lyndon B. Johnson. The years before the King assassination did not add up to the FBI's finest hour.

But the FBI was in the position of conducting an investigation which ranged far beyond the concrete evidence at hand. When the leads were in fact bogus ones, the Bureau was attempting to prove a negative in each case. Dr. King was a controversial figure. The possibilities of conspiracy were numerous. Yet a Justice Department task force that reviewed the FBI's efforts reported on January 11, 1977, that it was "satisfied the FBI did a credible and thorough job in attempting to identify any possible conspiracy or persons who could have been involved in the murder. . . . This does not mean that every allegation was pursued to an ultimate degree. Judgment based on experience dictated many of the decisions."

Meanwhile, Ray had told his story to the author, William Bradford Huie, who put it into a book, *He Slew the Dreamer* (Delacorte Press, New York, 1968). In the book, Ray provided an account of his escape from prison and of his subsequent activities prior to his arrest for Dr. King's murder. Among other things, Ray told Huie that the mysterious "Raoul" had furnished him with funds on a continuing basis for various undertakings.

The Justice Department team reported that "These matters were actively pursued by the Bureau but have never been corroborated. . . . Nor have they been corroborated by private inquiries of writers and journalists. It is the Bureau's opinion that

Ray most likely committed on a periodic basis several robberies or burglaries . . . in order to support himself. Ray's criminal background does lend credence to this theory."

On the other hand, the task force was critical of the FBI's failure to pursue more vigorously the theory that Ray was given aid and comfort by his family. Its report noted that the Bureau took the line that it is not unusual for a fugitive to be in touch with family members, but that such contact is not generally pursued without some evidence or direct participation in a crime. However, given the furor over the King murder, the task force concluded that the FBI was negligent in the small attention it paid Ray's family.

The Bureau discovered that Ray's brother, Jerry, had visited him in the Missouri State Penitentiary three or four times and had borrowed money from James on at least one occasion during his confinement. Another brother, John, visited or attempted to visit James Ray at the prison on at least nine occasions; the last visit took place on April 22, 1967, the day before Ray escaped. The Bureau also learned that while in prison James Ray had a fellow prisoner send a money order to a fictitious company in St. Louis. The money was mailed to the address of Carol Pepper, the Ray brothers' sister; James Ray told the inmate who sent the money that it was a way of getting money out of the prison.

James Ray was seen by several people in St. Louis, where John Ray was living, and in Chicago, where Jerry Ray lived, during the period immediately following his escape. It was in Chicago that James Ray bought a car on June 5, 1967, and he had worked in a restaurant in nearby Winnetka. Ray's employers told the FBI that James had received several calls from a man claiming to be Ray's brother. Jerry Raynes, father of the three brothers, told the Bureau that John and Jerry had mentioned that James was in Chicago during the summer of 1967.

Jerry Ray denied to FBI agents in several interviews that he knew anything about James's travels or his source of funds. Yet the Bureau learned that on August 25, 1967, James Ray (using the name John L. Rayns) transferred his 1962 Plymouth to Jerry in Chicago. At the time, James was making his way from Canada to Birmingham and he told his brother he had "several thousand dollars." Meanwhile, an informant told agents Jerry told him he had recognized the photograph of Eric Starvo Galt as that of his brother, James.

So the task force wondered in print at the FBI's failure to hold Jerry on charges of aiding a fugitive, or even to confront Jerry with the facts it had discovered.

"The task force found the credibility of Jerry's denials to be suspect," said the report. "In light of this low credibility and critical passage of time which has allowed the statute of limitations to run, we concluded that the FBI abandoned a significant opportunity to obtain answers from family members concerning some of the important questions about James Earl Ray which still remain."

So in early 1977, with the conspiracy theory still hanging like laundry on a line, the House Select Committee on Assassinations launched an investigation of the murders of Dr. King and President Kennedy. When, in the fall of 1978, the committee finally brought its inquiry to an end, the King "mystery" was still flapping on the line.

13

Inquiry Without End

One's first impulse was to feel sorry for Ray. Now fifty years old, he was thin almost to the point of emaciation. He seemed weary, and his face wore lines of anxiety.

Early in March 1978, after the House assassinations panel had concluded its investigation of the Kennedy murder, a man named Russell G. Byers, who described himself as a former St. Louis automobile parts dealer, got a member of the staff on the telephone. Byers wanted to tell the committee all about a conspiracy to kill Martin Luther King. Shortly, Byers was interviewed. If true, his story would be sensational.

Byers claimed that he was approached sometime in late 1966 or early 1967 by a "business associate" named John Kauffmann, who invited him to a meeting with a patent attorney, John H. Sutherland. Byers identified Sutherland further as a member of the conservative Southern States Industrial Council, and a leader of the racist White Citizens Council of St. Louis. According to Byers, Sutherland told him that a group of businessmen would pay him $50,000 to kill Dr. King. Byers said he declined the offer, but learned later that the payoff was made to James Earl Ray.

Committee investigators learned that both Kauffmann and Sutherland had died, Kauffmann in 1974 and Sutherland in 1970. In checking the two men's backgrounds, they found the men had been members of the American Independent party and were active supporters of the campaign of Governor George C. Wallace in his candidacy for the Presidency. A Wallace campaign office in St. Louis was located in a house across the street from a tavern operated by James Ray's brother, John, and their sister, Mrs. Carol Pepper. Interviewers found that Kauffmann was often in the tavern and that he talked freely about his $50,000 offer for the assassination of Dr. King.

Then on August 3, the New York *Times* reported that the FBI had received a report in 1974 that a Missouri businessman was "the individual who made the payoff to James Earl Ray after the killing" of Dr. King. The *Times* said it got its information from FBI documents released under the Freedom of Information Act to Harold Weissberg, a private investigator of assassination matters, and to the *Times*. According to the *Times* story, the documents included an FBI control agent's account, dated March 19, 1974, of an informant's report to him in late 1973. The account said the informant was given the information by Russell G. Byers in the fall of 1973. To the House committee, Byers identified the individual who paid off Ray as John Kauffmann.

The *Times* story was an embarrassment to the FBI because the Bureau admittedly had not pursued the Byers account. An FBI spokesman explained that the control agent's report had not been properly disseminated within the Bureau and thus did not come to light as part of the FBI's "assassination material" until five years later.

Whatever, the Bureau's memorandum made fascinating if somewhat inchoate reading. It quoted the informant as reporting that "during the fall of 1973 [lengthy deletion] Beyers [sic] talked freely about himself and his business, and they later went to [short deletion] where Beyers told a story about visiting a lawyer in St. Louis County, now deceased, not further identified, who had offered to give him a contract to kill Martin Luther King. . . . Sometime later [lengthy deletion] this individual advised [short deletion] that Beyers truly is a 'very treacherous guy,' cautioning him [the agent] to stay away from him, he wanted to stay away from him if he wanted to stay out of trouble."

It was indeed a sensational story. But months of digging by committee investigators failed to find any corroboration for Byers's tale. The suspects were dead, and no evidence was forthcoming that anyone with a usable name offered James Earl Ray even a thin dime to murder Dr. King, much less paid him for the grisly assignment. "The evidence tends to paint the outlines of a conspiracy," said Democratic Representative Louis Stokes of Ohio. "But such evidence is not proof." The committee found several persons with direct links to the Ray brothers who also had direct or indirect links to Kauffmann and Sutherland, but that was all.

Nevertheless, the committee pursued its search through most of Washington's bright autumnal weather of 1978. Everybody believed to have had any contact with the King case—from former Attorney General Ramsey Clark to former members of a black activist Memphis youth group—was heard. James's brothers, Jerry and John, took the witness chair. So did James's former and current lawyer and FBI agents. If nothing else, the hearings showed that Dr. King's murder was still very much on the official mind 10 years later.

Mark Lane, James Ray's latest lawyer, a conspiracy buff and self-described protector of civil liberties, met with Representative Stokes and District of Columbia Delegate Walter Fauntroy. Lane was accompanied by the Reverend Ralph D. Abernathy, who headed the Southern Christian Leadership Conference for eight years after Dr. King's death. After the meeting, Abernathy told reporters: "The information that Mr. Lane revealed is that it was former FBI agents and off-duty FBI agents who took the life of Dr. King."

That was a shocker, even after all the rumors and published reports that Hoover's FBI waged a 10-year feud with Dr. King— and after making due allowance for the avid, publicity-seeking Lane's reputation for florid hyperbole. Committee members were properly skeptical, but the allegation had to be looked into, and it was.

Within a few days, to the surprise of no one possessed of even the meanest intelligence, the committee announced it had found no evidence that the FBI was involved in Dr. King's assassination. At that time, the public learned that Lane reportedly told the committee Delegate Fauntroy had said the panel had evidence of the Bureau's involvement in the murder.

In an opening statement, Fauntroy denounced Lane as a "consummate pitchman . . . who thrives on publicity—good or bad. Mr. Lane's repeated attempts to spitefully use the death of Dr. King and to spitefully use those who were associated with him in life require that I remain silent no more." And Andrew Young, then American Ambassador to the United Nations, was called before the committee to deny Fauntroy had told him of an alleged FBI assassination squad, as Lane had alleged.

But the hearings did add to the lore of an FBI feud with the black civil rights leader with testimony by a former insider at the Bureau. In an appearance tinged with pathos, Arthur Murtaugh, a former FBI agent in Atlanta who retired to turn college professor, testified that the Bureau conducted "a 10-year vendetta" against Dr. King and then botched its investigation of his murder by ignoring the possibility of conspiracy.

Murtaugh twice broke into tears, and his voice frequently quavered as he recounted the campaign of wiretaps and dirty tricks—since admitted by the FBI—designed to discredit Dr. King and reduce his influence among blacks. "It is not with pleasure that I sit here and tell you things about an organization I spent a lifetime with," he told a hushed audience.

Murtaugh said the Atlanta office assigned 15 agents to the campaign, and that the electronic surveillance operation produced "about 40 or 50" cabinets of files on Dr. King's telephone conversations. After the assassination, the investigation was assigned to the Bureau's Intelligence Division instead of the Criminal Division.

"It just defies reason that the same people who have engaged in a 10-year vendetta against Dr. King should investigate his murder," Murtaugh told the committee. He said the investigation was made routine as soon as James Ray was identified as the assassin and as a fugitive to be apprehended. "The idea that anyone beyond Ray could be involved was pooh-poohed from the very beginning," he said. "The Bureau decided 24 hours after King was killed that it was not a conspiracy."

But the FBI then had its day in court. Robert Jensen, the agent in charge of the Memphis field office at the time of the murder, testified that several conspiracy theories were investigated, including the possible involvement of the Mafia, the Ku Klux Klan, or a Communist government. Jensen told the committee the FBI also checked the movements of James Ray's brothers, John and Jerry. "The interviews," he said dryly, "were not fruitful." In the end, he said, there was never any evidence developed that anyone other than James Ray was involved.

It was a tedious job the committee had set for itself: To

review in detail almost every question students of the King case
had ever raised about the civil rights leader's death. In effect, the
committee was playing a game of chess with assassination buffs,
but the game was deemed necessary because the unanswered
questions wove a sinister story.

G. Robert Blakey, the committee's chief counsel, told the
story this way: "Ray is broken out of prison, either as assassin or
patsy. He is given financial support, plastic surgery, a car and a
gun, while arrangements are made for a ticket out of the country
and a false passport. Meanwhile, King's security is withdrawn,
and he is felled by one deadly shot. The escape of the assassin is
facilitated. Ray is caught, convicted or framed, but in any event
silenced."

One of the toughest questions involved the lapse in police
security in Memphis that left Dr. King virtually unprotected.
When he arrived in Memphis the day before his death, Dr. King
was given a four-man security detail. That detail was withdrawn
the next day, an hour before his death.

Frank Holloman, then the city's Director of Fire and Safety,
testified the security squad was sent home because Dr. King
didn't want any police protection. "He said he was among
friends," Holloman told the committee. At any rate, Dr. King
protested the security arrangement when he arrived in Memphis,
and the next day Dr. King's party had tried to lose its police
escort on a drive through the city. So the chief of the detail was
told to terminate the assignment.

Then there was Edward Redditt, a black former Memphis
police detective, who was assigned to surveillance of Dr. King but
was relieved shortly before the fatal shot was fired. Redditt told
the committee his job was to spy on Dr. King rather than to
protect him. He claimed he was removed from the assignment for
his own protection, because black groups had made threats on his
life. Nobody, including Redditt, seemed to know who had ordered
that he spy on Dr. King.

Anyway, the *pièce de résistance* served up by the House
hearings was the appearance of James Earl Ray, at his side the
bearded, hungry-eyed Mark Lane. A heavy blanket of security
pervaded the hearing room. Seventeen United States marshals
were in the room. Marshals and Capitol police guarded the
corridor outside. Ray was escorted to the witness chair by seven

other marshals. Representative Richardson Preyer of North Carolina, the former federal judge who was presiding, ordered the spectators to remain seated and stationary when the witness was moving in or out.

One's first impulse was to feel sorry for Ray. Now fifty years old, he was thin almost to the point of emaciation. He seemed weary, and his face wore lines of anxiety. Gently, he patted the high wave of hair above his forehead. Younger, he could have been a lost child.

Ironically, Ray was placed under oath before testifying. The procedure seemed out of place. He was serving a 99-year sentence for the King killing, and he had been charged with breaking out of prison and other crimes. The man could not have been concerned about another prison sentence for perjury or contempt of Congress.

His voice at first was clipped, with an occasional nervous jerkiness, as he read his 38-page statement. The tone suggested defiance. But as time passed, he seemed only to want to be finished with it.

"I did not shoot Martin Luther King, Jr.," said Ray, who long before had recanted his confession. "The plea was procured by fraud."

Predictably, the essence of Ray's testimony was that he had been duped and caught in a trap by the mysterious "Raoul," who he said had helped finance his travels through the United States, Canada, and Mexico in 1967–68. But he could offer no corroboration for that claim. Indeed, he said again, as he had said to the author, William Bradford Huie, that he didn't even know Raoul's last name.

Ray testified that he met Raoul in Canada and that they worked together smuggling goods from Canada to the United States and from the United States to Mexico. He said he knew Raoul for nine months up to the day Dr. King was murdered, that he took cash from him, drank with him, and played with him, but never asked the man his last name.

"I assumed he was a crook," Ray said. "I never made no effort to know him too well. That's an easy way to get killed."

In any event, Ray said he and Raoul "broke contact" in early 1968. Ray then took a correspondence school course—"a locksmith or rather, a lock-picking course," he said. While taking the course, he remembered that he had answered an advertisement in a Los Angeles newspaper placed by a woman who called herself a "nympho-something." Ray's smile was small. "Of course, I had been in jail six years," he said.

Ray and Raoul got together again in March 1968. At Raoul's urging, Ray said, he bought a 30-06 rifle and cartridges and delivered them to Raoul in Memphis the day before Dr. King was killed. On the day of the murder, he claimed, he went window-shopping and made several stops at saloons, and was having his car serviced at a gas station when Dr. King was shot. Later, when he tried to return to his roominghouse, he found it surrounded by police and drove away.

The next day, the committee took out after James Earl Ray. Representative Preyer ran the session in the manner of the trial judge he once was. Representative Stokes, a veteran criminal lawyer, conducted the cross-examination.

Stokes set out to demonstrate through questioning that Ray had stalked Dr. King in Atlanta, where the civil rights leader lived, a few days before the murder. Ray had taken special care to insist he didn't go to Atlanta after buying the rifle in Birmingham, Alabama.

Asked by Stokes about that statement, Ray held to it. "I know I didn't return to Atlanta," he said. Then he leaned back and said quietly: "If I did, I'll just take responsibility for the King case right here on TV."

Stokes called for committee exhibit F-59. It was a poster-size reproduction of two laundry tickets showing that Eric Galt—the alias Ray was using—dropped some clothes for cleaning at a laundry in Atlanta on April 1, 1968, three days before Dr. King was murdered.

Stokes read from an affidavit supplied by a clerk at the Piedmont Laundry in Atlanta. In it, the clerk described James Earl Ray as the "Eric Galt" who came to the shop on April 1. Ray looked at the tickets, his brow heavy. "I think this is an important area," he said.

But after the lunch break, Ray told the committee: "Those laundry tickets must be mistaken. I went into the laundry, but not on April 1." Now, his face drawn, he seemed flustered.

And now Stokes brought his questioning back to the ubiquitous Raoul. Could Ray give the committee the names of any people who could testify to Raoul's existence? Ray gave the question some thought, then said there were three such people. But he could name only one of the three.

Quietly, Stokes read a summary of a statement from the witness saying that the only times he had seen Ray, Ray had been alone.

After that, it was somewhat anticlimactic.

Ramsey Clark, Attorney General at the time of the King murder, told the committee the Justice Department didn't take control of the investigation because it would have worsened relations—already strained—between him and J. Edgar Hoover. But Clark testified that although "there was a quality of racism in Hoover's attitude toward Dr. King, the FBI investigation of the killing was thorough. The FBI's reputation was on the line. Failure to perform would have had profound impact on public confidence in the FBI." So all Clark did was "keep myself informed and make an occasional suggestion. The FBI was given a free hand." He said that although the Bureau investigated various conspiracy theories, "I don't recall any presentation of evidence that ever implied the direct involvement of another person."

Ray's former lawyer, seventy-eight-year-old Percy Foreman, informed the committee that Ray admitted to him there was no such person as Raoul. Ray, he said, believed that it would be a defense for him if he could plead conspiracy. "I told him there was no such person as Raoul," Foreman said. "He admitted that. I asked him why he picked the name Raoul, and he said it was the name of a bawdy house operator in Montreal he had held up."

"Do you ascribe racism as his motive?" asked Representative Floyd J. Fithian, Democrat of Indiana.

"Indubitably and completely," Foreman replied. "Ray thought racial conflict between blacks and whites in America was imminent and he wanted to fire the first shot. To him, the shooting of Dr. King was the Pearl Harbor of that war. He intimated to me that he would be the white hope."

When Jerry Ray, forty-three, was called to testify, committee counsel aired the theory that Raoul might be one of James Ray's brothers. "When you come down to it," he said, "the Raoul theory that seems to fit is that the mysterious accomplice might actually be one of Ray's brothers, Jerry or John, or a composite of the two of them.''

Jerry, James's fast-talking younger brother, denounced the allegation in short, furious words, and accused the committee of unfair tactics. One of his two attorneys, Florynce Kennedy, a black who openly called her client "a redneck racist," charged that the committee seemed bent on ignoring any information that might exonerate the Rays.

The committee had to get a writ from the United States District Court in Washington to permit John Ray, forty-five, to testify. John Ray had been arrested a few days earlier and booked on suspicion of burglary and assault with intent to kill in a St. Louis case.

Police said John had walked into a house on the South Side of the city, brushed past the two children of one Jesse Evans, and started looting the premises. The children ran out and called their father, who was visiting nearby. Evans, his brother, and a friend rushed to the home and tussled with the intruder, but he managed to escape their combined clutches.

So John Ray turned up at the hearing wearing a well-ripened black eye. He denied any role in the assassination. He denied taking part in five separate bank robberies in the St. Louis area. He explained his conviction for a sixth bank holdup as a frameup. But John Ray did describe himself as "a moderate seg- regationist," although he couldn't remember a remark attributed to him in an FBI report. A Bureau informant had quoted John as saying after Dr. King's murder: "What's all the excitement about? He only killed a nigger . . . King should have been killed 10 years ago."

At that, the committee figuratively threw up its hands. Before adjourning, Chief Counsel Blakey announced that the panel could find no evidence that James Earl Ray was paid to assassinate Martin Luther King, Jr. Ray, said Blakey, probably financed his flight from Memphis with cash obtained from an Illinois bank robbery. And, as the spectators filed out of the last public hearing, Louis Stokes put it this way: "I'm not sure, given the passage of time, that we proved conclusively that there was a conspiracy."

In its final report, filed on July 17, 1979—two and one-half years and $5.4 million after launching its investigation—the committee used a little stronger language. It reiterated that James Earl Ray fired the single rifle shot that killed King, but the report added that "on the basis of circumstantial evidence . . . there is a likelihood" that the murder was the result of a conspiracy.

The committee's conclusion was couched in convoluted language. It was based on speculation that while serving time in prison Ray heard of the $50,000 bounty offered by a "St. Louis group" for King's life and suggested that Ray "may simply have acted with a general expectation of payment after the assassination. Or he may have acted, not only with an awareness of the offer, but also after reaching a specific agreement."

In short, the report echoed Louis Stokes's finding but—committeelike—used more words to do so. The case of the United States versus James Earl Ray provided just enough material to keep the plot buffs busy well into the twenty-first century. As for all those reports of FBI and CIA involvement in the assassination, the committee virtually gave both shops a clean bill of health. Virtually, because its report said the FBI's counterintelligence program helped create a climate in which King's assassination was possible. This was what lawyers are fond of calling a "safe" theory—one that could never be proved or disproved, absent evidence that would stand up in a court of law.

14

Don Juan in Philly

How, he asked, could the woman on whom he had lavished money, jewelry, a house, "four cars, or three, a Mustang, a Torino," how could she tell the grand jury she had never done any work for the wage she drew as a state-paid assistant to him? He had paid her with his gifts to her, "for the work you did."

After he dropped out of high school in Philadelphia, Buddy Cianfrani got a job as a sometime messenger for the Democratic machine's tougher technicians in the rough-and-tumble Second Ward on the steamy South Side. "I hafta go into politics," he used to say. "Lookit me. I can't talk Harvard. You think any of those English Protestants are gonna elect me president of some bank? I gotta make myself a big shot where I can."

His square name was Henry J. Cianfrani, but in later years he liked to boast that in his neighborhood "they wouldn't know who Henry was." So he was always Buddy, a mixture of toughness and sentimentality, the kind of young man with whom South Philadelphia could be comfortable.

So it was one of those things that, in afterthought, seemed inevitable when Buddy Cianfrani became Democratic chairman, or boss, of the Second Ward. He spoke his neighborhood's language, political and ethnical. And he had that toughness bestowed on so many by a hard life at the bottom. He owned the Second, and he ran it efficiently, which is to say that—even as in the WASP-ish Republican wards—his patronage mill ran smoothly and he had important contacts in both city and state. He added to his power by serving two terms in the Pennsylvania

House of Representatives, and expanded it still further when he was elected to the State Senate in 1966.

Buddy Cianfrani could deliver the goods for other, more important politicians, too. During the 1966 campaign, he asked his ward to support Robert Casey, who was running against Milton Shapp for the Democratic gubernatorial nomination. Casey defeated Shapp, 2790 to 522, in the Second. When Shapp and Casey ran against each other again in 1970, Cianfrani supported Shapp—and Shapp won, 2220 to 335, in Buddy's Second.

Cianfrani went on to become chairman of the Senate Appropriations Committee, a post that made him the second most powerful Democrat in the state. As the man who directed the disbursement of money, and thus power, he was a figure to be reckoned with by party officeholders, office seekers, and a Philadelphia Establishment that could ill afford to scorn a politician who could veto its pet projects.

Governor Shapp recognized Cianfrani's stature. He tried to appoint Buddy's uncle, Louis Vignola, presiding judge of the Traffic Court, serving at the Governor's pleasure. Buddy had his uncle send the appointment back. Shapp was informed that Buddy wanted his uncle appointed to a fixed five-year term, placing him beyond Shapp's reach. Buddy got what he wanted.

Cianfrani had chutzpah in the most shameless sense. He was, after all, "The Big Cannelloni." He was strong enough not to give a damn what some people thought of him. With the support of John R. Sills, then patronage chief of the Democratic City Committee, Buddy nominated one Rocco Frumento as a state cigarette tax agent in 1971. Because Frumento was a convicted felon, the Shapp administration balked. But Frumento got the job after Buddy informed Shapp that otherwise he would block passage of the pending state income tax bill.

Frumento went on to become an alternate delegate to the 1972 Democratic National Convention in Miami Beach. He also went on to become implicated in a cigarette-smuggling scheme. And Helen Sills, John Sills's eighty-year-old wife, who had certified Frumento's application for the state job, ended up with a $14,000-a-year job on the state's payroll. Frumento was murdered in what Philadelphia newspapers called "gangland style" in February 1976.

Buddy Cianfrani had become a legend. He claimed his legislative salary of $18,500 was his only source of income, and he said he reported taxable income for the four years 1972–76 totaling $42,144. But there were stories that he dropped as much as $1000 in a single day at the racetrack, and he openly associated with purported Mafia figures. He was also a well-known womanizer whose appreciation of the opposite sex was not dimmed when he entered his fifties.

Cianfrani was married in 1946 and fathered three daughters. But he separated from his wife in 1956 when he launched an affair with Mrs. Vera Domenico, a slender, five-foot blonde of impeccable grooming. He built a house, Lady Land, for Mrs. Domenico in Cherry Hill, New Jersey, a two-story brick Colonial with the mandatory manicured lawn and swimming pool, enclosed by a seven-foot-high redwood fence. He and Mrs. Domenico lived there together from time to time. Between those idylls, Cianfrani dallied with numerous damsels in Harrisburg, the state capital, and Philadelphia.

Meanwhile, Buddy Cianfrani found himself under the eye of the law in the person of a Mister Clean lawyer named Walter Phillips. Phillips had been named a special prosecutor to investigate political corruption—a way of life in Pennsylvania—and in 1974 Phillips looked into Cianfrani's extralegislative affairs.

Phillips's first look-see involved maintenance workers at a state highway yard in Nicetown. It seemed that some workers were stealing metal signposts and selling them to junk dealers. Disgruntled workmen tipped off Phillips's investigators that the yard also was a center for cigarette smuggling and suggested that Cianfrani was involved in the racket.

Phillips prosecuted one man from the yard and eventually sent him to prison for five to ten years. But the prosecutor couldn't find anything on "The Big Cannelloni." At least, he couldn't find any witnesses who were willing to offer him anything more than gossip. Meanwhile, some of Phillips's investigators started poking into a stale file which contained reports that Cianfrani had received payoffs for getting would-be physicians into medical schools. In 1975 there were indications that a Florida businessman had paid $17,500 in an unsuccessful effort to get his son into Temple University Medical School. Investigators fingered a suburban Philadelphia dentist and a nightclub operator in the city as Cianfrani middlemen.

Then an FBI agent told the Phillips team he had discovered that one Martin Abrams appeared to be living beyond his means. Abrams was a $12,000-a-year supervisor for the Philadelphia Housing Authority, but he drove an expensive car, had bought five expensive boats, and maintained a fancy city apartment and a cottage at the seashore. The FBI man said there was evidence that Abrams was taking a cut for carrying medical-school payoffs to Cianfrani and to the Speaker of the Pennsylvania House, Herbert Fineman.

Abrams was tailed by FBI agents but led them nowhere. So the Philadelphia dentist was called before a grand jury, where he invoked the Fifth Amendment against self-incrimination. Phillips went to Robert P. Kane, the state attorney general, and asked Kane to grant the dentist immunity to get him to testify. Kane refused to do so.

Cianfrani, meanwhile, had been boasting that he would "strangle that bastard"—Phillips. Cianfrani and Kane were friends and political allies. Phillips was fired in March 1976 after Kane charged he had leaked information about the immunity issue. Out with Phillips went the payoff investigation; the prosecutor's office lasted only until the state legislature—led by Cianfrani—cut off its funds.

Other guys in white hats now interposed themselves on the scene. One was Neil J. Welch, who took over the FBI's Philadelphia field office in 1975 and launched a campaign against white-collar crime. He was joined a year later by David W. Marston, who arrived in Philadelphia as United States Attorney. Marston called in the chief of his corruption unit, Alan Lieberman, and told him to investigate the medical-school plot involving the Florida businessman. Lieberman checked with the FBI office. Did anyone around there know anything about those payoffs? The answer was yes and no. Under Welch's prodding, the FBI was surveilling the activities of a convicted drug trafficker who was reported to be a Cianfrani middleman. Agents came up with empty hands on that one, but in August 1976 the FBI decided to employ some tips its men had dredged up to try to build a case against Martin Abrams.

One of Neil Welch's informants was Philip Gagliardi, an alleged killer, who was on the Housing Authority staff. "Pump your pal Abrams," Welch ordered Gagliardi. With a small tape recorder taped to his skin, Gagliardi pumped. He and the recorder listened as Abrams boasted that he had become rich as a bagman for Cianfrani and Speaker Fineman. "I collected $37,500 from a couple of rich jewelers who wanted Cianfrani and Fineman to get their kids into the veterinary school at the University of Pennsylvania," Abrams claimed. Abrams named names and dates; he was a man who seemed to have total recall.

Fed to FBI Agents Jim Perry and Gregory McLean, this information touched off a grand jury investigation. Abrams was subpoenaed to testify. He told Gagliardi, still wearing his "body wire," that his lawyer had urged him to "be a stand-up guy." Abrams vowed that when it was all over, "I'm going to see both of them [Fineman and Cianfrani] and say 'I saved your asses and I want to better myself.'"

So Abrams went before the grand jury and took the Fifth Amendment. Alan Lieberman persuaded the judge to grant Abrams immunity from prosecution. Immunity is granted only if the witness tells the truth. Now compelled to testify, Abrams lied; he denied he ever took any payoffs. So Lieberman had a solid perjury case against him, but neither he nor Welch wanted to fool with the small fry Abrams. They wanted Fineman and Cianfrani, and Abrams would be a much more effective witness against them if he were not a convicted perjurer.

So Perry and McLean went back to Abrams. They took a hard line during a two-and-a-half-hour meeting at Abrams's apartment on September 22, 1976. They were tough verbally, contemptuous. They played one of the tapes Gagliardi's "body wire" had recorded. They showed Abrams a photograph of a Detroit hit man called "Alley Oop," and said Abrams was on "Alley Oop's" list. Abrams didn't budge. He figured Cianfrani and Fineman would protect him, and he had heard that Marston was going to be fired.

Abrams went on trial in November on the perjury charge. The Gagliardi tapes were played and Perry and McLean testified about their conversations with Abrams. Abrams folded and pleaded guilty. He was to get a light sentence, then a change of identity if he cooperated in further prosecutions.

Swiftly, then, the federal lawmen built a case against Fineman. It was a solid case, they felt, although based in large part on Abrams's credibility. They had much less on Cianfrani, even though Abrams had told of making payoffs to both legislators. In the Fineman case, there was correspondence and third-party testimony alleging that Fineman had attempted to destroy evidence that he had taken the money. But that kind of material was lacking in the Cianfrani case. Cianfrani preferred to do his talking on the telephone. His was a "one-on-one" case. If Cianfrani denied taking the payoffs, the jury would have to decide whose story was more credible—Cianfrani's or Abrams's. And, of course, Abrams was a confessed perjurer.

Meanwhile, the Cianfrani idyll with Mrs. Domenico had been jarred by Cianfrani's infidelities. First, Mrs. Domenico learned he had been having an affair with a young woman named Patricia Arney, a free-lance writer and a committeewoman in Cianfrani's Second Ward. She learned later that Ms. Arney had an abortion after becoming pregnant by Cianfrani; it seemed Ms. Arney became angered by Cianfrani's hypocrisy in pushing an antiabortion bill and had told all to the Philadelphia *Inquirer*.

Then, at Lady Land, Vera Domenico received a telephone bill showing a call to a telephone number she didn't recognize. She dialed the number and spoke to a woman who identified herself as Laura Foreman. According to Mrs. Domenico, they had an unfriendly chat. Cianfrani had met Ms. Foreman shortly after she became the *Inquirer*'s political writer in late 1974, and the two became lovers in mid-1975. In his Santa Claus role, Cianfrani showed his compulsive generosity. He bought her a $3000 fur coat, furniture, house plants, tires for her sports car, and gave her $10,000 in cash.

By this time, Mrs. Domenico and her sister-in-law, Evangelina Domenico, had been put on the State Senate's payroll, and over a two-year period received paychecks totaling more than $25,000. Digging by Agents Perry and McLean produced gossip that neither woman did any work for the Senate or any other legislative unit.

Neil Welch's men also learned that Cianfrani had had an earlier love affair with a young woman who was a graphics artist and that he had installed her in a $340-a-month townhouse on Philadelphia's posh Society Hill. The artist also became pregnant but refused to have an abortion and gave birth to a baby girl.

As a result, there was a series of ugly confrontations between Cianfrani and Mrs. Domenico, one of which ended with Cianfrani throwing a wad of money at her. A neighbor in Cherry Hill quoted Mrs. Domenico as saying that Cianfrani had spat at her, "thrown things at me, and knocked me in the face." She was furious at Buddy's infidelities with younger women, and told a friend: "He lost me a long time ago when he put me on the level of those pigs."

There was also a disturbing report making the rounds of South Philadelphia that Cianfrani allegedly had tried to put out a gangland contract on Mrs. Domenico's life. According to street-wise types, Cianfrani had asked Mrs. Domenico for a picture of her as a keepsake but instead allegedly had passed it on to two hit men. The alleged contract was said to have been vetoed "from on high." Gossipers later reported an incident involving Mrs. Domenico's Italian greyhound. She was said to have complained that the dog became violently ill after eating hamburger meat bought by Cianfrani.

No solid leads were found to support these unpleasant rumors, but the FBI's investigations did dig up something on another payoff case. This one involved the owner of a pharmacy in South Philadelphia named Julius Mingroni.

Mingroni was a friend of both Cianfrani's and Mrs. Domenico's, an affable young man known as "Jules." The story was that he wanted to apply for admission to the Philadelphia College of Osteopathic Medicine (PCOM) and that he had asked Cianfrani to use his influence in his behalf. Mingroni had told one Dr. Joseph Zappasodi, a New Jersey osteopath, that he could get into PCOM if he paid Cianfrani $10,000, and Zappasodi told investigators he had advised against it.

But Mingroni went ahead anyway. Allegedly, he and his father drove to the South Philadelphia apartment where Vera Domenico then was living, and there Mingroni handed Cianfrani a large paper bag filled with money. Mrs. Domenico, it was reported, helped count the money, and when Cianfrani was satisfied with the count he told Mingroni he was "a cinch to get into PCOM."

Meanwhile, Fineman was indicted for taking payoffs and for obstruction of justice. But when they tried the case in May 1977,

Fineman was convicted only of obstruction of justice. As Marston, Lieberman, and Welch had always suspected, Abrams's credibility was the problem. It was now imperative to strengthen the case against Buddy Cianfrani. A series of chats with Mrs. Domenico was clearly indicated.

Agents Perry and McLean drove out to Lady Land to visit with Mrs. Domenico. It was the first of several calls they made on her during the spring of 1977. They were straightforward, but polite and considerate; Perry acted the role of a father figure. Where they had hit Abrams hard, they stroked Cianfrani's *innamorata*. Mrs. Domenico was willing to talk, although she was obviously in fear of Cianfrani's violent temper. She reminded the agents that Cianfrani had a lot of dangerous friends.

She spoke of Cianfrani's gifts to her—the cars, the house, the jewelry. She blew hot and cold. One day she would talk so much the agents kept having to interrupt her; the next day she would clam up, sorry about what she had told them.

But Perry and McLean knew they had to beef up the case against Cianfrani. They kept going back to Mrs. Domenico. During one weekend, Perry spoke with her 24 times on the telephone. She told the agents of the Jules Mingroni payoff. For the first time, the FBI had an independent account of that segment of the case against Buddy. Mrs. Domenico also told them that she and her sister-in-law, Evangelina, had been ghost workers on Cianfrani's committee payroll.

It was inevitable, then, that Mrs. Domenico finally should agree to let the FBI tap her telephone and plant a bug in her living room. No incriminating tape had been available in the Fineman prosecution. The FBI now had a chance to produce one on Cianfrani.

With the tap and bug in place on June 9, Mrs. Domenico went before the grand jury under subpoena. In keeping with an understanding she had with Marston and his assistant, Gregory Margarity, she took the Fifth Amendment. (Margarity had been assigned to the case because Lieberman was still working on Fineman's appeal.)

At 4:32 P.M., Mrs. Domenico called up a Cianfrani flunky, Frank Gerace, to report on her appearance before the grand jury. Gerace already was well informed.

"They're gonna tell ya you'll go in, and they'll immunize

you; that's all," he said. "Then they'll tell ya the next, ah, Friday to be ready with the answers."

Mrs. Domenico: "Oh, I see."

Gerace: "Do ya understand? What you and him [Cianfrani] have discussed. He wants to have breakfast with you."

Mrs. Domenico laid down the law: "He's only gonna talk to me if he talks respectfully. Otherwise . . . I don't even want to be in his company. I told you he nauseates me. Now if you can get him to control himself. . . ."

Gerace: "Yes, I will."

Later that day, Mrs. Domenico told Gerace Cianfrani had ordered her to "fire my attorney," and that she was going to be given a drug to "make me throw up," to avoid testifying.

"So I said to him who told you to give me a drug," she told Gerace. "He said a couple of lawyers said to give you a drug, make you throw up and postpone it a week until Marston's thrown out."

Cianfrani called her again. He told her not to worry about her testimony, because "I'm getting all kinds of information. . . . I'm gonna make sure you're protected." Fearful that his phone might be tapped, Cianfrani said: "On this phone, I want you to cooperate 100 per cent with them."

Having been granted immunity, Mrs. Domenico testified freely about Cianfrani's activities. At the same time, she managed to string her former lover along, a strategy she apparently believed was a life-or-death necessity. But her cover was blown by Cianfrani's lawyer, the ornate, polished Nicholas Nastasi, a good Republican, a member of the prestigious Union League, an aficionado of the philosophers Étienne Gilson and Jacques Maritain, a connoisseur of vintage wine.

Nastasi used all his considerable legal competence to wrest from the prosecution an affidavit that included a brief summary of Mrs. Domenico's testimony to the grand jury. He telephoned Cianfrani. "I'm shocked," he told his client. Distraught, Cianfrani called Mrs. Domenico.

"All I'm asking you is if you said the following things," he said. "You know what you said. You told them you worked for me, you only been to Harrisburg once in your life, you don't even know where the committee is, that I have other people on my payroll also. I bought you the house, you were living in the house, you were living with me while you were paid. I did pay for all the work, you know, to have the pool and a whole bunch of stuff done."

She denied it. But, she said, "Is that serious?"

Cianfrani rambled on. "Well no, not serious, not serious. Why would that be serious? God Almighty! That's, that's great!"

Mrs. Domenico: "Is it criminal?"

Cianfrani: "Sure is, on my part, sure is. Almost like Hays the way you worded it." (Wayne L. Hays, an Ohio congressman, was ruined when his girl friend revealed he had put her on his payroll to keep her handy for romantic trysts.)

Then on July 8, Cianfrani received a copy of Mrs. Domenico's testimony enclosed with a letter from Nastasi. He was furious, and drove to Lady Land.

Mrs. Domenico was in a tizzy. She had switched off the FBI's hidden tape recorder. She had to switch it back on. So she sent Cianfrani out to the patio to check a tree she told him was leaning dangerously and was about to fall into the swimming pool. While he was gone, she switched on the recorder; Cianfrani's footsteps were recorded on tape as he returned to growl that the tree "didn't bend an inch."

"Oh thank God," said Mrs. Domenico. "But it did bend, didn't it?"

Cianfrani sent his "go-fer," Gerace, out for a roast beef sandwich for a hungry Vera Domenico. She was grateful. "You know how many, many times I'm eating butter and macaroni," she told Cianfrani. "You know, God must have sent you because I'm so tired of eating macaroni."

Cianfrani spoke to her in anguished tones. "I, I, I'm not going to get nervous. So eat, eat your roast beef sandwich when it comes. But talk to me first."

The scene was all hammed up, a theater of the absurd. From the background, the recorder picked up voices on a TV program, "To Tell the Truth." Vera stared at the oil portrait above the mantel of Cianfrani in formal dress, looking down on what was his romantic retreat from the legislative world, the world of deals, of "arrangements," of muscling votes.

How, he asked, could the woman on whom he had lavished

money, jewelry, a house, "four cars, or three, a Mustang, a Torino," how could she tell the grand jury she had never done any work for the wage she drew as a state-paid assistant to him? He had paid her with his gifts to her, "for the work you did."

His voice grew weary as he spoke about mounting legal fees. "Vera, they're using us," he said. "Everybody is robbing. . . . And you told them Evangelina got paid for not doing any work."

But Vera Domenico didn't want to talk about her past testimony to the grand jury. She wanted help, advice. She wanted to know what she should say at the next grand jury appearance.

Then she brought up the subject the FBI was interested in. What was she going to say "about what the prosecution wants to know about that bagful of money?"

Domenico: "They're going to subpoena me again. . . . They're not happy with Jules [Mingroni]. They know something about Jules, that I was there for the pay. They said that me, you and Jules was there and paid you off in front of me."

Cianfrani: "They knew there were four people there."

Domenico: "But they didn't say four people were there."

Cianfrani: "Well, they don't know. They're guessing. Vera, they're guessing."

The discussion was about a meeting in April 1970 in Mrs. Domenico's South Tenth Street apartment, at which FBI investigators said Mingroni paid off Cianfrani for pushing his application to osteopathic school.

"Jules's father was never there," Cianfrani told her.

"Jules's father was never there?" Mrs. Domenico's tone was incredulous; she wasn't buying that. "Who was the old man that was in there? That came with the bag of money. Somebody knows something. There was an old man in my dining room on Tenth Street with a bag of money and you said it was Jules's father. . . . It was me, you, Jules, and Jules's father."

Cianfrani's voice sought to reassure her. "Vera, Vera, Vera, keep calm. Vera, don't crack. Believe me, they don't know anything, Vera."

Vera said she wasn't cracking, "but they're going to call me back, Buddy. Suppose they have tapes of the payoff."

"Listen to me," said Cianfrani. "Please let you rest, and me rest, so we can beat this federal investigation. Why do we keep pounding this over and over? Don't you ever pop about it."

Frank Gerace returned with the roast beef sandwich. Vera Domenico bit into it. "Let me, let me eat this roast beef sandwich, and do me a favor . . . please go away, Buddy."

"Now I was crazy to come here," growled Cianfrani. He was right the second time. Listening to that tape, Agents Perry and McLean were sure their case against Cianfrani was clinched. They told Mrs. Domenico so and tried to get her to enter the federal witness-protection program. She refused. But later—as it were—she got religion. In the protective custody of an FBI agent who was a Mormon she went off to make a pilgrimage to Mormon headquarters in Salt Lake City.

Buddy Cianfrani, at fifty-four, still gravel-voiced and hearty, was indicted on September 23, 1977, on 110 counts of racketeering, mail fraud, obstruction of justice, and income tax evasion. A little more than three months later, on December 30, he unexpectedly pleaded guilty to the racketeering, mail fraud, and obstruction-of-justice counts and *nolo contendere* (no contest) on four counts of income tax evasion. On February 15, 1978, he was sentenced to five years in prison for the racketeering violation and five years for mail fraud, the sentences to run concurrently. He also drew five years' probation on the obstruction-of-justice and income tax evasion charges.

But Cianfrani had revenge of a sort. David Marston, the United States Attorney who prosecuted his case, was fired by President Carter in March 1978, two months after it was disclosed that a Democratic congressman had telephoned Carter and asked him to "expedite" Marston's dismissal. The congressman, Joshua Eilberg of Philadelphia, pleaded guilty on February 24, 1979, to a federal conflict-of-interest charge and was sentenced to three to five years' probation and a $10,000 fine. Eilberg was charged with taking a payoff of a size beyond the wildest dreams of Buddy Cianfrani. Alan Lieberman, one of Cianfrani's prosecutors, told a federal court in Philadelphia that a law firm set up by Eilberg got $100,000 in legal fees from Philadelphia's Hahnemann Hospital after helping the hospital win a $14.5 million federal grant in 1975.

TO MAKE
A
BUCK

15

The Balmy Bank Robbers

"Yeah, I think I could kill them. What have I got to lose? The Supreme Court did away with the electric chair. I can kill them all and when the cops come in, just throw down my guns and surrender. What have I got to lose?"

In November 1978, John Wojtowicz was paroled after serving a little more than five years for his part in an attempted robbery of a Chase Manhattan Bank branch in Brooklyn. He told reporters he would celebrate his parole by seeing his wife, Carmen, and his children, then ten and eight, and by visiting "Ernie Aron and George." Aron was Wojtowicz's lover at the time of the bank heist, and later adopted the name Liz Eden after a sex-change operation. George was Wojtowicz's prison sweetheart.

A touch offbeat, most people would say. But so was the holdup of that bank at Avenue P and East Third Street, in which threats were followed by slapstick comedy and, finally, sudden death.

Tuesday, August 22, 1972, had been a routine day at the bank when closing time came and the last customers were departing. As each customer left, the door was locked by Calvin Jones, a uniformed but unarmed guard. But two of the "customers" didn't leave. As Robert Barrett, the bank manager, was examining a loan application, he looked up to see a sandy-haired young man with a round, almost baby's face standing at his desk.

"Are you Mr. Barrett?" asked the young man.

"Yes."

Barrett didn't catch the man's name, but he got the message

from the .38 revolver in the "customer's" hand. "Freeze," Barrett was told. "This is a holdup. I'm not alone."

He wasn't. A second man carrying a briefcase was invading the tellers' section. Within seconds, he started filling the briefcase with currency. The second man was John Wojtowicz. The man holding a gun to Barrett's head was Salvatore Naturile.

The telephone rang on Barrett's desk. He looked at Naturile, an eyebrow raised. "Answer it," Naturile ordered. The caller was Joe Anterio, a personnel officer in the bank's downtown head-quarters. Anterio said he wanted to transfer a teller to another branch.

"Hell no!" snapped Barrett. Then he told Anterio to give the promotion to a teller who had been sacked a few months earlier because he was suspected of dipping his hand into the till.

"By God, you're talking real funny, Bob," Anterio said. "Is something wrong there?" Barrett's face took on the look of a man who wanted his way and refused to argue about it. "Yep," he growled, and hung up. The "Yep" was a prearranged signal that the bank was being held up.

"Fine," Naturile said. "You're smart not to try to tip off anybody."

By this time, Wojtowicz had filled his briefcase with what later was found to be $37,951 in cash and $175,150 in traveler's checks. By this time, too, the cops were on their way. Within a few minutes the first prowl cars had arrived. More police followed, and a gaggle of FBI agents, until more than 200 lawmen were on the scene. Reporters and hundreds of curious onlookers joined the mob.

Inside the bank, Naturile yelled: "All right. We're stuck with you people. We're gonna keep you here until the cops let us go. You're all hostages, and the only rights a hostage has is to do what he's fucking well told." He grinned. "Just call me Sal. We can all be friends if nobody does anything foolish."

Wojtowicz looked around at the frightened bank employes. "That's right," he said. "We don't wanna hurt anybody. Just cool it. You can call me John."

And indeed, there was, incongruously, an air of gentleness about the two robbers—Sal, who couldn't have been more than eighteen or nineteen years old, and John, with his creased, lived-in, friendly face.

Shirley Ball, a fifty-year-old teller, was full of thoughts. She was shaking. She hoped it didn't show; you could never tell what a bank robber would do to someone who looked nervous. I don't know which way to turn, she thought, they're stuck with us and we don't want to get on their nerves.

Worse, she had to go to the bathroom—really go.

"Please John," she said. "I've just got to go to the john."

John Wojtowicz looked at her hard for a moment, then let his mouth relax. "Okay," he said. "Let's go, you and me."

Mrs. Ball was scared. But she told herself this was no time to be prudish. She walked fast to the ladies' room, John following. But John just looked over the place, told Mrs. Ball, "Make yourself comfortable," and walked out. Back in the office he announced: "If anybody's got to go, okay. We're civilized, and we don't know how long we're all gonna be here. But no tricks."

John was the boss. Now he told the nine hostages they could make unlimited phone calls to family and relatives. Mrs. Ball called her husband at his office. He told her he'd get there as soon as he could. "You can't come in," she told him. "I'll just stand outside," he told her. Somebody turned on a radio and live coverage of the holdup blared into the bank.

Shortly, a telephone call came from the police. They wanted to talk to one of the stickup men. John took the phone. He said he and Sal were willing to negotiate. But the bottom line was a jet airliner that would take them out of the country. The official caller said he'd get back to them.

"Just a minute," John said. "I wanna see my wife." He was told that might be arranged. "I'll let one hostage go if you let me see my wife. His name is Ernie Aron."

"*His* name?" the cop asked. "It's a man?"

"Yeah, it's a man, so what," John said. "We're married. Three hundred people came to the wedding. They got poor Ernie penned up at Kings County Hospital; they think he's crazy." So a squad car was dispatched to the mental ward to pick up a twenty-six-year-old male wife.

There were boos and cheers from the crowd outside when Ernest Aron arrived, wrapped in a soiled hospital robe, haggard, uncertain. He was hustled into the police command post in a nearby barbershop. John released the first hostage, guard Calvin Jones.

Ernie phoned John. "I don't want to see you," he said. "It's all over. I told you that before."

John pleaded with him: "But Ernie, I did this for you, so you could have your operation. Why are you afraid of me?"

"I'm not afraid of you," said Ernie. "I'm just done with you." He hung up.

"How about that Ernie?" John said to the bank manager, Barrett. "He wouldn't even come in here. We were married, by a priest."

So John Wojtowicz accepted a substitute he described as "another homosexual." The friend was escorted to the door of the bank by an FBI agent, who held him by the back of his belt so he couldn't dash in and join the party. As the crowd outside let loose with boos and hisses, the friend greeted John at the door with a kiss.

John got a call from Ed Kirkman, a reporter for the New York *Daily News*. Identifying himself only as John, Wojtowicz gave Kirkman a long interview.

He told Kirkman that he "and a couple more" gunmen, armed with shotguns, a .303 British Enfield rifle, and a bomb, invaded the bank after the customers had left, "so no innocent bystanders would get hurt. We waited while the last one left, she was a lady carrying a baby. Then we pulled out our guns and stuck up the place. We got $29,000."

John claimed that the gunmen had gotten information from an employe in the bank's main office that they could get between $100,000 and $200,000 if they hit it at five minutes to three. He went on:

"We were just about to go out when the stupid cops pulled up in front of the bank. Can you imagine pulling a radio car in front of the door of a bank being stuck up? Everything would have been all right if they had come a couple of minutes later. The cops surrounded the bank. I told a lieutenant that if they tried to crash in, the people are dead.

"Yeah, I think I could kill them. What have I got to lose? The Supreme Court did away with the electric chair. I can kill them all and when the cops come in, just throw down my guns and surrender. What have I got to lose?

"I'm a homosexual. I told the cops to get my wife. . . . Then we'll negotiate. What the hell have they got to lose? We know they'll catch us eventually but we'll stop and talk and maybe release a few hostages at a time until we know where we're going. . . . If the cops fire a shot, we'll return it and everybody will be dead.''

Robert Barrett and Shirley Ball, thoughtful people with an intelligent curiosity, by then must have had time to wonder about Sal and John, their sudden captors. What kind of young men were they? Would they really kill? Where did they come from?

Naturile came from what conventional society would call the dregs. The youth, who sported a faint blond mustache, had lived a silent, lonely life. Sal drifted at an early age to New York City, where he was arrested repeatedly for offenses ranging from possession of burglar's tools to grand larceny to possession of dangerous drugs. He always identified himself to police as Donald Matterson of Jersey City.

Sal, in fact, was a petty outlaw, never violent but always trying to beat the system, a struggler in a rootless life, unwanted even in the sleazy bars and pool halls he frequented. He had been out of jail only six months when he met John Wojtowicz in a Manhattan homosexual saloon, one of the many he turned to as a refuge from his directionless life. He found comfort there because he was accepted even though he insisted he was "straight."

John Wojtowicz had had a chance to do something with his life. He was a sometime athlete who played softball. He had a dilettante's interest in politics. He graduated from high school with a 97 percent average, a superb student of mathematics and mechanical drawing. It was inevitable that he should take a job in a bank and find a girl friend there, fun-loving Carmen Bifulco. He called her "Mouth"; she called him "Dingbat." They were engaged just before John was drafted and shipped to Vietnam, and married when he returned to Brooklyn a year later.

John was temperamental, sometimes indignantly so. Carmen couldn't take that, so eventually she and the two children moved in with her parents. John went back home and started making the rounds of homosexual gathering places. There, he was an exhibitionist and somewhat of a swaggerer, but good company; he always could make people laugh.

Then he met Ernie Aron and fell in love. Ernie was always demanding gifts, a bracelet here, a new suit there, more spending money. John was annoyed, but compliant. And finally they were "married" by an unfrocked Catholic priest after Ernie had tried to commit suicide. But they were given only a "blessing." The former priest who celebrated the ceremony told them he wouldn't perform a homosexual marriage because it was an unnatural alliance. He assured John and Ernie that a blessing was a union between two people who promised to be loyal to each other.

Three hundred guests attended the "wedding," including John's mother and Aron's father. There was a lavish buffet, and John had bought Ernie a wedding gown. A "straight" wedding couldn't have offered any more formal detail. Four months later, John and Ernie split. Ernie wrote John a letter, explaining: "I'm sorry but I won't be able to see you tonight as by the time you read this note I'll be in Florida. . . . I just can't take it any more." Ernie wanted to be a woman, physically.

On the weekend before the robbery, John and Ernie had a reunion, and their last fight. Ernie took an overdose of barbiturates and collapsed. Friends called an ambulance and he was whisked to Kings County Hospital.

The hours passed. Barrett's assistant, Mrs. Dolores Goettisheim, kept making coffee for all. Negotiations for the release of the hostages continued off and on. Richard J. Baker, chief assistant to John F. Malone, FBI Regional Director, had arrived on the scene to direct strategy. Baker, fifty-one, neat in a pin-stripe suit, a tall, affable man with thinning gray hair, was stalling for time. Experience had taught him that with the passage of time the chances increased of wearing down an adversary, and then options developed. Baker was looking for an opening.

So Baker kept John Wojtowicz talking, on the phone and through the bank door, opened for their negotiations. He turned down none of John's demands, but kept telling John calmly that arrangements to devise the machinery to put those demands into practice were complicated and time-consuming.

"Baker's got terrific judgment," said Denis E. Dillon, chief of the Brooklyn Federal Strike Force Against Organized Crime.

"He knows how to deal with people. His support was of immense help to us in developing cases against Mafiosi, particularly against members of Joe Colombo's gang."

So time did pass, and as it did the order went out to cut the bank's telephone lines and put a halt to John's publicity campaign. Baker wanted John to be relaxed, but he didn't want the gunmen to be too comfortable; he wanted them to be anxious to get out and thus easier to deal with. And he was telling the truth when he told John the lawmen were trying to make arrangements for the gunmen's getaway. Officials of Hansa, a charter airline, had been contacted about providing an airliner, and Baker's men and the police were working on plans to transport John and Sal to Kennedy International Airport on Long Island.

As the day darkened into night, the hostages tuned in a baseball game between the New York Mets and the Houston Astros. The air conditioning in the bank went off. John and Barrett went down to the basement and tinkered with the controls without success. Back upstairs, John shoved a desk against the basement door and knocked his gun against the desk. A shot rang out and the hostages dove for cover under tables and chairs, but the bullet imbedded itself in the floor.

Outside, the crowd of curious was joined by two women. One was John's mother, Mrs. Theresa Wojtowicz; the other was Mrs. Clyde Saunders, mother of twenty-year-old Joan Saunders, one of the hostages. Other relatives and friends of Wojtowicz's and the hostages also were in the throng. Both women prayed, mostly in silence, but sometimes aloud. "Oh Lord, have mercy!" Mrs. Saunders cried. And Mrs. Wojtowicz, her fists clenched, kept calling out: "Merciful God in heaven, help my son and all those other people in there with him."

At one point, the FBI's Baker went into the bank and spent a half-hour conferring with John Wojtowicz and Salvatore Naturile. He told reporters the meeting was "a wide-ranging series of discussions over many different propositions. We're trying to draw up contingency plans. It all takes time."

That was shortly after 10:00 P.M. Inside the bank, John scurried about nervously. Shirley Ball kept thinking he might be going crazy. But she told herself he was all right, that he tried to be nice. She didn't mind him calling her "Mouth" because she was so talkative. And yet she shivered when John and Sal kept telling the hostages they'd kill them if necessary.

"I'm supposed to hate you guys, but I've had more laughs tonight than I've had in weeks," Barrett told John. Barrett sensed a kind of camaraderie in the atmosphere. Once John spotted a police sniper outside. "Whaddaya think of that sonofabitch!" he yelled. "He really wants me, he wants me in the worst way." Barrett smiled. "Yes, I guess he does, John," he said.

John told the bank manager he hated his father, and that he was devoutly religious. "There's gotta be a God, to take care of the good people on this earth," he said. John also confided to Barrett that he favored capital punishment, but he was puzzled by the system. "Now," he told Barrett, "I can shoot you and they won't give me the gas chamber. But if I shoot a cop, I get it. Now I wonder: if I put a gun to your head and another gun in your hand and made *you* shoot the cop, would you get it?"

At about two o'clock in the morning, a small negotiation was successful. An FBI agent delivered three large pizzas to the bank's door.

"Go open the door," John told Shirley Ball. "Take the pizzas and pay the guy." He gave her a package of dollar bills labeled "$1000." Mrs. Ball dropped the package on the sidewalk and the dollar bills fluttered about. The crowd cheered as three FBI agents dutifully retrieved the money.

"What about it?" Mrs. Ball asked one agent. "Enough is enough. Do you want to trade eight lives for two? Don't stretch our luck, give them their demands."

"We're doing the best we can," the agent replied. "We'll get you out."

Meanwhile, a couple of agents were bringing up Mrs. Ball's husband, Harry. He had been waiting outside for eight hours. Mrs. Ball and her husband embraced while John Wojtowicz held a bargaining session with United States Attorney Robert Morse. When John turned to go back inside, Mrs. Ball followed him.

"I could have just walked off," she told the other hostages, "but I couldn't have lived with myself afterwards."

John was worried about Robert Barrett. "You got something? You need a doctor?" he asked Barrett; the manager had told John earlier that he was a diabetic.

"I'm okay," Barrett said. "I drank some orange juice."

But John insisted that Barrett be examined by a doctor in a car outside. The doctor told Barrett he seemed all right, "But now we'll drive you to the hospital for a cardiogram."

It was Barrett's chance to leave the bank and never return. But he waved off the doctor. "I'll be okay," he said. Then he went back inside, grinning. "I bet you never thought you'd spend the night with your boss," he told the hostages.

"The women can go with Sal and me," John said. "We'll take them to Moscow or Tel Aviv, anywhere they want to go."

Shirley Ball spoke up. "I don't want to go to Tel Aviv," she said. "What if an Arab catches me on my way there?"

"Well, wherever you want to go, girls," said John.

It was not until 3:30 A.M., more than 12 hours after the gunmen invaded the bank, that the FBI appeared to capitulate. There had been protracted dickering about how to get to Kennedy Airport and win freedom for the hostages, and finally an airline limousine pulled up outside with an FBI agent at the wheel. Ten minutes later, John Wojtowciz emerged from the bank, a rifle slung over his shoulder.

First he approached a group of plainclothes police standing at a corner a few yards from the bank. "I want all you cops across the street," he yelled. The cops stood there. "Don't you know what across the street means?" yelled John. The cops moved across the street. "Now all you people with guns, I want them on the ground," John yelled. The guns were dropped.

"That son of a bitch," one cop said. "Can you believe it?"

Then John walked over to the limousine, frisked the agent-driver, and searched the inside of the vehicle, as anguished relatives of some of the hostages watched from down the street.

"Okay," said John. Then, just after 4:00 A.M., he hustled seven of the eight hostages and Sal Naturile into the limousine. A teller, Mrs. Josephine Tuttino, was left behind in the bank. The FBI agent, who jollied the passengers as they climbed aboard, was alone on the front seat of the first of five rows of seats. Alone in the second row was FBI Agent Fred Fehl. Sal Naturile was flanked by two hostages in the third row; there were three hostages in the fourth row; and John Wojtowicz sat between the last two hostages in the fifth and last row.

"What's your name?" John yelled to the driver.

"Just call me Murphy," was the response. He turned his head to look back to Naturile, who had a gun pointed at the driver's seat. "Hey, careful with that gun, Sal. Hold it a little higher, huh? We hit a bump and I'm gone. I don't want to die."

Then Murphy addressed the rest of the passengers: "You want the windows up, I'll open the windows; you want them down, I'll close them. Whatever you want, just ask for it."

The limousine took off for the airport, followed by two dozen FBI and police cars, red lights flashing. The motorcade streamed down Rockaway Boulevard and was passed through a chain link fence across the airport service road at New York Avenue. Civilians at the gate were ordered to leave. In his fifth-row seat, John Wojtowicz hugged his rifle.

At the airport, the motorcade sped toward the Hansa plane, idling on runway 22R in a remote area of the huge flying field. The jet had just returned from Pittsburgh, where it had delivered 4000 pounds of mail, and it had been stripped of its 12 passenger seats.

The limousine stopped. John and Sal now seemed more relaxed, as though they could already taste freedom, but the hostages were tense. As they waited for the plane to draw near so they could almost step from the limousine into the aircraft, Murphy made jokes about bad flying weather in Peking. Then he announced: "I'll see if they've put the food on the plane," and got out of the limousine.

His passengers could see Murphy talking to a cluster of lawmen. Then he walked back, followed by Richard Baker and Louis Cottell, chief of New York City's Detective Bureau. Murphy climbed into the limousine and took his place behind the wheel. The limousine windows were open to the cool of the August morning.

Baker walked up to the limousine and, through a window, talked with Fehl about the size of the plane and about the refueling process, about to get under way. The time had come for Murphy to put into execution "The Baker Plan."

Over his shoulder, he asked Baker: "Will there be food on the plane?" He was saying, in code, that Naturile's gun was up, that he could take him now.

"Yes," Baker replied, meaning he could take Wojtowicz.

Murphy smoothly lifted a .38 revolver from under the floor mat, spun in his seat, and in one quick motion grabbed Naturile's gun and shot him fatally in the chest. Meanwhile, Baker reached into the limousine and seized the barrel of Wojtowicz's rifle as the bandit sat there, stunned.

The hostages piled out of the limousine to freedom and safety. "We're all right," Barrett said. "That is, we're alive."

But Sal Naturile, eighteen, was dead on arrival at Jamaica Hospital. The slug from Murphy's .38 had torn through his left lung and his heart.

John Wojtowicz, twenty-seven, pleaded guilty to a robbery charge on February 16, 1973, and a month later was sentenced to the 20-year prison term from which he would be paroled in November 1978.

There remained one surprise development to be dealt with in this offbeat case, this criminal farce which ended in sudden death. Two days after Wojtowicz's sentencing, a third member of the bandit team stood before a judge's bench. His name was Robert Westenberg, twenty-eight, and he surrendered to the New York office of the FBI in October 1972. Westenberg confessed that he had gone into the bank with Naturile and Wojtowicz on that August afternoon, but discovered his courage was pure Dutch and walked out again and went home.

"I decided I couldn't go through with it," Westenberg told the judge before he was sentenced to two years in the pen. Sal Naturile, his remains sharing a grave with those of his father in a New Jersey cemetery, should have been so chickenhearted.

16

Nightmare of a Senator

"Then he told me he had dealed with a Senator who was shot and robbed. He told me the Senator was an old man. I asked him why did he do it. He just laughed."

"I'm sorry to say we have absolutely nothing to go on." The speaker was L. Patrick Gray III, Acting Director of the FBI, on the telephone to President Nixon. It was just before midnight on January 30, 1973, and Nixon wanted action. "Bring in those thugs," he told Gray.

A few hours earlier, Senator John Stennis, Democrat from Mississippi, had arrived at his home in a pleasant, tree-lined neighborhood of Northwest Washington. He parked his white Buick Electra on the street and got out; he felt his seventy-one years after a long day at his office and a Capitol Hill reception.

Suddenly he was accosted by two black youths, one of them with pistol in hand. "This is a holdup," he was told. "Let's have all your bread." Swiftly, the Senator was relieved of 25 cents in change, his wallet containing about twenty dollars, and a gold wristwatch engraved with his initials.

"Okay," said the youth with the pistol. "I'm going to shoot you anyway." He fired two shots from the small-caliber gun. One of the shots ripped into Stennis's left thigh midway between knee and hip, struck the bone but didn't break it, and then fragmented. The second bullet plowed into the Senator's left side close to the lower ribcage. It passed through the mid-portion of the stomach and then through the pancreas.

Inside the Stennis home, the Senator's wife had heard her husband drive up—recognizing the sound of the engine. Then she heard two pops, as though made by firecrackers. She opened the front door to see Stennis staggering up the sidewalk to the house, calling her by name, "Coy!"

"Call for help," Stennis told his wife. "I've been shot."

She helped him into the house and onto a sofa in the living room, then went to the telephone. A few minutes later, a District of Columbia Fire Department ambulance arrived and administered first aid. At Stennis's request, he was then taken to Walter Reed Army Medical Center (where he had been treated previously for a colon problem).

At Walter Reed, Stennis was wheeled into the emergency room, and a team of six senior military doctors, experienced in treating gunshot wounds, went to work. The surgery took more than six hours; it was almost three-thirty on the morning of January 31 when Stennis was taken to the recovery room. A few hours later, a hospital bulletin described the Senator's condition as "very serious"—the term used to reflect the "most critical" cases. But Maj. Frank Garland said Stennis's vital signs—heartbeat, pulse, blood pressure, and respiration—were stable. The prognosis, he said, was "guarded," but he added that Stennis was conscious and "resting comfortably." He said it did not appear that any of the wounds would have a permanent effect, although there was always the danger of infection resulting from damage to internal organs.

John Stennis, one of the most powerful men in Congress, Chairman of the Senate Armed Services Committee, opponent of gun controls, survived the attack to return to his job. Meanwhile, the FBI found a big and maddeningly complicated assignment on its hands.

Although Washington police joined the Bureau in a massive joint investigation, the prime responsibility was the FBI's under the 1971 Congressional Assassination Statute, which makes it a federal offense to kill, kidnap, assault, or attempt to kill or injure a member of Congress. Thus, the Bureau got most of the heat generated by Nixon, who called the attack on Stennis "senseless," and peppered Director Gray with phone calls and memos urging swift apprehension of the assailants. Nixon also ordered Attorney General Richard G. Kleindienst to prepare strong new proposals for gun control legislation, although the President had never been a leader in that particular crusade. On Capitol Hill, numerous legislators—not all of them hunting headlines—called for new and tougher anticrime laws.

Four days after the shooting, FBI agents interviewed John Stennis at Walter Reed. The Senator struggled to be specific, but the sum of his contribution was general; he could say only that the two assailants were black males, both about sixteen or seventeen years old, both slim and about five feet eight inches tall. He remembered that one of the youths wore a light blue jacket, and he said he believed he could recognize them if he saw them again. Finding the pair was another thing; Stennis's descriptions fit thousands of young blacks in the Washington area.

So the search was focused on known offenders, youths with arrest records for crimes of violence, especially those who had been caught while up to no good in the genteel Upper Northwest section of the city. In the same neighborhood, FBI agents and police interviewed officials and teachers of Wilson High School and Deal Junior High School, both only five blocks from the Stennis home.

Anonymous letters and telephone calls received at FBI headquarters instructed the Bureau to check up on civil rights activists. These faceless informants were sure that Stennis had been attacked because he was, as one caller put it, "a lifelong enemy of integration and Negro rights." But the FBI rejected such suggestions. Investigators were sure that the assailants were street toughs looking for money. Unlike the cars of most members of Congress, Stennis's Buick license plates bore no inscription identifying the owner as one of Capitol Hill's elite.

The Senator's son, John Hammond Stennis, a Mississippi state legislator, did express bewilderment, however. Although not theorizing that his father was shot because of who he was, the younger Stennis told FBI agents: "Why he was shot is the question. He had given him his billfold. The robbery was accomplished, there was no reason to shoot the victim."

But Washington police, familiar with crime trends in their city, quoted statistics showing that in recent years street robbers, especially younger ones, had attacked their victims even where there was no resistance. An FBI informant passed along street talk that Stennis's attackers had tried to kill him "so the dude wouldn't be alive to identify them."

In response to the wide publicity given the shooting, numerous tipsters called the FBI with "positive" identifications of the robbers, but hundreds of leads were followed to dead ends. However, investigation of the leads produced the arrests of eight fugitives in unrelated cases, and the recovery of several handguns used in assorted crimes. And by the end of February 1973, FBI agents and police had interviewed more than 800 persons, including suspects and streetwise men and women the lawmen believed might lead them to the offenders.

At that point, the lawmen knew literally nothing about a case that had gained nationwide attention. They didn't know how the two attackers had made their getaway, although the assumption was that they had done so by car. The problem was they couldn't find anybody who had seen a car that could have figured in the gunmen's escape. The streets of Stennis's neighborhood seemed to have been deserted on that early evening of January 30.

There was, to be sure, the night an underground FBI agent was sipping a beer in a ramshackle ghetto saloon. Swapping small talk with one of the customers, he mentioned that another regular had been picked up by police on a rape charge.

"Ah, Shorty didn't do that girl," he was told. "The fuzz picked up the wrong guy as usual."

"How do you know?" the agent asked.

"How do I know?" was the reply. "Because Shorty was shooting crap all that night, that's how I know. Besides, Shorty don't go around hurting folks. He just steals a little here and there."

"Shorty's a harmless crook, then," the agent remarked.

"Hell yes, not like some people who shoot their mouths off around here."

The agent's interest perked up. "Like who, for instance?" he asked.

"Oh, like some people. Like a dude the other night I never saw before and ain't seen since. He sound like he came from outside the territory. A big mouth. A big mouth with a suit with a vest and a yeller shirt and tie."

"A big-mouth dude," the agent remarked.

"Yeah, he sure talked big. Said his name was Ty, or Pie, maybe. I never knew him. Nobody knew him. He claim he made some bread in a stickup, then shot the sucker. Why he shoot the

sucker after he got his bread is what I'd like to know. You get
your bread and you split, is the way. Don't make no sense to
shoot a sucker.''

"Did he kill the sucker?" the agent asked.

"No, he claim not. Claim he read in the paper the man was
living. Claim the man was a big shot, but he didn't say who.
Nobody here gonna ask any questions about who. That way you
might be the next who.''

Later, when his informant had left, the agent tried prudently
to pick up more information about the big mouth. But everybody
he talked to claimed he or she knew nothing about him. The agent
couldn't press them, but he was convinced that Ty or Pie was
indeed a passing stranger. None of them admitted knowing the
man's name, although the bartender said it "might have been Ty,
or something like that.''

The agent hung around the bar for several nights thereafter,
but Ty or Pie didn't show. What he had heard, then, was not
much of a lead, even of the flimsy variety. But the boasting of Ty
or Pie went into the investigative record. You never could tell.

Indeed you never *could* tell. A few days later, police were
called to quell a husband-wife brawl in a shabby Northeast
neighborhood. While they were subduing the husband, the wife
screamed a threat to tell police about his "shooting a Senator.''

Constabulary ears snapped to attention. "What's your name,
son?" one of the cops asked. "Fuck you!" the husband told him.
He was relieved of his wallet. In it, a driver's license identified
the husband as Tyrone Isaiah Marshall, eighteen years old.

Husband and wife were hustled to a precinct station, and the
FBI was notified. It seemed happily possible that Tyrone Marshall
was the Ty or Pie the underground agent had learned about and
duly reported for inclusion in the docket of the Stennis case.

Taken to separate rooms, the Marshall couple was questioned
for more than five hours by police and FBI agents. Mrs. Debra
Marshall denied she knew anything about the Stennis shooting
and said the police "must have been hearing things" if they
claimed she had threatened to expose her husband's part in the
crime. Tyrone Marshall said he had "never even heard" of the
crime.

During the questioning, however, police got a search warrant for the Marshall residence. There they and FBI agents found a .22-caliber pistol and six .22-caliber bullets. The handgun was taken to the FBI laboratory, where the Bureau's painstaking scientists reported that its barrel markings matched those on the two bullets taken from Senator Stennis's body.

Tyrone Marshall had been held, meanwhile, on a charge of assaulting his wife "with a stick," and his wife had been released. Marshall had been scheduled for arraignment that day in Superior Court on two charges of robbing two different women on December 14, 1972, and on the following January 3. That arraignment was postponed so Marshall could be held on the Stennis charges. Magistrate Jean S. Dwyer refused to set a nominal bond, as requested by Marshall's court-appointed counsel. "For an eighteen-year-old, he has either been very busy or very unlucky," she said of Marshall. She held him under $50,000 surety bond.

At the FBI, the handgun was traced through federal gun registration forms to a combination general store-gunshop in La Grange, Georgia, to one Derrick Holloway of a Northeast address in Washington. Agents picked up Holloway, who told them he had lent the gun to Tyrone Marshall and then had driven Marshall and his brother, John, around Washington, looking for a likely robbery victim. He claimed he waited in the car while the Marshall brothers robbed Senator Stennis and Tyrone Marshall then shot him.

Holloway and John (J. B. for "Johnny Boy") Marshall followed Tyrone Marshall before Magistrate Dwyer's bench. Like Tyrone Marshall, they were charged under the Congressional Assassination Statute. John Marshall's bond was set at $25,000 and Holloway's at $10,000. The FBI notified the magistrate that Holloway had "indicated" in a sworn statement that he would testify for the prosecution.

On March 28, 1973, a few days less than two months after the Stennis shooting, the Marshall brothers and Holloway were formally arraigned. All pleaded not guilty to an eight-count grand jury indictment charging armed robbery, assault with intent to kill, attempt to assault a member of Congress, and attempt to kill a member of Congress. By then, the FBI and police had interviewed 1100 persons in one of the most intensive manhunts in Washington's history.

II

Senator John C. Stennis looked across the courtroom to where Tyrone Marshall was sitting. "I believe that's the man who held the pistol," said Stennis.

The identification was made out of the presence of the jury because the prosecution had previously agreed Stennis "would not or could not" identify Marshall. Stennis later said he believed he could do so and was permitted to testify with the understanding that none of his remarks would be divulged to the jury.

Anyway, Stennis got the chance to tell his story to Judge Joseph C. Waddy, for whatever influence that might exert on the judge's charge to the jury at trial's end. It is far more likely, however, that Judge Waddy was merely paying a courtesy to the distinguished victim of a brutal crime.

Prosecutor Roger Adelman asked Stennis: "Can you recognize anybody at the defense table as the man with the gun?"

Stennis leaned forward, looking at Ty Marshall. "I think so," he said. "To this extent. I've been noticing this gentleman as I have been sitting here. Based on what I've seen of this gentleman sitting here and, more especially, since he opened his eyes, he has many of the features of the man I dealt with that night—the man with the gun. . . . I do believe that's the man who had the pistol."

As the trial progressed, the evidence against Ty Marshall piled up. FBI witnesses told how the attack gun was traced to Marshall's hand. It was sold by the Georgia shop to one Tommy Lewis Thornton, who told agents he bought the gun for his cousin, John Webster of Washington, who was visiting him at the time. Webster testified he brought the gun to Washington and sold it to Holloway for $40, in mid-January.

Other witnesses were traced through investigation and interviews by the underground FBI agent who first learned about Ty or Pie in a ghetto saloon. They included street-corner friends of Ty Marshall, four of whom told the court Marshall had boasted of the shooting in such diverse locations as the Psychedelic Haven Record Shop and the Turkey Thicket playground near Marshall's home.

The testimony of one of the four youths was especially

chilling. George Hutchinson, nineteen, said he had an "all right" relationship with Ty Marshall and that they frequently exchanged confidences. He testified he and Marshall were leaving the Turkey Thicket playground one day when Marshall turned to him and said "he wanted to tell me something, but he wanted me to promise not to tell nobody. Then he told me he had dealt with a Senator who was shot and robbed. He told me the Senator was an old man. I asked him why did he do it. He just laughed."

There was also Otto Brocks, nineteen, who said Ty Marshall told him on a street corner one night about a week after the shooting that he, his brother John, and Derrick Holloway had "pulled a hustle." He was asked what happened to the victim of the hustle. "He [Ty Marshall] said the man was shot," Brocks replied.

There was Emmett Howard, eighteen, who testified that on the day after the shooting he was in the Psychedelic Haven with Marshall and that Marshall reported that "he and J. B. [Marshall's brother] approached this man and asked him for his wallet and he started hollering and carrying on and he shot him."

"Who shot him?" asked Assistant United States Attorney Steven W. Grafman.

"Tyrone," Howard replied.

There was Michael Ginyard, nineteen, who quoted Ty Marshall as saying: "I shot the dude."

And, finally, there was John Thomas, an employe of the District of Columbia Sanitation Department. He testified that he overheard a sidewalk argument between Ty Marshall and his wife in which Mrs. Marshall accused her husband of shooting the Senator. Marshall, according to Thomas, didn't deny the accusation, but stepped back and told his wife: "You crazy. That [meaning Thomas] might be the police you tellin' that to."

But Ty Marshall still had a partial out. While his trial was in progress, his brother John had pleaded guilty to having participated in the Stennis holdup. John's admission of guilt came just five days before his twenty-second birthday, and thus made him eligible for sentencing under the more lenient provisions of the Federal Youth Corrections Act. Had he not changed his plea, John could have drawn three consecutive life terms as an adult. As it was, he was sentenced to 15 years in prison, with the provision that he could be released at any time corrections officials decided he had been rehabilitated. So, at the most, John Marshall would serve 13 years, under another provision of the act requiring his parole two years before the maximum time was served.

So Ty Marshall, by then nineteen years old, followed his brother's example. He suddenly pleaded guilty, undoubtedly influenced by the government's announcement that Derrick Holloway had been granted total immunity in exchange for his agreement to take the witness stand against Ty Marshall. That meant Holloway was home free.

Judge Waddy accepted Ty's plea over the objections of government attorneys, who contended that the judge had the option of continuing the trial to a conclusion they were confident would result in a jury verdict of guilty, therefore making Ty subject to a longer prison sentence. But Waddy interpreted the law to mean he had no discretion other than to accept Ty's plea. He called in the jury and announced that the case had been disposed of.

Then Judge Waddy asked the prosecution to inform the court what additional evidence Holloway would have provided. Prosecutor Grafman obliged with a virtual minute-by-minute chronology of the events of January 30, 1973, when John Stennis barely escaped death:

About 6:15 P.M., Holloway dropped in at the home of the Marshalls. He showed John Marshall his gun. Ty Marshall appeared while they were admiring the pistol, and said: "Let's go riding," a phrase understood in their ambience as meaning that the three go out and find someone to rob. The trio drove off in a Dodge Dart Swinger owned by Holloway's mother and crossed from the city's Northeast section to the richer Northwest area, where they began looking for a "hit." They saw an elderly woman about to enter an apartment building, but by the time they changed course to intercept her she had disappeared into the building.

A few minutes later, the three youths saw an elderly white man—Stennis—passing them in a white car. "Let's get him. Let's get him," Ty Marshall called out. While Ty and John Marshall were robbing Stennis, Holloway waited for them in the car, parked at a nearby street corner. He heard two shots fired.

And when Ty Marshall returned to the car for the getaway he told Holloway: "The old man was making too much noise so we had to shoot him."

After the robbery, the trio drove around downtown Washington for a while and then attended a lecture at the Founding Church of Scientology. The next day, Holloway heard a radio newscast that Stennis had been shot. He called Ty Marshall and asked: "Do you know that man you shot was a Senator?" Ty laughed. "So what?" he said. "He's just a fucking white man."

After Grafman's recitation, Judge Waddy asked Ty Marshall why he was entering the guilty plea. Stammering, Marshall replied: "Because . . . they have . . . too much evidence . . . on the charge . . . on the conviction."

That seemed to be that. But Ty was not about to stand still for a tidy cleanup of the Stennis shooting. When he was ushered into court for sentencing, he brought with him another surprise. He asked Judge Waddy to let him withdraw his guilty plea. He said the government had been "unfair" to him because he had been told that no one charged in the crime would be given immunity from prosecution.

There followed an interlude of two weeks, granted to permit Ty's counsel to prepare a proper motion and to discuss the change-of-plea request with the youth's parents. Finally, however, Ty Marshall made his last trip to the courtroom.

There, Judge Waddy rejected the attempt to change the plea as "frivolous and without substance." He read extensively from two separate presentence reports that Ty Marshall be sentenced as an adult. Then he sentenced the youth to concurrent 10 to 30 year prison terms under the Congressional Assassination Law, and to another one-year concurrent term on a charge of carrying a dangerous weapon.

Any other penalty, the court said, would be "incompatible with the welfare of society. Marshall has shown no remorse for the shooting, no desire to change his behavior, and appears to have developed a sense of self-immunity to accepted customs of laws and society."

"I ain't accepting that sentence," Marshall shouted. Then he began struggling with three United States marshals and had to be forcibly removed from the courtroom while his father roared sternly from a bench in the rear: "Tyrone!"

17

The After-Hours Tax Cop

But what chilled Kenny was the black box, about six by eight inches, above the door. His captor taped two wires to the boy's ribcage, and two others to his legs, and hooked all four to the box. "If you yell out, or if anyone comes in except me, 115 volts will go through your body," the man told the boy.

He was thirty-nine years old, a husky man just under six feet tall. He wore a neatly trimmed beard and mustache, and was well groomed; his appearance was dapper, just missing foppishness. Throughout his trial, his demeanor was calm, as though he wasn't particularly interested in the proceedings. But he broke down and sobbed when a California jury found him guilty of kidnapping.

The man's conviction ended the FBI's dogged investigation of what had seemed to be the perfect crime. Its pursuit of the kidnapper had taken just four days less than three years, and at times more than 300 agents were deployed in that wearisome, bone- and brain-numbing search for the abductor of eleven-year-old Kenny Young of Beverly Hills, California.

It was a problem that began shortly after midnight on the morning of April 3, 1967. Mr. and Mrs. Herbert Young had returned to their home after visiting friends. They checked on their five children and found them all sleeping soundly. "Let's go to bed," Young said, yawning.

Sometime later, perhaps an hour after the Youngs had retired, a car turned into their driveway. A man got out and climbed the outside staircase to the second-floor deck. He found the sliding glass door to Kenny's room—where the boy slept alone—unlocked.

Slipping into the room, the man shook the boy awake. Kenny uttered the beginning of a scream, shut off when the man struck him four blows on the head with something heavy. "Shut up or I'll kill you," the man told the little boy, now stiff with terror. Then he gagged Kenny and blinded him with adhesive tape, dropped an envelope on the bed, and marched the boy down the steps and into the car. The Young household slept on in the dark silence.

Holding Kenny down on the front seat with one hand, the man took a walkie-talkie from the pocket of his jacket. "All clear?" he asked of the device. "All clear," came the answer.

The boy shivered, but not because he was dressed only in undershorts and socks. His shaking annoyed the man. "Do you know what they can do to people like me?" he asked. "They give us capital punishment." Then he bound the boy's arms behind his back and drove off.

The ride took about half an hour. It ended at a location where the man carried Kenny up five steps to a landing and then forced him to walk up a second flight of seven steps that felt like concrete. After leading the boy into a room, the man pushed him face-down onto a mattress and removed his blindfold. Blinking, Kenny saw that he was in what looked like an L-shaped room, which apparently had no windows. The man was busy; he plugged Kenny's ears with wax and tied his hands and feet to the bed-frame. Then he removed a pair of black gloves and departed.

The Youngs' six-year-old son got up about 6:00 A.M., followed presently by their three-year-old adopted daughter, and their two other sons, eleven and thirteen. Shortly before eight o'clock, as Young was dressing, his wife came upstairs. "Everybody's had breakfast but you and Kenny," she told him. Kenny had gone to bed the previous night with a headache after a big day. Mrs. Young went to his room to see if he was awake and to give him an aspirin if needed. She found only the envelope on the empty bed and opened it, then returned to her husband.

"Look at this," she said. "It must be a joke."

Young read the note his wife had found in the envelope. It was a typed carbon-copy message, partially blurred: "Do not call the police or your missing merchandise will be vindictively destroyed. . . . Give a reasonable explanation to all interested parties concerning the absence of this merchandise. We need

$250,000 in hundreds only. Be at the pay phone at the Standard Station, northeast corner of Westwood and Ohio, at 6:00 P.M. on Wednesday."

Young felt first a surge of anger, then a cold fear. He ran to Kenny's room and found bedding strewn on the floor, the glass door open.

"I don't think this is a joke," he told his wife, struggling against the catch in his throat. The couple embraced, weeping. Young was also trying to think. Finally, he said, "I'm going to call the police. I've got to."

He telephoned a man he knew—Police Chief Clinton H. Anderson. Within five minutes, Anderson arrived with Detective Chief John Hankins and three police officers. Anderson had left orders to alert Los Angeles authorities and the FBI.

The thirty-five-year-old Young was well-to-do. He was president of both Gibraltar Financial Corporation, a holding company, and its subsidiary, Gibraltar Savings and Loan Association, of Beverly Hills. His father-in-law, Sydney R. Barlow, had founded and continued as major shareholder of both institutions, which had assets in excess of $400 million.

But large amounts of cash sometimes are not readily available even to the wealthy. So Young arranged to borrow $100,000 of the ransom from the Beverly Hills National Bank, putting up stock as collateral. His father-in-law put up the other $150,000. Since Young had to have the money all in $100 Federal Reserve notes, he had to take the senior officer of the bank into his confidence and explain what he was doing with the small fortune. He arranged to pick up the money just before leaving for his rendezvous with the kidnapper.

That was in mid-afternoon of Monday, April 3, a little more than 48 hours before Young was scheduled to deliver the ransom to the kidnapper. The FBI was standing aside, in keeping with its longtime policy of doing nothing to endanger the life of a kidnapping victim. The Bureau neither approves nor disapproves the payment of ransom, leaving that decision up to the family.

Meanwhile, Kenny Young's captor had returned. He had the boy bend over the bed with his feet on the floor while he close-clipped his dark hair down to the scalp. "We want that adhesive blindfold to stick tight, don't we?" he said to his victim.

With the blindfold off during his haircut, Kenny found that the room in which he was being held was rather large, its floor covered with a reddish brown asphalt tile, its walls a light green shade. It contained a TV set, a small radio, and an end table at the head of the bed holding a tall lamp. But what chilled Kenny was the black box, about six by eight inches, above the door. His captor taped two wires to the boy's ribcage, and two others to his legs, and hooked all four to the box.

"If you yell out, or if anyone comes in except me, 115 volts will go through your body," the man told the boy. Then he cooked up bacon and eggs for his captive and served them with toast and milk. "I'm a lousy cook," the man said, "but I used to be married and I had a little girl." He told Kenny there were others involved in the kidnap plot. "I tied up the other four people and I'm taking the money for myself," he said.

Waiting for Wednesday, the boy's parents got little sleep. FBI agents and police checked Kenny's room, the outside staircase, and the driveway, but they found no fingerprints, nothing that could be called a clue. The letters of the ransom note were too fuzzy for any attempt to trace the typewriter. Lawmen agreed the note was written by an intelligent, educated individual, but were puzzled by one misspelling, perhaps deliberate. "I have your merchandise," it said. And then: "Don't let our competators [sic] get it."

Wednesday finally came. Wesley C. Crabb, the FBI agent in charge, told Young to follow the kidnapper's instructions to the letter. About the rendezvous, he told Young: "We'll have our men spotted throughout the Los Angeles area. Make the conversation as long as possible so we can try to trace the call. Try to remember every detail. Under no conditions will we do anything to jeopardize the safety of your son. Our work begins after his return."

There were half a dozen phone calls. Twice the phone rang, then went silent. Four times, when Young picked up the receiver, no one answered on the other end. Crabb told Young: "If he doesn't call, just go to the rendezvous he named; he'll be expecting you."

The kidnapper never called. But Young's 1965 Cadillac had undergone a transplant. A microphone and tape recorder were concealed in the car by FBI experts, so adroitly that Young himself failed to find the bugging device during a half-hour test search. Then, shortly after five o'clock Wednesday afternoon, wearing black slacks and a blue golfer's shirt, as directed by the kidnapper, Young left his home. He stopped at the bank to pick up the ransom, stashing it in a tan overnight bag, then continued on toward the service station. A .38-caliber pistol was holstered behind his right thigh in case of trouble.

Young reached the Standard station at about 20 minutes to six. He took his position outside the phone booth and alternately stood and paced. He chewed gum. The telephone in the booth rang at exactly six o'clock, and Young picked up the receiver. "Go to the corner of Sepulveda and Moraga," a voice ordered. "There's another Standard station there, with a telephone booth. Goodbye."

At the second station, Young waited an interminable 40 minutes before a 1965 white Chevrolet—license plate NBD770— drove up. The driver motioned Young to follow. The two cars sped north about a mile and a half on Sepulveda Boulevard and under the San Diego Freeway. At a barren area strewn with gravel north of Sunset Boulevard, the white Chevrolet stopped. Young pulled up behind, then swung around in front at the driver's orders.

He saw a rangy male get out of the Chevrolet and walk deliberately, easily, confidently up to his car. The man was about five feet ten and appeared to be in his twenties, a dark man with an olive complexion and thick, black wavy hair. It looks like a wig, Young told himself. The man wore black gloves and wraparound sunglasses. One hand was inside his jacket, as though holding a gun; the other hand was free.

"Give me the bag," the man said, his voice rasping.

"We can't keep this quiet any longer," Young said. "There are too many people calling and asking questions. How is my son? When will I get him back?"

The man spoke between tight lips. "Your son is fine. You'll get him back tonight. Go straight home and wait for a call from your boy." Then he drove off.

Young returned home a little after seven o'clock, and he and his wife sat together next to the phone. A couple of FBI agents tried to reassure them by emphasizing that everything had gone like clockwork and that the kidnapper had no reason to harm Kenny. They waited, and waited, nagged by fear.

About three-thirty the next morning, the doorbell rang at the Santa Monica apartment occupied by John A. Negrey, a forty-three-year-old bachelor and aerospace engineer, and Ed Bawell. Groggy, Negrey answered the bell. Outside the door stood a small boy dressed only in undershorts, his head shaved, a strip of tape fastened to his forehead and his wrists taped with adhesive.

The boy's voice was small. "I've been kidnapped," he said. "They got away. Can you let me in?"

Negrey looked at the child. The figure before him was too pathetic to be playing a prank at that time of the morning. He let the boy in, an arm around him. Then he fretted that the kidnappers might be nearby, and he made sure the door was locked. Aroused by the noise, Bawell walked out of his bedroom. "You look pretty calm," he told the boy. "Better call up your folks."

Kenny Young walked over to the telephone and dialed home. "Dad, I got away and I'm all right," he reported, his voice matter-of-fact. "I'm awfully tired. Would you come and pick me up?" Negrey took the phone then, and told Young his son was all right.

Ten minutes later, the doorbell rang and eight FBI agents arrived; Kenny's parents had been persuaded to let the lawmen precede them, just in case. The Youngs arrived almost on the agents' heels and took Kenny into their arms. "Hi, Dad. Hi, Mom," Kenny said. "I'm sure glad to see you."

Later, the little boy told FBI agents he had been given four sleeping pills before the kidnapper left for the rendezvous. Then, sometime after the delivery of the money, he had been taken from the hideaway and left in the rear seat of a sedan parked in an underground garage in the Negrey-Bawell apartment building. He had been warned to remain there for half an hour; he waited as long as he could, then wriggled loose from his bonds and hurried upstairs.

"I wasn't scared," Kenny said. "No, I *was* scared when he showed me the gun. And I didn't like that black box."

Now the FBI could go to work—but from square one. The clues were meager, and probably misleading because the kidnapper had shown a professional touch in everything he did. He had used a fuzzy carbon copy as his ransom note, a copy that even the scientists at the FBI laboratory found too messy to yield any distinctive markings. There were two tape recordings of the man's voice, obtained by Young when they talked over the phone at the first gas station and again during their face-to-face encounter. But the kidnapper's "flavor" strongly suggested he had disguised his voice.

Kenny's description of his captor differed from that given by his father. Kenny said the man was about thirty-nine; his father said he was in his twenties. To Kenny, his captor was six feet or taller; his father said he was no taller than five feet eleven. To the father, the kidnapper looked as if he weighed about 180 pounds; to Kenny, he was about 200 pounds. The man the father talked to had thick, black wavy hair; Kenny said he had blond or brownish hair.

Mexico City police wired a report that the kidnapper had been seen south of the border by several citizens, and that other civilians claimed $100 ransom notes had shown up in the country. Two days later, the reports were called false by Mexican authorities.

On April 10, Los Angeles police found the white Chevrolet abandoned at a Canoga Park, California, shopping center. FBI agents hurried to the scene. They found the car had been stolen, as authorities had suspected all along, and that its license plates had been altered with orange paint and bits of metal. The thief also had modified the car with special switches that deactivated the brake lights and the overhead interior light. An analysis of dirt vacuumed from the car's floor revealed earth that contained both freshwater and saltwater diatoms—minute, shell-like particles that are virtually indestructible. Experts at the California Division of Mines and Geology told the FBI that such diatoms occurred together in only one place in southern California: the abandoned Grefco Mine Laboratory, near the Palos Verdes Hills between Santa Monica and Long Beach. The kidnapper, then, had been at the old mine, but no one knew whether that information was significant. It went into the file as a never-can-tell item.

Wesley Crabb, the Bureau's agent in charge, was intrigued by a vagrant thought and put it up to his men at a conference on progress. "It may sound crazy, but I'm convinced the kidnapper came from a law enforcement background," he said. "Maybe a cop who went wrong, or even somebody higher up. Look at it this way: The guy approached Young's car like a cop—standing by the doorpost to avoid being struck if the driver suddenly flung the door open. How many people besides lawmen know about the use of overhead and stop-light turn-off switches? We use them and so do the police to black out our cars during night-time surveillance operations. The section where the money changed hands was a dead zone for radio transmission. Law officers know that. I don't think the average guy, or hoodlum, does. Let's add that as a possible to the kidnapper's profile."

Moreover, the FBI knew by now that they were hunting an especially wily fugitive. To confuse his pursuers, he had operated widely over different Los Angeles suburbs, stealing the car at one end of the San Fernando Valley and ditching it at the other, abducting the boy in Beverly Hills, arranging the ransom meeting in the Westwood area, releasing Kenny in Santa Monica. As Crabb put it: "He's been acting like a cop who knows how cops think." And none of the ransom money had surfaced; obviously, the fugitive knew how fast currency serial numbers were distributed to banks in every American community.

As the months passed, a small army of FBI agents was purposefully deployed in the Los Angeles area. They investigated more than 200 suspects and talked to all of them. They checked on the activities of former law officers and private detectives who had been involved, or were reported to have been involved, in assorted shady enterprises. They canvassed apartment buildings and flophouses. They interviewed used-car dealers and dealers in guns. They talked to underworld informants, and went underground themselves in an effort to pick up gossip that might give them a lead. And they got nowhere.

And then, on September 29, 1969—more than two years after the kidnapping—there was a short story in the newspapers about the arrest of one Eugene Patterson, an ex-convict, for the armed robbery of a supermarket in Alhambra. Two days later, Patterson was identified as one of two men who had held up a theater the previous September. It was what lawmen called a "nothing" story, routine stuff. And, routinely, Agent Crabb asked the

Alhambra police to let him know if Patterson said anything interesting. But it was the thirty-eighth case in which Crabb had shown this routine interest, with no results.

Anyway, Lieutenant James Harton, chief of detectives on the Alhambra police force, was hoping to find that Patterson had an accomplice when he spent several days cultivating a palship with the ex-con. The supermarket and theater jobs bore the hallmark of a strategist, a planner, and Patterson was just a plain-wrapper heist man with a gun. Harton was looking for the brains behind the jobs, the leader who knew about cash on hand at the two places and where personnel were distributed at various times of day.

So Harton supplied Patterson with cigarettes, street talk, and an ear for the prisoner's tales of his adventures during other stickups that had landed him in various jail cells. Patterson liked Harton; he called him "a right cop," and was fond of asking: "Hey Lieutenant, what's a nice guy like you doing packing a badge like that?"

This day, Harton brought Patterson a couple of packs of cigarettes. "Thanks a lot, Lieutenant," Patterson said. "Missed you yesterday. Something big going?"

Harton sighed a practiced sigh. "Nothing," he said. "Deuces and treys. Routine." He sat back and sighed again and stared hard at Patterson.

Patterson walked to the door of the cell, peered up and down the corridor, then walked back and sat down on the other end of the cot. He looked at Harton. "Look, Lieutenant," he said. "I know what you want. The guy that did the master-minding on the two jobs. I'd really like to tell you about the man. But I wouldn't be doing you no favor, believe me. You couldn't handle it because this guy is big, you couldn't touch him. He's really high up, high up in the U.S. government."

Then he leaned forward and went on in a half-whisper: "Look pal, you've got me on this market job. You know it and I know it, and I got parole violation to go with it. I'm going back and I know it. But you know that the right word in the right place can make a lot of difference in there, a lot of difference in how you got to do that time—easy as possible, or awful hard. I need some kind of friend to put down a good word, Lieutenant, and that's why I'm not conning you about this guy when I say you can't touch him."

Harton cleared his throat. "The man planned the jobs?" he asked.

"Yeah, but you can't touch him."

"Who could touch him?"

"Not you, not your chief, not even Chief Davis down in L.A. The only ones who could touch him would be the FBI."

Harton got up from the cot and stood there looking hard at Patterson. "Suppose I get you the FBI, and they come right in here with me. If they tell you they can touch him—and keep him out of reach of you after they do—will you lay it out for them?"

Patterson coughed nervously. "Get them, Lieutenant," he said. "Get those people, and I'll tell them who master-minded the jobs."

Crabb dispatched three agents to the jail. They listened quietly while Patterson told about how the two robberies were planned down to the last second, the last step the robbers took. The man who did the planning, he said, was Ronald Lee Miller, a special agent in the Intelligence Division of the Internal Revenue Service.

Miller, thirty-eight, was arrested that same day in October on a warrant charging him with the market and theater robberies. Before going to the Federal Building in Los Angeles with Harton and another detective, the FBI agents contacted the Internal Revenue Service's Internal Affairs Division and were assured of full cooperation.

The police and agents waited outside the supervisor's office. By prearrangement, the supervisor sent Miller out with two other IRS agents to do special surveillance duty at Los Angeles International Airport. The two other agents knew the score, for obvious reasons of security.

As Miller and the two other IRS agents left the building, Harton stepped forward. He identified himself, verified Miller's identity, then: "You're under arrest, Mr. Miller," he said.

After Miller was booked, police and FBI agents searched his elegant condominium apartment on a quiet residential street in Van Nuys. There, they found hundreds of wigs, beards, and mustaches, theatrical makeup materials, and even artificial scars.

They found 14 guns of all sizes and calibers, guard uniforms, police uniforms, postal uniforms, and burglary tools.

Miller was sacked from his IRS job when he was booked on robbery charges. As far as Lieutenant Harton and the Alhambra Police Department were concerned, their job was done; they had nabbed Patterson's leader-accomplice. But Crabb and his agents wondered whether they had finally landed their man, too—the kidnapper of Kenny Young. Although Miller denied all the charges against him, and there was no tangible evidence linking him to the Young case, his alleged criminal involvement and his law enforcement background fitted the profile built up by the Bureau's long investigation. And, as an IRS agent, Miller was in a position to obtain such personal information as Herbert Young's access to ready cash, his address, and his unlisted telephone number. The FBI wanted to know more about him.

It was bizarre. Crabb had to force himself to believe that Miller could have moonlighted as a kidnapper, just as Miller's IRS colleagues were shocked into virtual disbelief by Patterson's allegation that Miller was a stickup man. Miller's record was excellent; he seemed a model of the compleat federal agent. He *looked* like a lawman. He *talked* like one.

Moreover, the dapper, self-confident Miller, an IRS agent since 1964, was a man whose loyalty and integrity had been beyond reproach. He had served as a bodyguard in California for President Nixon and, before that, for Vice President Hubert Humphrey—assignments reserved for the pick of the IRS crop. He was a crack shot and a judo expert, and, as a former makeup artist for a Hollywood studio, he was unerring at spotting disguises. He was considered highly knowledgeable in surveillance techniques, typewriter evidence, and operations of Swiss banks where money could be deposited under a numbered secret account. Younger colleagues remembered how he kept reminding them that hot cash could be kept away from the law by having it picked up by a courier from a Swiss bank.

There was more fodder for the FBI in the testimony of Miller's superior, Donald F. Bowler, chief of the IRS Intelligence Division in Los Angeles. Bowler testified at Miller's preliminary hearing that two of his agents had told him "a couple of years ago" that Miller might have been involved with criminals. As

Bowler recalled, the substance of what he was told was that "some files had come to light in another investigation in which there were allegations about Mr. Miller's association with people who were in armed robbery activity." Bowler said he discussed the allegations with Miller and Miller's explanation persuaded him that Miller was clean. He also noted that Miller had been working on tax fraud cases and on that assignment he was authorized to carry a gun.

Patterson's testimony at the hearing was no help to Crabb and his men. He said he had been involved with Miller since 1962, but his contribution to their joint activities was summed up in his casually voiced statement: "We were just stealing together, was all."

In any case, Miller was in safekeeping; he remained in jail when he said he couldn't get up the premium of $1875 on his $18,750 bond. Crabb told himself he wouldn't get up bail, either, in Miller's shoes. A kidnapping suspect would not want to suggest that he had even relatively meager resources when $250,000 had been collected in ransom money.

So, with six months to go before the three-year statute of limitations ran out on the kidnapping case, the FBI pursued its theory that Miller was the prime suspect. A team of agents began questioning Patterson about his relationship with Miller, urging him to try to reconstruct his activities during late March and early April two years before. Patterson denied knowing anything about the kidnapping of Kenny Young, but the agents kept after him. They interviewed him daily; amiable, patient, making of their questioning a social occasion. Telling of his partnership with Miller, Patterson said they had teamed up in about 30 robberies. He named days, hours, and places—even individual long-distance calls placed by Miller from hotel and motel rooms to persons Patterson couldn't identify.

Other FBI agents checked Miller's work record. On each date and at each time named by Patterson, Miller was off work—either on a regular day off, or sick, or away from the office "following up a tip." The long-distance calls checked out; telephone company records verified every call Patterson had mentioned.

Then, worn down or concluding he had nothing to lose by

telling everything, Patterson started talking about "a big one, a really great big one," Miller had pulled somewhere, "I don't know where or what."

His friendly inquisitors pressed Patterson. What did Miller say about the "big one"? Patterson said he wasn't sure, but that Miller once mentioned that he felt "insecure about having large amounts of cash stashed all the way across the ocean."

Yes, Patterson finally admitted, Miller had talked with him about a kidnapping. That was on February 12, 1970—four months after Miller's arrest on the robbery charge. Patterson said Miller showed him a list of names, including Herbert Young's. He went on, talking fast now:

Miller drove Patterson in a government car to the abandoned Grefco Mine and told him it would be an ideal place to hold a kidnap victim. On the night of April 2, 1967, Miller and Patterson drove in two cars to Beverly Hills. Miller handed him a walkie-talkie, stationed him at a street corner, and told him to call a warning if anybody appeared. The next day, Miller gave him $1000 in $20 bills. "He didn't say why he was giving them to me," Patterson said.

The question was whether Patterson's story would hold up in court. He was the only witness against Miller, and the statute of limitations had less than two months to run. Crabb and his men needed corroborating evidence.

Miller denied everything, laughing scornfully at his "amateur" questioners. Among other things, he denied he had driven Patterson to the Grefco Mine in a government car. But IRS records showed that Miller had use of car 90110, a 1963 Plymouth, between April 2 and 7. Agents located the car and laboratory technicians took scrapings from its wheel wells and the undersides of its fenders. Analysis showed that the scrapings contained particles of freshwater and saltwater diatoms—those diatoms the California Division of Mines and Geology had identified as occurring only at the site of the Grefco Mine.

FBI artists altered several photographs, including Miller's, by adding the wraparound sunglasses and hair described by Herbert Young. Asked if he recognized the kidnapper of his son, Young promptly pointed to Miller's picture. On a gamble, agents interviewed Patterson's common-law wife. Their first questions produced no results. But then, out of the blue, she told them that before the kidnapping she had picked up a telephone extension and heard her husband and Miller discussing "where to hide the kid."

Back to Miller went what he called his "private sleuths." He laughed. He told them that at 6:55 P.M. on that Wednesday evening when the ransom money changed hands he was interviewing an automobile dealer on an IRS matter 30 miles from the barren freeway site. "Check my office diary," he said. The agents did so, and the diary verified his story. The auto dealer confirmed Miller's visit to him. But when pressed, he remembered that he actually had talked with Miller in the early or mid-afternoon, *not* in the evening.

A Los Angeles grand jury heard the evidence against Miller and returned an indictment on the kidnapping charge on March 31, 1970, just four days before the statute of limitations expired.

Patterson told all to the grand jury:

That on March 27, eight days before the kidnapping, he drove Miller to San Fernando, where Miller boldly stole a 1965 white Chevrolet, used during the kidnapper's confrontation with Herbert Young, while it was being serviced at a gas station.

That Miller took a license plate (TPD770) from a parked Volkswagen in Encino and used pieces of it to alter the letter-number combination of the plate on the white Chevrolet from NBJ885 to NBD770.

That Miller didn't tell him the job was related to their earlier conversation about a possible kidnapping, and that he didn't see the Young boy in the car when Miller drove off.

That when the two men met the next day he asked about the success of the job and Miller told him it was none of his business and that he was better off not knowing about it.

That after news stories about the abduction appeared, he asked Miller if he "did it," and Miller denied any involvement.

That sometime later, Miller told him he had kidnapped the Young child and confidently predicted that the FBI would never solve the case.

Crabb asked Patterson after the indictment why Miller had picked him as a lookout during the kidnapping, despite the obvious security problem.

"How come he trusted you?" Crabb asked.

Patterson smiled. "Well, I had protected him before," he said. "I did time for one of our jobs together and I didn't snitch on him." He paused, and frowned. "But when your boys kept asking me questions, day after day, month after month, I decided kidnapping a kid was different from sticking up a store."

Miller, whose tenure with the IRS had given him a basic education in the law, waived a jury trial in the robbery cases and chose to take his chances with Judge H. Burton Noble. After the publicity produced by his indictment on a kidnapping charge, he obviously believed a judge would be more detached than a panel of citizens who had fed on his notoriety.

But the prosecution held a full house of evidence. Two employes of the theater, where Miller was charged with picking up $5680 in cash, identified him as the holdup man. Mrs. Terri Torri, cashier at the Shopping Bag market, identified Patterson as the man who relieved her of about $10,000 when she admitted him to her office because he was wearing the uniform of an armored transport company and she thought he had come to pick up the receipts of the day before.

And then the still dapper Miller, courtly and confident, heard Patterson testify that Miller had furnished him with a phony uniform, a gun, handcuffs, and a dummy money sack, and directed him to the cashier's office. Patterson said he and Miller used a stopwatch to check the timing when they made three "professional dry runs" before the robbery.

It was no surprise, then, when Judge Noble sentenced Miller to 10 years to life in state prison on the two charges. No mention was made in court of the kidnapping charges for which Miller was to be tried a month later.

That trial lasted more than a month—from September 10 to October 23, 1970. As expected, the state's star witness was the kidnapping victim, Kenny Young, whose testimony was vital to the prosecution's argument that he had suffered "bodily harm" at Miller's hands and that Miller thus was subject to the death penalty.

Kenny, by now fourteen, told the jury that the first thing he remembered after falling asleep was that "someone was taking me out of bed." He said he started to scream, but was hit over the head four times with what he later learned was a gun, and was told that he would be killed if he screamed.

That tore it. After deliberating for six hours, the jury returned a verdict of "kidnapping with bodily harm," a verdict that called for either death or life imprisonment without parole. A few days later, the jury recommended a life term with no parole. On November 2, 1970, Miller was sentenced to life. But the court reduced the jury's recommendation banning parole, ruling that the sentences for robbery and kidnapping, to run consecutively, should effectively keep Miller in prison for the rest of his natural life.

Eugene Patterson had been an invaluable state's witness. Besides, he was already serving a prison term. So all charges against him were dropped.

Earlier, Judge Raymond Choate had "suggested" that a long step toward rehabilitation might be taken if Miller were to disclose how the $250,000 ransom could be regained by Kenny's father. But by the spring of 1979, not one of the $100 ransom bills had surfaced. Wherever those Federal Reserve notes had been secreted, they were no good to anyone—barring an incredible genius who could come up with an impossible means of altering their serial numbers.

18

A New Fence in Town

*Down the street, the thieves stood in long lines
waiting to use the pay phone at the Amoco station. They
jostled for places, quarreling over seniority, and both
men and women occasionally traded punches. Some
relieved the tedium by picking the pockets of their underworld colleagues.*

What happened in the underworld of Washington, D.C., in October 1975 was inevitable. Thieves were stealing millions of dollars' worth of expensive equipment from office buildings—private
and governmental—all over the Capital. The loot included sophisticated computers and other electronic equipment as well as
typewriters, calculators, and even tons of letterheads and envelopes, from empty offices, loading docks, and freight elevators.
Employes lost their purses, wallets, and paychecks to the round-
the-clock intruders. Fences, professional and amateur, were
swamped with stolen goods.

So it was no surprise when men who openly described
themselves as Mafiosi from New York City muscled in on the
racket. They were husky, mean-looking men, and they prowled
the Fourteenth Street and T Street "crime corridors," making
their low-spoken pitch to the traffickers in larceny—petty and
grand—who mingled with the junkies, dope pushers, and general
hustlers on trash-cluttered sidewalks and in fetid alleys.

One of those who listened to the pitch was Tee Brisbon, who
was dissatisfied with the low prices paid by the local fences. At
the moment, he had nothing to sell, but he wanted to case the
"foreign" operation. So he went along with a couple of the scouts

to a warehouse located in a light-industry neighborhood just off bustling Bladensburg Road, a crumbling low-rent ghetto.

Once inside and up a flight of stairs, Tee Brisbon found himself in a big room furnished with a long counter and an assortment of battered straight-backed chairs. One of the scouts introduced him to the man standing behind the counter.

"Meet Pat Larocca," he told Tee. "He'll take good care of you." Larocca beamed. "Call me Pat," he said.

Jovial and expansive, Pat explained the "security" setup. "You don't take any chances coming here," he told Tee. "We only let in one guy at a time, or two or three if they all have the same business. I don't want you interrupting anybody else's business, and you don't want anybody interrupting your business. This is the P.F.F. Corporation, like the sign outside says, and we got the cops fixed. We're businessmen, we do things right."

Larocca turned off his smile. "And in case anybody gets any bad ideas, we got security on weekends, too," he said. "This is a Mafioso armed with a shotgun. He had his tongue cut out in a gang war. He's crazy. He never sleeps, he just shoots people."

Tee was also introduced to Mike Franzino, a burly six-footer who didn't smile. "We're Pat and Mike, like in the joke," Pat said.

Tee was impressed. The P.F.F. Corporation seemed to be a nice, safe place, and Tee liked nice, safe places when he was selling his merchandise. So he said he'd be back when he had some "goods." Pat said that was fine. "But when you come back, it'll be different. You hafta phone us ahead of time from the pay booth outside the Amoco gas station at 25th Place and Bladensburg Road. Then I'll call you back, or somebody will, and you can come on in."

Back on Fourteenth Street, Tee oozed enthusiasm when he told his friend, James Alfonso Washington, about the P.F.F. "They down from New York to organize D.C.!" he said gleefully. "That where the big money is. They sound like they pay big."

Washington had some expensive movie equipment, and he wanted top price for it because he had barely escaped with it when a night watchman barged into the store he was robbing. He went along with Tee, who made the required phone call, and they were admitted to the presence of Pat and Mike. Pat checked the merchandise. "It's pretty good stuff," he said. Then he offered $150 for it. Washington could hardly repress his delight; that was at least $50 more than he could get from a local fence. He snapped up the offer.

"We pay high prices," Pat said comfortably, "because with our connections we can *get* high prices." He paid Washington in crisp $10 bills, then gave Tee and Washington each one of his business cards bearing the P.F.F. telephone number.

Tee Brisbon and James Alfonso Washington spread the good word among the street people. In turn, the street people spread the good word among other brethren. Soon, there was a parade of thieves to the warehouse and the scouting expeditions were discontinued. Sellers brought their friends and their friends brought their friends to do business with the generous but tough, no-nonsense buyers at the P.F.F. Like Tee Brisbon, they found comfort in the stern security of the place. They could depend on the Mafia to protect them.

As one of the thieves told a pal, "Man, this is just like on television. You should hear those dudes talk Italian."

And indeed Pat and Mike sprinkled their talk as they worked with a variety of Italian phrases. Pat was always yelling comments that sounded like "Ay, Mike, bacha-ma-gu, besamacu, me-dee-chi, me-dee-chi." And Mike would yell back: "Ay, Pat, simpatico, simpatico."

Sometimes, Pat and Mike would break out a bottle of Jack Daniel's Black Label bourbon or a gallon jug of wine, and their guests would drink out of real glasses. It was so *social*. "You make money, we make money, so everything's all right," Pat told them. "The capo of capos in New York is happy. The capo is the boss, the Don. He's a genius. He thought up the idea of having a calculator and office machine repair shop downstairs as a front. Send your friends. But no stoolies or else. . . ." He whipped a forefinger across his throat.

Pat showed them the scar on his head, parting his shaggy black hair. "See, I got shot in a gang war in New York. I don't hear so good in one ear. Speak in this ear," he said, tugging at his right ear. "Speak up loud. I'm Pasquale Larocca. What's your name?"

And Pat would grin when most of the thieves answered with

nicknames—"Squirrelly" or "Zorro" or "Weasel" or "Pumpkin Head." He'd tell them, "Good, play safe." But when a seller gave him a proper name, Pat tapped him gently on the chin with his big paw. "Good," he'd say. "An honest man." Then he'd erupt into one of his explosive, roaring laughs.

II

Mike stepped into a phone booth in a Peoples Drug Store hard by the White House and dialed a number. Outside, a light drizzle fell on the late November scene. He was put through to Nick F. Stames, Washington Bureau Chief of the FBI.

"You're right on time," Stames said to FBI Agent Michael Hartman, a.k.a. Mike Franzino. "Anything new?"

"Just a routine call-in," Hartman said. "Everything's going fine. We're doing a land office business and it should continue. We get new people every day. We got some good fingerprints from those booze glasses and the counter and doorknobs and other places."

"Received," said Stames. "They're in the lab. Okay, let's run this operation as long as we can. We want to get as many in the corral as we can. Good luck—and study your Italian."

Michael Hartman hung up, and then—as Mike Franzino— went back to work on one of the more ingenious projects in law enforcement annals, a turnabout on the criminal community that ran for five months, eventually produced 188 arrests, and brought about the recovery of 3500 pieces of property valued in excess of $2.4 million. P.F.F., Inc., nicknamed "The Corporation," actually stood for Police-FBI-Fencing, Incognito. It was a cooperative effort involving the Washington Metropolitan Police Department; the FBI; the Law Enforcement Assistance Administration; and the Alcohol, Tobacco and Firearms Division of the Treasury Department.

That project had its genesis in a conversation between FBI Agent Robert Lill and Lieutenant Robert Arscott of the Washington police, who was in charge of investigating office thefts in the downtown area. Thefts in the Capital had become epidemic, but they were hard to stop because such larceny offered few clues or witnesses. Trying to stop it, city police and federal lawmen were falling all over one another because a single crime could involve several agencies. Meanwhile, businessmen and insurance companies were howling about the high cost of thievery.

"For God's sake!" Lill complained. "I showed up at one government building to check on a burglary and found three different city police squads, the Federal Protective Service, and some internal government security force all grilling a poor guard. I could barely get in the door."

Arscott agreed. He was a veteran cop who had been similarly frustrated many times. What was needed, he said, was a cooperative campaign against the thieves that wouldn't have lawmen getting in one another's way all the time. He had talked about the problem from time to time with one of his detectives, Robert W. Sheaffer, Jr., and told Lill: "Bob's an idea man. I'll call him in."

Sheaffer, young and aggressive, did have an idea. Why not disguise a detective as a fence? Thieves needed buyers for their loot, and a fence got to know a lot of them in a very short time. As Sheaffer put it: "This guy contacts our fence and, zap! we've got a confession on the spot."

Lill and Arscott decided to give it a try. They got their superiors to share the costs, and in August 1975 a city detective named Vincent Tolson, dressed in a mod suit, set up business as Al White in a little office at 1625 K Street, Northwest, in the heart of the city's commercial sector. The word was put out on the streets that White's firm, Urban Consultants and Research, Inc., was interested in buying stolen goods. A half-dozen FBI agents and police staked out the office, waiting for Tolson-White to take his customers into a nearby alley where they could be photographed receiving money for their loot. It didn't work; apparently the neighborhood was too white collar. So the office was moved two blocks to a new storefront on L Street, in a section frequented by prostitutes. Still no go.

The big wheels at both the FBI and the police department were getting nervous. After all, they were spending money taken from tight budgets. So they ordered Lill and Arscott to get some expert advice on fencing operations. They agreed the man to see was Capt. Francis R. Herron of the New York City Police Department, known as the best fake fence man on the East Coast.

Accompanied by FBI Agent Hartman and Police Sgt. Karl Mattis, Lill and Arscott drove to New York and met with Herron.

Briefly, what Herron told them was they were all wrong, that a one-man operation wouldn't work. "You've got to have backup people," he said. "You never know when someone is going to try to take you off. You've got to control everything in the operation with manpower and organization."

Back in Washington, Urban Consultants was shut down. Then Lill and Arscott opened their campaign for a large-scale, well-financed operation. It took a couple of weeks, but they finally raised $67,000, contributed more or less equally by the FBI, the Washington police, and the Law Enforcement Assistance Administration. Their new illicit purchasing establishment would be organized to the last pencil.

They rented the warehouse off Bladensburg Road and did considerable renovating on the second floor. Their customers were to be received in a room within a room. Behind the false walls, there were hidden TV cameras, an evidence-processing area, and alarm equipment. Microphones were concealed at strategic points in the inner, customer's room. The chance of a surprise attack was virtually eliminated. When the front door, which was unlocked during business hours, was opened, it set off a high-pitched, flutter-noised alarm audible only inside the P.F.F. office. Having mounted the stairs, the customer was instructed to show his face in a plexiglass window of the door before the electric lock was buzzed to let him in. As the customer entered, the undercover man behind the counter would check a mirror on the opposite wall to see if there was a gun in the visitor's back pocket.

Two men armed with sawed-off shotguns would patrol the passageways on deep carpeting that kept the noise down. Microphones were hidden in dead electric outlets on the counter. There was also a dead telephone on the counter; when the buyer needed time to think, he was to scratch the back of his head, signaling a colleague to push a button that rang the phone. Then the buyer would pretend to talk to a Mafia crony in New York while he gathered his wits. If anything looked suspicious, any of the lawmen could summon the others to go into action by triggering a silent alarm system of red Christmas tree lights. Every member of the team was armed, and all were crack shots.

Agent Lill and Lieutenant Arscott did the casting for the two leading roles in the continuing performance of what Lill called

"The Thieves' Follies." Detective Patrick J. Lilly got the role of
Pat Larocca because he had an excellent record as an undercover
man and "could con a wino out of his wine." Agent Hartman, big
and muscular, whose repertoire of facial expressions and threatening demeanor "make me look like the meanest man in town," was
a natural as Mike Franzino, Pat's partner. Mike stood by with a
shotgun at the ready during the transactions to emphasize his
function as "The Enforcer."

There were six undercover men in all—four from the D.C.
police, and one each from the FBI and the Alcohol, Tobacco and
Firearms Division of the Treasury Department. They had all
grown beards and their hair was long and uncombed, their language tinted with what they believed were Italian accents and
sprinkled with cuss words and obscenities. While the six ran the
"store," other lawmen from their own outfits and from the Secret
Service, the U.S. Postal Service, and the suburban police depart-
ments backed them up by tracing the stolen goods.

Pat and his men worked 16-hour days in the unheated
warehouse, subsisting mostly on fried chicken and assorted sand-
wiches. Occasionally, when business was slow, Mike cooked up
meatballs on a hot plate. This gastronomic largesse also was
lavished on special, big-stealing customers when they spoke wistfully of the good smells emanating from Mike's pot. They had to
wait, however, until Mike prepared their orders—meatballs containing a minimum of meat and a maximum of hot sauce, pepper,
and mustard.

"Have a meatball," Pat would urge his guests. "You hurt
Mike's feelings if you don't eat his food." The customers looked
at "Mean Mike" fondling his shotgun, and fell to. But there were
no calls for seconds.

Down the street, the thieves stood in long lines waiting to use
the pay phone at the Amoco station. They jostled for places,
quarreling over seniority, and both men and women occasionally
traded punches. Some relieved the tedium by picking the pockets
of their underworld colleagues. They smoked pot, and there was
the occasional glint of a heroin syringe. The P.F.F.'s unlisted
phone number was scrawled on the wall of the phone booth, along
with such messages as "Annie, a good lay," and "See Ben, the
lawyer." Somebody left a dead raccoon in the booth.

Pat and his men had to be on constant guard against robbery and mayhem. One day three especially aggressive holdup men got tough with Pat over the price he was offering for a heart-lung resuscitator from Prince George's County's General Hospital. "You shit, you're lookin' to get killed," one of the men told Pat.

The men had been frisked, but Pat knew that even the best frisking job sometimes missed a cunningly concealed weapon. "Quiet!" he roared. "Show some respect for the organization." On cue, there came from the back room a fearsome "Italian" shout, followed by the sound of a pump-action shotgun being cocked. The three men took their money and fled.

From time to time, Pat and Mike interspersed their amiable shop talk with threats. "Don't get tough around here," they'd warn customers who seemed too truculent. "You know what we do to fuckers who get tough. We have to kill them, because they might get sore enough to go to the rollers [the cops]. We pay good money to have them hit. It's too bad, because some of them have kids, but it has to be done."

Pat laughed when customers gave him phony proper names or nicknames, but he turned them over to Mike before doing business with them. And Mike would brandish his shotgun and make them show driver's licenses, social security cards, and give their dates of birth.

"Where'd you get the pearls?" Mike asked one customer.

The man explained he had lifted them from a "mark" in Detroit. "I hadda shoot him," he said. "But he didn't die, the mother-fucker." His ID was written on a clipboard and recorded on television film.

Pat and Mike and their fencing colleagues urged their clients to tell them stories about how they beat the system. "You guys hafta impress me," Pat was fond of saying. "The way you keep beating the rap. You could be Mafiosi. Tell me more."

One customer, who wanted to be addressed as "Slim," told his listeners how easy it was to burgle government offices during working hours. "I go into those places four, five times a week," he bragged. "Nobody bothers me." He had brought with him a sophisticated computer unit he claimed he had just lifted from the Department of Health, Education, and Welfare.

"I went into this office where I'd been before," he said.

"The thing I wanted was this thing. It was on top of a filing cabinet. There were all those women typing and that kind of crap in little places with walls of glass on top of metal below them. They could see me, but they never bothered me. I picked up a big cardboard box full of papers and stuff and dumped it out on the floor.

"It was a fucking big machine, like you say you want. One of the women leaned over the glass and looked at me, but I told her I was just getting a box, and I gave her a smile and she went back to work, typing and looking down at what she was doing. Nobody asks you any questions in those offices, especially if you're black like me. They don't want to get in trouble for bothering a black, not in D.C.

"I had a lot of trouble with this machine. It was too big, and when I put it in the box the walls came apart on the box. Goddam, I was sore. I grabbed a big plastic trash bag and put the machine and the box in it. The bag tore a little and part of the machine showed, but shit, I had to take it that way.

"I carried the bag down the corridor and down two flights of stairs and I was making for the outside door when a white man stopped me. He said excuse him, and I liked to drop dead. What the hell did he want? But he picked up a piece of string that was sticking out of the bag and put it back in. I said thanks a lot, but then he told me to wait a minute and I was ready to slam him, but he went and stepped on one of those rugs that has something in it to open doors, and the door opened and I blew the place."

Pat looked at him with practiced wide eyes. "Goddam, you're slick," he said. He paid Slim $230 for an IBM machine worth about $3000. Slim said something Pat pretended not to hear. He leaned his head over the counter, down close to one of the mikes hidden in a dead electrical outlet. "Speak up," he told Slim. "Right into this ear." Slim told the mike: "Oh, I was just saying I also stole about 40–50 women's pocketbooks this month. Took them right off the desks, and nobody noticed me."

Pat's eyes really rolled in his head when one customer walked in with $1.2 million in Treasury checks. "Where the hell did you get these?" he asked. "What are you, a master crook?"

The man was pleased at the praise. "Wait'll you hear," he said. "I just walked into HUD [the Department of Housing and Urban Development] and walked around a while and pretty soon I came to this room with the door open and I went in and there was nobody there, and there was this big vault in the wall with the door open, so I went in the vault and took as many checks as I could carry."

That thief, like so many other P.F.F. customers, was on parole, in his case from an armed robbery sentence. "All you have to do is tell them you're gonna go straight and get a job and they let you out," he told Pat. Some parolees told their parole officers they were working for P.F.F. Pat got several calls from parole officers, checking on the parolees. He told them the men did indeed work for P.F.F. But not one parole officer thought it necessary to make a personal call to the warehouse to verify the information.

Thirty P.F.F. customers asked Mike Franzino, the FBI agent working incognito, if he would get them jobs as hit men for the Mafia. Looking hard at them and listening to the boasting, Mike concluded that most of them would kill for the P.F.F. for as little as $50 per corpse. Indeed, one of the volunteers, George ("Sonny") Logan, a slender thirty-six-year-old whose uniform was a turtleneck sweater and a leather jacket, confessed for the video cameras and the microphones to the murder of a Prince George's County dope dealer. He even described the two guns he used.

Mike checked the homicide report and, when Logan returned, Mike asked him: "How many times did you shoot this Gilbert Parsons?" Logan said that as he recalled it was about six or seven times. That's what the homicide report said. Its description of the guns also agreed with that Logan had given. And perhaps Logan had a personal motive for killing Parsons; he told Mike he started using heroin when he was twelve years old and had kicked the habit "maybe 16 or 17 times."

One youth asked Pat how he could get into the narcotics trafficking racket. "We don't mix fencing with junk," Pat told him. But Pat wanted to be obliging. He sent the youth to meet "a man wearing a full-length pink suede coat, one earring, and a tattoo on his right forearm" on a Baltimore street corner. "Man, that's some dude," said the youth admiringly.

He was back two days later to complain that the contact didn't show up. Pat told him he must have gone to the wrong place, and sent him back to Baltimore. When the man in the pink coat again failed to keep the rendezvous, the customer gave up. He told Pat: "I've had enough of this trash. I'm going to work for a living." Mike patted Pat on the back. "Pat, you saved a soul," he said.

There was the customer who was also an informant for the Prince George's County police. He tipped his contact there that there was "a dynamite fencing operation in Northeast Washington." Pat heard about it from one of his own informants. The next time the customer visited the warehouse, Pat picked up the dead phone on the counter, dialed, and then had a brief conversation with the nobody on the other end of the line. "Well, we'll have to hit him," Pat said, and hung up.

Pat called Mike over and gave him the assignment.

"Do you want him completely taken out, or just mangled?" Mike asked.

"Take his head off," Pat ordered.

The customer left in a hurry, went to a phone booth, and put in a call to his Prince George's police contact. "Hey, I was wrong," he told the policeman. "That place is Northeast, all right, but it's up in New England somewhere. I got it wrong. I thought the dude meant Northeast Washington, D.C."

P.F.F.'s haul included 1500 credit cards, 225 typewriters and calculators, 700 savings bonds, 70 television and stereo sets, 18 automobiles and trucks, three electric ranges, an $800 bearskin rug, and an electrocardiogram unit. One customer brought them a total of 80 District of Columbia welfare checks, stolen by a welfare employe who arrived at the warehouse in a D.C. government car. Some checks lifted from the mails were delivered by a Postal Service employe in the government jeep he used on his delivery rounds.

Lieutenant Arscott had some fun with the automobiles, all stolen. From time to time he'd drive one to the stationhouse of the police district from which it was stolen, leaving it in the parking spot reserved for the district commander. Meanwhile, Nick Stames, in charge of the FBI field office, checked on the $1.2 million Treasury checks stolen from HUD. He discovered that although HUD stopped payment on the checks a week after they were found missing, officials there never reported the loss to the FBI or police.

"Some security," Mike remarked. "It's a wonder those HUD people didn't send engraved invitations to all the crooks in town, telling them to come on over and help themselves."

By then, toward the end of February 1976, the time had come for P.F.F. to issue its own invitations. Word was passed to its clientele that "the Don" was so pleased with the fencing operation in the old warehouse he had given Pat Larocca a promotion. In appreciation, Pat was going to throw a party for his Washington customers who had helped him earn a "well done" from the capo of capos. The big boss himself was coming down from New York for the shindig, so the guests were told to leave their guns at home—"the Don" insisted on tight security. Also, they were directed to call first from the phone booth at the Amoco station. There would be girls, and lots of fun.

Thus on Saturday night, February 28, well-dressed men and women lined up at the phone booth, some of them bribing others to get to the head of the line. As they got the OK from Pat or one of his henchmen, the guests strolled down to the warehouse where the P.F.F. paid the highest prices in town for stolen goods.

Pat was impeccable in his ruffled formal shirt and maroon dinner jacket as he stood by the door. Some of the guests had been invited by word of mouth; others held Mafia business cards on which was scribbled: "7:45 P.M., Saturday, February 28, 1976." Jovially, Pat thanked the guests for showing up. "This is my chance to impress the Man," Pat told them. "The Don wants to meet you." He was sure they wouldn't mind if one of his men frisked them. "The Don," he explained, "is very security conscious."

Docilely, the guests submitted to the search, then were admitted to the party in groups of no more than four. "We have to be careful," Pat told them. "We don't want any cops crashing this party. Somebody might get arrested.

"See, there's your old friend Mike, still holding his shotgun, even in a tuxedo," Pat cried. "Mike is security conscious, too." "The Don" sat imperiously in a corner, occasionally smiling as one of his minions kissed his ring. Pat introduced him as "Don Corleone." Everybody but the thieves knew the capo of capos as Sgt. Karl Mattis of the D.C. police.

"And now before we start to party, I have a surprise for

you," Pat announced. "I have a really funny thing to tell you. I'm a cop. You're under arrest." At the same time, one of the false walls collapsed and the room suddenly became alive with armed lawmen, some in uniforms, some in flak jackets with the word POLICE stamped on the backs.

"Hey Patty, that's some joke," one of the guests yelled. "That's real funny, Patty."

Pat grinned. "It's real funny, but it's not a joke," he said. He kept on the grin. "Don't anybody make any moves. We call this a BYOB party, for Bring Your Own Bail."

And so it went, as the P.F.F. wound up its business. After their arrests, guests were taken by teams of uniformed officers to an adjoining warehouse where they were handcuffed to a chain secured to a steel beam. One outraged guest was a pimp from Maryland who had been hired to provide girls for the party and had been given a $100 down payment. When he strolled into the room he was accompanied by three elaborately dressed women and carried a Winchester rifle he had brought as a gift for "the Don." He was charged with violating the Mann Act, a federal law which prohibits taking a woman across a state line for illicit purposes. Another customer brought his own handcuffs. He had been arrested for robbery and had escaped from the district stationhouse.

In all, police, FBI agents, and other lawmen scooped up 60 suspects at the party. That night and the next day, a little army of more than 500 police and FBI agents swept up another 123 on warrants for crimes from purse-snatching to murder. Eventually, 170 of those nabbed were convicted and sentenced to prison terms. One who was acquitted was George ("Sonny") Logan, who confessed to the murder of Gilbert Parsons, the dope pusher, on videotape. His defense argued that Logan had lied to impress men he believed were Mafia hoodlums.

Four days after the party, Mike Franzino, a.k.a. FBI Agent Mike Hartman, was doing some cleanup work at the warehouse when a customer strolled in with a pocketful of government checks to sell. Mike paid the man $150, then tossed a newspaper on the counter.

"Hey," he said. "You read about the big fencing ring that was really run by the rollers?"

"Yeah," the customer replied. "I was wondering if it was you guys."

"It was," Mike answered. "I'm an FBI agent and you're under arrest."

That unfortunate customer was the next to last to call at the offices of the defunct P.F.F., Inc. A scout car sent to pick up the would-be purveyor of government checks was just pulling into the driveway of the warehouse when a youth from Maryland called from the Amoco pay booth to say he had some merchandise to fence. The scout car was pulled into the warehouse garage, and shortly the youth was admitted to the "business office."

Mike bought the loot. Then the young man asked: "How about me getting a job as a hit man?"

"I'll put you on the phone with the Don so you can apply to him," Mike said. He dialed a number and handed the phone to the customer

"Hello," said the youth.

"Hello," said a man's voice on the other end of the line. "This is Lieutenant Robert Arscott of the Metropolitan Police and you're under arrest."

Bewildered, the youth put down the phone. "Can they really arrest you by phone?" he asked Mike.

"He did, didn't he?" said Mike.

19

Alarm in Portland

"Our intent is to either collect $1,000,000 or to make you people wish to hell we had."

Even in an age of senseless violence, the bad news seemed unbelievable to the people of Portland, Oregon, during that week in October 1974. Then there was a why-weren't-we-told feeling.

They were told on October 16 that dynamite damage had been found along the power lines of the Bonneville Power Administration. They were told also that an earlier dynamiting had damaged transmission towers near Maupin, in central Oregon, but that the FBI had asked that the explosions not be publicized until its agents had a chance to conduct a quiet, undercover investigation.

When all the news was out, the public learned that eleven transmission towers had been ripped by explosions between September 28 and October 18 in an area within a 100-mile radius of the city. Three towers had been toppled; the remaining eight were less severely damaged. Unexploded bombs were found on three more of the 65-foot towers, part of a 12,000-mile network of transmission lines that were the backbone of the Pacific Northwest's economy. The damage was estimated at $250,000.

Police and FBI agents found that the bolts had been removed from the towers' supporting legs. They found traces of dynamite, and there were the remains of electrical blasting caps, several six-volt batteries, and a timing device. Clearly, what had happened was sabotage. The acts of a lunatic, or lunatics, perhaps, but acts that imperiled the daily lives of hundreds of thousands of human beings.

Shortly, these acts of sabotage were confirmed. On October 18, the BPA received a letter from one "J. Hawker," who claimed to be the saboteur—or chieftain of a sabotage band. The three-page letter was turned over to the FBI field office, and a copy was read at a news conference by Don Hodel, administrator of the federally owned utility.

"Our intent is either to collect $1,000,000 or to make you people wish to hell we had," said the letter. "The extent of damages resulting from the demolition of your power lines is incidental. Our primary objective was to impress any potential nonbelievers that we mean business. Whether or not the towers we hit will be the beginning or the end is strictly up to you people. We have the men and equipment to keep as many towers down as is necessary to force compliance with our demands."

No deadline was set, but the letter warned: "There will be repercussions if we feel you are stalling."

"J. Hawker" gave explicit instructions for delivery of the million-dollar ransom, and told the BPA to announce its readiness "to deliver" by placing a classified ad in the Portland *Oregonian*, the Seattle *Times,* and the San Francisco *Examiner.* The ad was to read: "I would like to inform Mr. J. Hawker that our company is willing to complete our business agreement. Would he please notify by writing to: Names—and address—."

Payment of the $1 million was to made in $800,000 in $50 bills and $200,000 in $20 bills. After the ads were placed, the BPA was told it must be ready to dispatch two of its pickup trucks without canopies, each containing two men, to a designated location. The trucks were to be accompanied by an Oregon State Police pickup truck carrying two men dressed in state police uniforms. All three trucks were to be equipped with 23-channel Citizen Band radios, and each of the four BPA men would carry a walkie-talkie with at least two channels, a compass, a three-cell flashlight, and a stopwatch. The ransom would be carried in one of the BPA trucks, "in any type container."

Finally, "J. Hawker" described what he called his "terrorist organization." Its members, he wrote, were "thoroughly experienced at this type of operation—and they are government-trained, believe it or not. If you are entertaining an illusion of apprehending our pickup men, forget it. An attempt will lead to: 1. Your delivery men will be killed. 2. We will black out the entire Portland area and vicinity (or both).''

Administrator Hodel told the news conference that the letter contained too much detailed information to be ignored as a prank. Julius Mattson, agent in charge of the FBI's Portland field office, added: "We're taking this very seriously. It's the only way you can treat it until it's proven otherwise."

But Hodel announced that the BPA would refuse to meet the extortionist's demands. Instead, he said, the utility had decided to offer a reward of $100,000 for information leading to his capture. At the same time, he admitted that the extortionist "apparently has the capability to carry out his threat. If they are determined to do it, they could knock out power to Portland and the nearby vicinity." He warned hospitals and other institutions to check their emergency generating systems.

Faced with the blackmailing of a four-state power delivery network, the people of Portland—targeted as the hostages—generally preserved a calculated calm. They were concerned, but not scared. But there were the predictable exceptions. Airlines reported numerous cancellations of reservations to the city, and an increase in tickets sold to other localities a safe distance away. People left town on sudden vacation trips and to visit sick relatives.

Neighbors called police to an address in what the elitists would call a middle-class neighborhood, reporting a domestic brawl. The cops found a man and wife sitting in their unlighted living room, glaring at each other. The wife had the beginnings of a black eye.

"We had a fight," the wife reported. "This idiot kept making me turn off all the lights to save electricity. He beat up on me."

The husband appealed to the gendarmes' sense of civic responsibility. "I was just trying to be a good, patriotic citizen," he told them. "Everybody should try to conserve energy in a crisis like this."

The wife was asked if she wanted to prefer charges. "Oh hell no," she replied. "Leave us alone. This way I don't have to see his face." Laughing, the cops departed.

But official Portland was not amused. While calling for public calm, officials at all levels of government reacted quickly and positively to the threat, drawing up emergency plans for a blackout. The police department placed members of the force on instant alert to control looting and violence. In some cases, plans for evacuation and transfer of people to other localities were made. Searches were undertaken to locate generators that could be pressed into service for use at hospitals, nursing homes, jails, and other basic facilities that didn't have their own power sources. Temporary solutions were discussed for problems that might occur in the water supply system and in the treatment and disposal of sewage.

Business and industry generally reported that their operations could survive minor shutdowns without serious loss. An exception was the area's substantial aluminum industry. Officials pointed out that restarting of aluminum reduction pipelines after a power failure would be enormously expensive. A Reynolds Metals spokesman said that restart costs at its plants in nearby Troutdale, Oregon, and Longview, Washington, would be as high as $7 million.

"There is no cause for public panic," said an editorial in the *Oregonian,* Portland's morning newspaper. But it added that until arrests were made and guilt fixed, "there could be no assurance that there will not be more attempts to disrupt transmission lines. . . . Unless caught soon, the dynamiters may lie low for a while and strike again when the heat is off. New attacks might not be in the Portland area. Other Northwest cities and areas are equally vulnerable."

The *Oregon Journal,* Portland's afternoon daily, expressed concern that the dynamiters "may trigger a flock of crackpots to engage in similar evils, the way D. B. Cooper—first of the skyjacking parachutists—inspired a collection of airplane hijackers." In the Cooper case, the FBI received a number of crank letters from persons claiming to be the extortionist.

It was not unexpected, then, when the *Oregonian* received a letter signed "J. Hawker" which said the extortionist had suspended operations because of bad weather. The letter seemed authentic. Attached to it was a verbatim copy of the first note from the saboteur. This time, the author explained that the threat against the BPA was directed at the "U.S. Government, since BPA is financially affiliated with the federal government."

There was also what amounted to an announcement that the extortionist was not acting alone. Under the typed "J. Hawker" signature were two lines: RVOVN, and, in parentheses, REORGANIZED VETERANS OF VIET NAM. Perusing the letter, FBI Agent Bill Williams recalled that during the Civil War there was a guerrilla band known as the "Jayhawkers."

The BPA's Hodel was not sanguine about the safety of the utility's power network. He admitted that no amount of policemen or National Guardsmen could protect the thousands of BPA towers, most of them in rugged country. "There's little we can do to protect them," he told a press conference. "We can't put a man on every tower in that kind of mountain country."

And from Maine to Hawaii, other utilities officials took a look at their own security systems after receiving crank phone calls that they might be the next victims. There was grumbling about environmentalists who had forced a nationwide trend to locate steam power plants farther and farther away from user cities. Hodel told reporters: "The threat here points up the need for having at least some steam plants located near the population centers. Having such facilities would discourage further attempts to make power systems out in the countryside targets for extortion."

In any case, Hodel stuck to his decision not to pay ransom. "If we ever pay even one penny of blackmail, there isn't one power system in the United States that's safe," he said. His office was flooded with telegrams and phone calls from utilities across the country endorsing his position.

Characteristically, the FBI declined comment on its investigative efforts. But Julius Mattson, directing the Bureau's team, was convinced "J. Hawker" would continue his campaign to cash in on his sabotage by dynamiting more transmission towers or other equipment.

Drawing on his training and knowledge of terrorist tactics, Mattson figured that "J. Hawker" might be cocky enough to believe the BPA would change its mind about paying ransom if still more of its property were damaged. "Extortionists know about the importance of money," he told his men. "They know there are pressures to pay up to avoid costly destruction. This J. Hawker sounds like one of those guys who is always sure he can win by turning up the heat. Look at it this way, he wouldn't have embarked on this blackmail scheme if he didn't think he could come up with a million bucks for his pains."

So Mattson borrowed four small planes from the Bureau of Customs (since renamed the Customs Service). An FBI agent and an Oregon State Police officer were assigned to each aircraft, and they joined local police aboard BPA helicopters in an aerial search of the Mount Hood and Mount Tabor countrysides. Meanwhile, ground crews were doubled, working on foot and by car on a spot check of tower locations. BPA and law enforcement costs were running at more than $20,000 a day, but the idea was that "J. Hawker" would move cautiously when he saw that almost everywhere he could go was under surveillance.

Sure enough, "J. Hawker" showed his annoyance. The FBI received a second letter from him five days after the first one was delivered. "J. Hawker" reiterated his demand for a million-dollar payoff and warned that it would be "dangerous" if the BPA and FBI refused to cooperate. He threatened more damage to the transmission lines and said if the authorities didn't do business with him he would "destroy the Bull Run watershed by a fire nobody could put out."

The mass surveillance continued. Meanwhile, Mattson placed classified ads in the personal columns of the *Oregonian,* the San Francisco *Examiner,* and the Seattle *Times*—as "J. Hawker" had demanded. The ads read: "Mr. C. Baker would like to contact colleagues in R.V.O.V.N." They listed a Portland post office box number and a telephone number—for a special FBI line.

Now a third letter was received—delivered, by one of those Postal Service mistakes that had half the country aroused, to a private citizen never identified except as "an educator." It seemed that the "educator" had formerly rented the box 53 used by the FBI in its classified ads. Turned over to the Bureau's field office, the letter was found to consist of six typewritten pages, giving detailed instructions for communication between the extortionist and the authorities. Communication with "J. Hawker" was to be established through a Citizens Band radio linkup and the use of a special "J. Hawker" code. The code was similar to Morse, but with alterations.

For example, the message "Stop and wait for further instruc- tions" was a CODE THREE and was transmitted as dash-dot-dot- dot. The message "Disregard your last previous instructions" was a CODE SIXTEEN and was transmitted as dash-dash-dot-dot. In all, there were 21 coded messages.

Mattson was impressed. The guy is no dummy, he told himself. This is no junkie or pool hall wise guy, but somebody with technical knowhow and a sense of thoroughness. Probably a frustrated electronics tycoon. He was not surprised, then, when Dr. Paul R. McHugh, head of the psychiatry department of the University of Oregon Medical School, concluded that the vocabulary in the letters indicated an educated person. McHugh also speculated that the writer had been in military service and that his tendency for self-dramatizing might be his Achilles' heel. "He's doing too much talking," said McHugh. "He's boasting."

At any rate, Mattson concluded that since "J. Hawker" intended to communicate through CB radio, he might be effectively traced through direction finding (DF) equipment. He arranged for a loan of a DF kit from the Federal Communications Commission.

According to "Hawker's" instructions, FBI agents from the Portland office were to establish radio contact with him on October 29, between 8:00 A.M. and 1:00 P.M. Arrangements were made for cover by cars of the site "Hawker" had selected for the ransom drop the FBI had no intention of making.

All efforts to establish communication were fruitless until just before one o'clock, when contact was made. No voice was heard. Instead the agents heard what sounded to them like animal or bird calls. Moreover, the FCC equipment was not sensitive enough to establish a hold on "Hawker's" position.

"Goddammit," raged Mattson. "Here's the FCC with all kinds of sophisticated stuff and its DF won't work. Probably it's the first time, and it had to happen to us."

Actually, a DF is a relatively simple radio receiving device which permits the detection of the direction from which radio waves emanate. It consists of a coil antenna mounted on a freely rotating vertical axis and, of course, a radio receiver.

"Any kid could build one these days," Mattson fumed. "The FCC must have hired a real dumb kid to build this one."

In any case, there was nothing to do but phone FBI headquarters in Washington and request shipment of one of the Bureau's DF's. At least we check them regularly, Mattson told himself. The DF arrived in due time in the charge of Special Agent James W. Greenleaf.

"I'm the nurse," Greenleaf told Mattson. "In case you guys make this poor thing sick."

Out went the FBI–Customs–Portland police team again. And again they established contact with "Hawker"—this time on October 30. With the new equipment, agents were able to calculate "Hawker's" relative position. But "Hawker" stopped transmission before his exact location could be determined.

Again on November 4, the FBI monitors pinpointed "Hawker" to within a two-block area. As the agents closed in, they saw a blue-gray Plymouth sedan equipped with a CB antenna drive off. Once more, "Hawker" ceased transmitting, and the Plymouth disappeared. Frustrated, Mattson ordered a check on all similarly described cars registered in Oregon.

Then on November 11, the FBI office received still another letter from "Hawker." It again instructed the agents to establish radio contact between 8:00 A.M. and 1:00 P.M. the next day and to be prepared to deliver the million dollars to a spot near Mount Tabor. FBI men were dispatched by car to cover the countryside around Mount Tabor and a section of Southeast Portland. The DF equipment was checked. Every possible drop site was marked on the agents' maps.

The coded sounds, animal or bird, were monitored again. This time the DF located "Hawker's" exact position. As the surveilling cars headed for the spot, agents saw a blue-gray Plymouth sedan pulling away from the side of the road. The driver, a male, was holding a radio and antenna outside the car window. As transmission continued, a female passenger in the back seat turned and looked out the rear window. She turned back and appeared to say something to the driver. He turned and looked to the rear, then quickly pulled in the radio and antenna.

Moments later, the agents' car pulled alongside the Plymouth, and the driver was ordered to pull over. He nodded affirmatively, but continued to drive on. Gunning the engine, the driver of the agents' car pulled ahead of the Plymouth and cut in front of it. The Plymouth stopped.

There was no fuss. Both the driver and the female passenger complied when ordered to step out of the car. The driver was identified as one David Winsor Heesch, thirty-four, and the passenger as his wife, Sheila Arlene Heesch, also thirty-four, a pert brunette. In the car, agents found a .22-caliber Browning automatic rifle and a .22-caliber derringer pistol. Both were loaded.

Of collateral interest to the agents, baffled by the animal or bird sounds they had monitored on their CB receiver, was a hunter's duck call found on the floor of the front seat.

"We're a fine bunch of city slickers," said Greenleaf. "Not one in the whole crowd of us ever went duck hunting. Overeducated in the wrong things, that's the trouble with people these days."

Heesch, an unemployed truck driver, was arrested on a charge of mailing a threatening communication. Mrs. Heesch was charged with aiding and abetting her husband's violation. After their arrests, agents searched their home. In the refrigerator freezer they found carbon copies of the extortion letters, all signed "J. Hawker." Elsewhere, they seized various tools, .22-caliber ammunition, a map of Mount Hood National Forest, and a pair of binoculars.

On November 13, 1974, Heesch pleaded guilty to two counts of dynamiting Bonneville Power Administration high-voltage transmission towers, and to one count of mailing a threatening letter. Mrs. Heesch pleaded guilty to one charge of mailing an extortion letter, and to two counts of aiding and abetting the dynamiting.

Heesch, handsome and strapping, told reporters he got his high school diploma in the Army after dropping out of school in his senior year. He said he conceived the extortion plot six months earlier, and that he assembled the bombs in his home in rural Beaver Creek.

"What was your intent?" asked United States District Court Judge Otto J. Skopil, Jr.

"To extort $1,000,000," Heesch replied blandly.

Heesch and his wife, parents of two small children, six and four, appeared at an unusual hour-and-a-half session. Ordinarily in a guilty plea hearing, there is no testimony, only an explanation of the defendant's rights by the judge. But Attorney Howard Lonergan, representing the couple, told Judge Skopil his clients wanted to "relieve apprehension, and assure the community there were no other explosive devices set, and no other persons involved in the crime with which they are charged."

Heesch's testimony sought to exonerate his wife. He told the court she drove him to the Maupin explosion site, "but had nothing to do with the bombings. I told her I would do the bombings whether she helped me or not. She didn't help." In all, Heesch said, he bombed towers in Maupin, Brightwood, Hood River, and Dodge Park in the Mount Hood and Mount Tabor countryside.

Mrs. Heesch denied a prosecution suggestion she had been dominated by her "strong" husband. "David is a good husband," she told Judge Skopil. "I was never under any threat from him. He didn't force me to help him in anything."

But nothing man or wife said was of any help to them when they came up for sentencing on December 16, 1974, before United States District Court Judge Robert W. Belloni. Before imposing sentences, Judge Belloni offered both defendants an opportunity to make statements, but they declined. Then he sentenced Heesch to 20 years in prison for destruction of government property and illegal use of the mails. Charged as an accomplice rather than as a principal in the crime, Sheila Heesch drew a sentence of 10 years. Tears came to their eyes as they stood together before the bench.

But their day in court was not over. Heesch decided to make a statement after all. He told Judge Belloni: "Actually, there was not a threat to the people of this city. I had no intent to burn down the Bull Run watershed or stop the city's power supply." But the judge stopped him before he could continue.

However, Lonergan was permitted to answer a charge by United States Attorney Sidney I. Lezak that the couple had not made full disclosure of details of the plot. Lonergan said Mrs. Heesch had given full information truthfully. He added: "As for her refusal to take a lie detector test, I concur. I consider the polygraph worthless and downright deceptive, based on my own experiences with it."

Judge Belloni was unmoved, then. But the final curtain had not dropped. Five months later, he freed Mrs. Heesch by reducing her sentence to 14 months and announcing that the United States Parole Board could release her "at any time."

Judge Belloni said that at the time of the sentencing he was faced with "compelling considerations relative to the public safety and the potential magnitude of the crime. These considerations at the time overshadowed other knowledge that the court had of Mrs. Heesch, her devotion as wife and mother, her general character—which had been excellent—and the family needs that were very apparent."

The judge also said he had been faced with the possibility that other, unknown persons may have been involved in the sabotage and extortion plot. Subsequent investigation by the FBI, however, had convinced him that no one else was involved, he said. Besides, he said he was convinced that Mrs. Heesch's participation was coerced by her husband's "dominant role" in the marriage.

"The Heesch children are blameless, innocent victims in this case," the judge said. "I am persuaded that their suffering is significant and that their needs must be met more effectively than at present. It may appear to some that the court is unmindful of the trauma, damage and real potential for public disruption that appeared in the J. Hawker episode. To them, I can say only that the court considers each case on its merits."

Mrs. Heesch was released from prison four months later, on September 9, 1975. During her incarceration, another facet of the case had been closed. Because no unofficial citizen had provided information leading to the arrest of her and her husband, the $100,000 reward offered for their capture by the Bonneville Power Administration went unpaid.

INDEX

PACE UNIVERSITY LIBRARY
New York, NY 10038
Telephone 285-3332

TO THE BORROWER:

The use of this book is governed by rules established in the broad interest of the university community. It is your responsibility to know these rules. Please inquire at the circulation desk.

NOV 1980